NB
2/98

AMERICA'S COURT

❧ Also by Barrett McGurn ❧

Decade in Europe
A Reporter Looks at the Vatican
A Reporter Looks at American Catholicism

AMERICA'S COURT

THE SUPREME COURT AND THE PEOPLE

BARRETT MCGURN

FULCRUM PUBLISHING
GOLDEN, COLORADO

To Jan and the children,
Bill, Betsy, Andrew, Lachie, Martin and Mark

Copyright © 1997 Barrett McGurn

Book design by Bill Spahr

Cover photo: West facade of the Supreme Court of the United States
by Franz Jantzen. Collection of the Supreme Court of the United States.

Library of Congress Cataloging-in-Publication Data

McGurn, Barrett.
    America's Court : the Supreme Court and the people / Barrett McGurn.
        p.   cm.
    Includes bibliographical references and index.
    ISBN 1-55591-263-X
    1. United States. Supreme Court.   2. Judicial review—United States.   3. Separation of powers—United States.   I. Title.
    KF8742.M345   1997
    347.73'26—dc21   97-25254
                                                                                                              CIP

Printed in the United States of America

0 9 8 7 6 5 4 3 2 1

Fulcrum Publishing
350 Indiana Street, Suite 350
Golden, Colorado 80401-5093
(800) 992-2908 • (303) 277-1623

CONTENTS

FOREWORD

BY JUSTICE SANDRA DAY O'CONNOR

Barrett McGurn, who spent nine years at the Supreme Court of the United States as its Public Information Officer, has written a book about the Court from the standpoint of his view of the Court's work from the "inside." The result is a readable and enjoyable account of life at the Court day to day. McGurn is a journalist by training and experience. He brings to the book a journalist's style—easy to read, full of quotes and hundreds of human interest stories. No dull, long chapters here. Just lively accounts of the years of the Court under Chief Justice Warren Burger. There are even some stories new to me about my arrival at the Court in 1981. Here is the human touch, life at the Court drawn from personal experience.

It makes good reading for anyone who enjoys learning more about that remarkable institution—the Supreme Court of the United States.

Sandra Day O'Connor

Sandra Day O'Connor
Supreme Court Justice

PREFACE

"This is to introduce Barrett McGurn, a fallen away newsman."

Words of the Chief Justice of the United States at a meeting of the Supreme Court press corps, September 1973.

The Chief smiled amiably, happy with his pleasantry, and the news men and women stared bleakly.

Two of the most influential components of American life were represented at the little meeting, the High Court and the media, each acutely aware of the other, and each fated never to find full peace with the other.

For many in the media the Supreme Court was the most secretive and elusive part of the government, locked away behind marble walls, privately generating decisions affecting the course of national life.

For the Court the media were a puzzling mixed array, some thoughtful and serious, others superficial and sensational, too anxious to know upcoming decisions before final conclusions were reached, too willing to make headlines where no facts justified them, too prone to find fault with an institution of mere mortals shouldering some of society's greatest responsibilities.

Complicating the Court-media problem was the fact that the judiciary as the third branch of government is so different from the other two, the executive and the Congress. What the White House, the Senate and the House of Representatives do is conducted, step by step, in full view of the media with press officers soliciting further attention. The principals in both branches must stand for reelection and cannot do without media friendship.

The Supreme Court and all the hundreds of members of the federal judiciary below the Justices, by contrast, serve for life, absent impeachable offenses which, in two centuries, have never driven a Supreme Court Justice from office.

The Justices do not share with their governmental opposite numbers across Capitol Hill and in 1600 Pennsylvania Avenue the same constant need for press approval. In the Justices' view, what the public and, especially, the lawyers and the federal and state judges need to know is what they say in the scores of annual decisions and supporting Opinions. These cope with the main national problems, seen in the light of the nation's eighteenth-century Constitution, illuminated by the wisdom of previous judicial decisions in similar cases and measured against the laws passed by the national and state legislatures. In a Justice's ideal world, media coverage would be left at that, with news bulletins about decisions delayed until reporters could give them at least a sliver of the study that went into their creation in months of work behind the Court scenes.

In a competitive news world where a beat of a few seconds is a major victory, there is no way to realize such a Justice dream. Mangled early news reports, leaving permanent impressions, sometimes are the result.

Where great issues are involved and privacy and lengthy deliberation take on the appearance of sinister secrecy, curiosity and suspicion grow. News is what is novel, unexpected, paradoxical. With the Supreme Court serving as the national, secular conscience, anything wrong at the Court is a contradiction in perceptions, and grist especially for the mills of muckrakers. They, too, were drawn to the Court seeking what could be found, and increasing the Court-media tension.

A judge first and foremost, Warren Burger nonetheless knew from earlier years as a Republican activist that the media can be ignored only at one's own peril. Arriving at the High Bench in 1969, Burger was appalled by the Court's press relations. In the Courtroom there were six desks for the media, just in front of the bench. When decisions were announced, sometimes a dozen cases at a time, with hundreds of pages of Opinions, the total would be handed to the six. News wire representatives would cram them into vacuum tubes, dropping them to writers on the floor below. Sometimes crucial pages jammed in the pipes as the writers, with fingers crossed, hoping they had missed nothing essential, sent their flashes to hundreds of news rooms. Sometimes errors were egregious and Justices were horrified at what made its way into print.

For its first one and one-half centuries the Court had no press office. When the Court finally, in 1935, got a building of its own, a former reporter for the United Press, Banning Whittington, was hired as Press Clerk to serve the physical needs of an expanding resident press corps. Burger felt that more was needed, and a new Public Information Officer (PIO) was added to the Court's corps of a half dozen officers and executives to serve as a liaison between the bench, the media, the inquiring public and, occasionally, Hollywood.

For the new position the Justices wanted a newsperson who could understand the news world, but not one who was a lawyer. The latter might be tempted to explain the sometimes cryptic decisions, products of months of unpublished backs-and-forths among the chambers in quest of a majority of five. The lawyer-spokesperson's interpretation might take on a life of its own as the "real" decision of the Court and the Justices could not tolerate that. A career reporter, on the other hand, might at least comprehend the eternal news quest for what my old editors on the *New York* and *Paris Herald Tribune*s used to describe as "Whatever is important and interesting and, preferably, both at the same time."

In addition to being a nonlawyer and a reporter, the Justices wanted someone with a third qualification, completion of least five years also as a government spokesperson, someone who understood what State Department Spokesman Bob McCloskey once said: "Reporters and spokesmen have the same task, to explain what the government is trying to do. The spokesman has an additional job, to help the government succeed."

I had the first two requirements, a nonlawyer with three decades as a reporter and foreign correspondent and four terms as a press club President, and I had just completed the third: five years as a Press Officer for the United States embassies in Rome and Saigon and at the Department of State. "By a nose" it was enough to win out over 140 other applicants, and I was launched into a new career, old news colleagues on the one side and, on the other, the reality of the Supreme Court.

For the one, the Court would forever be a vessel of secrets.

For the other, nothing of importance would ever lie unwitnessed for long inside the goldfish bowl.

ACKNOWLEDGMENTS

There are many I wish to thank for making possible this study of the ever mysterious and often ill-understood American Supreme Court.

I am indebted to editor Mark Carroll for proposing the project and to publisher Bob Baron for supporting it.

In a special way I wish to thank my family for helping make the work a cottage industry: my wife, Jan, an erstwhile journalist, for enduring support as well as proof-reading, and computer expert son, Martin, for their vast assistance.

I am indebted to many others:

To retired Chief Judge Howard Markey of the other national court, the United States Court of Appeals for the Federal Circuit, for his view of the Court from a parallel judicial peak.

To Susan Goltz, who was one of the first persons called upon when the Justices decided they needed the help of another lawyer.

To Court Clerk Joseph Spaniol, for many pertinent suggestions.

To Court Clerk Michael Rodak for his unfailing good humor.

To my successor as Public Information Officer (PIO), Toni House, a veteran newswoman, for many shrewd insights into the Court of the past decade.

To the imaginative and innovative Dr. Mark Cannon, the first to serve as an Administrative Assistant to a Chief Justice, and the person who recommended me to be the Court's PIO executive.

In a special way I am indebted to those many Justices, living and some now dead, beside whom I had the good fortune to work:

Chief Justice Burger first of all, the night law student who dared to reform American judicial systems, bringing to the task all his physical and mental strength.

Byron White, whose quiet humor matched his extraordinary athletic and intellectual skills.

William O. Douglas, a crusty loner who became a warm friend of those he came to know well.

Lewis Powell, gentleman of the Old South.

Thurgood Marshall, inexhaustible raconteur and fierce fighter for human rights.

Potter Stewart, the reporters' warm sympathizer.

Cheerful Bill Brennan, the friend of those who needed friends.

Sensitive Harry Blackmun.

William Rehnquist, the Chief Justice of the 1990s whose firmly conservative ideas exist side by side with the happiest sense of humor and the most open and kindliest of manners.

Sandra Day O'Connor, whose grace, self-regard and competence ended forever the debate about whether women had a right to a place in justice's highest counsels.

Finally I wish to thank, too, the corps of journalists who covered the Court: Jack Mackenzie, Linda Greenhouse, Warren Weaver, Jack Kilpatrick, Glen Elsasser, Fred Graham, Nina Totenberg, Lyle Denniston, Charlotte Moulton, Betsy Olsen, Morton Mintz, Linda Mathews, Carl Stern, Tim O'Brien, Betty Wells, Frieda Reiter, Jack Anderson and so many others, many of them lawyers, all of them keenly intelligent.

Dealing with them as PIO was not always a happy experience, especially when the hunt was on for secrets that the Court could not share or when unfair barbs were hurled at the nine, but I never doubted that theirs, too, was an essential form of public service.

❦ Part I ❧

SECRETS

CHAPTER 1

UNITED STATES VERSUS ITS PRESIDENT

The title of the case was shocking: 73-1766, the United States of America, petitioner, v. Richard M. Nixon, President of the United States. The "73" was for the 1973 year term of the Supreme Court of the United States, which ran from the first Monday in October 1973 until such time as the Justices chose to end the term, generally nine months later.

The appalling nature of the presidential case only would have been deepened symbolically if Special Prosecutor Leon Jaworski had allowed another ten cases to proceed him on the docket. Then the last four numerals would have been 1776, the year of the nation's birth and one last irony.

Customarily the Justices started their summer recess before the July 4 holiday, but the late arrival of the President's case and pressures in Congress to impeach the Chief Executive convinced the nine to hear case 73-1766 after the usual closing date— on July 8, 1974, holding the term open until such time as a decision could be handed down.

For many inside the huge white neo-Grecian judicial temple at Number One First Street N.E. on Capitol Hill, and especially in the Justices' chambers and the Public Information Office, it was a time of uncommon pressure. It started in late 1973 when former aides of President Nixon were put on trial for obstructing justice in a Republican Party burglary of the Democratic Party headquarters in Washington's riverfront Watergate hotel and housing complex. The defendants said that secret tapes President Nixon had made of conversations might exculpate them regardless of how compromising the President would find publication of the salty, not to say scatological, exchanges.

On October 19, 1973, *Newsweek* magazine had a report that the "tapes case" might arrive that night at the Virginia farmhouse of Chief Justice Warren Earl Burger, a man who lived without Federal Bureau of Investigation protection, but who, nonetheless, struggled for some privacy. *Newsweek* was counseled rather testily to give up any idea of calling on Burger in the wee hours. The magazine agreed and missed no story. Nothing reached Burger at home overnight.

It was an opening skirmish without wounds, but it pointed up the tensions that often develop as the media seek full, instant accounts, and the Justices protect what privacy they can while also working against premature releases of information. Warren Burger was himself a key figure in the Nixon case. He had been appointed fourteenth Chief Justice by Richard Nixon at a time when the latter reportedly wanted someone at the head of the Court who was neither a product of the presumptively effete Northeastern law schools, nor one who would emphasize personal freedoms at the expense of society's basic law and order needs.

Burger had come from the ranks of mid-country Republicanism. A take-charge person and an early battler for those born without silver spoons in the mouth, he had campaigned successfully as a student in the obscure St. Paul, Minnesota, law school to get his fellow nighttime schoolmates equal standing with the more highly regarded daylight scholars.

Interested in politics, Burger had served as campaign manager for the ill-fated Harold Stassen during the Republican presidential primaries of 1952. At the party's convention, as the Minnesota governor's bid failed, Burger had made a decision that launched his national and international career. He threw the Stassen support to Dwight Eisenhower, helping assure the General's election and, in the process, caught the favorable attention of the Republican Party's national leadership. Herbert Brownell, who had managed the unsuccessful Republican try for the White House in 1948, became Eisenhower's Attorney General, head of the Department of Justice. He called Burger to Washington to be the Assistant Attorney General in what is now the Justice Civil Division. There Burger, the erstwhile night law student, oversaw a staff of two hundred lawyers.

From Justice, by an Eisenhower appointment, Burger went to the District of Columbia federal Court of Appeals, one of the most important of the second tier federal benches. Thence, as a defender of society's right of self-defense, Burger came to the attention of Eisenhower's former Vice President, Nixon, and in 1969, the latter named Burger Chief Justice. A new day in American justice after the arch-liberalism of Earl Warren seemed to be dawning.

Amidst the gradual phasing out of the Warren Court, Burger was joined by federal Appeals Court Judge Harry Andrew Blackmun, a lifelong intimate. The two had been members of the same St. Paul, Minnesota, Boy Scout troop. They had attended the same Sunday School class with Harry's mother as their teacher. When Burger married, Harry was best man.

With St. Paul and the cheek by jowl community of Minneapolis famous as the "twin cities" it was inevitable that the two Nixon nominees would achieve immediate, however unwelcome, media fame as "the Minnesota twins," with Harry the caboose on his old buddy's train.

For the slightly built, sensitive and proud Blackmun, having a Supreme Court Justiceship reduced in print to carbon copy status was not easy to take but, for the time being, it appeared that the conservative Nixon had created a hard core of support for his philosophy at the summit of American justice.

If indeed Nixon, as reported, wanted Justices uncontaminated by the Eastern establishment, Blackmun had only one drawback: He had taken both his undergraduate and law degrees from "effete" Harvard.

In short order there were four Nixon appointees on the post–Warren Court. William Hubbs Rehnquist, the highly traditional Assistant Attorney General, a Stanford Law School graduate and a former Supreme Court Law Clerk, went to the High Bench. So did Lewis Powell, an archetypal Southern gentleman, and past president of the centrally important American Bar Association (ABA).

Powell, a Richmond, Virginia, partner in the largest Southern law firm east of Texas, had perhaps a small stain on his mid-country escutcheon; he, too, had studied at Harvard. He had taken a master's law degree there but, balancing that, he was a proud son of the Old Confederacy and, at least, had gone to Washington and Lee University south of the Potomac for his bachelor of science and law degrees.

With Byron White, the immortal "Whizzer" of college and professional football fame, as a right-leaning moderate and thus a potential ally of the Nixon four, it was easy to see why many in the media saw the altered bench as the "Nixon Court," presumably a haven of last resort for the soon beleaguered President.

The Burger Court. Gone were the ailing Justices Harlan and Black, not yet there were Justices Steven and O'Connor. Left to right, seated: Justices Stewart, Douglas (the senior), Burger, Brennan and White. Left to right, standing: Justices Powell, Marshall, Blackmun and Rehnquist (the junior Justice and Conference doorkeeper). This is the Court that judged Nixon. Harris and Ewing, Collection of the Supreme Court of the United States.

One reporter in October 1973 came with a question: Has Chief Justice Burger assured the White House that the attack on the President would fail once it reached the Court?

From the Justice's point of view the mere suggestion that such a thing was possible was an outrage. The reporter was warned off the story as "irresponsible, ridiculous nonsense," and it died there.

More rumors and queries sprouted: Did the Chief Justice counsel Attorney General Richard G. Kleindienst against appointing a certain federal Judge as a special prosecutor for the Nixon case? If so, isn't that compromising? Shouldn't the Chief count himself out of the case?

The answer came in two parts: First, the Chief did not recommend anyone as prosecutor. On the other hand, the Chief never had made a secret of his conviction as the leader of the judiciary that the constitutional separation of powers among three governmental branches—legislative, executive and judicial—barred any federal Judge from taking a job in the executive without resigning from the judiciary.

For that particular Judge or any of the hundreds of others on the federal bench, acceptance of the prosecutorial assignment would mean an immense personal loss: abandonment of a lifetime appointment and an eventual full-salaried retirement.

It ended there. The mentioned Judge did not step in as the President's prosecutor, and Warren Burger did not gave up his place on the bench. The potential headline scandal melted away. Tapped instead as prosecutor was Leon Jaworski, a Texas Lawyer with Washington and international legal experience who had served recently on a presidential commission on law enforcement and the administration of justice.

A persistent suspicion was that Burger, as Nixon's appointee and presumed crony, was in periodic communication with Nixon aides such as the by-then-indicted John Ehrlichman.

The Ehrlichman balloon was punctured easily. So far as that presidential Aide was concerned, Burger never had any exchange with him except on one occasion when evidently baseless charges were leveled against one of the major officials of the Smithsonian Institution, Washington's complex of major national museums.

The Chief Justice, by law, is Chancellor of the Smithsonian, a side responsibility that Burger took seriously. An amateur sculptor and painter of some talent, he never resented the claims on his time that the collection of museums imposed. Burger knew the accused officer and was able to assure Ehrlichman, and any others interested, that nothing he had ever observed supported what appeared to be off-the-wall allegations. The matter soon died.

As for Nixon, his remarks in a "background" talk with reporters had resonated well with the Court when he said that the executive and judicial branches should operate at "arm's length" from one another. Far from having a buddy relationship with the man who had appointed him, Burger had seen Nixon only a few times in his life, generally in a receiving line or some other perfunctory manner. An exception was one occasion when the Chief called at the White House to hand in a document. Nixon received Burger but talked on the telephone the bulk of the time the two were together.

It was the night of the aborted military incursion into Cambodia, a quick in-and-out raid designed to clean out enemy positions across the Vietnam border. It was a presidential move instantly decried by peace activists as a widening of the disastrous Southeast Asian war. Despite the Chief Justice's presence, judicial matters were far from the President's thoughts that night.

The columnist Jack Anderson, a premier Washington muckraker and governmental naysayer, may have heard of the encounter. He wanted to know whether the heads of two branches of the government had been "meeting privately several times in the past four months," and was assured that they had not. One more suspicion of collusion at the government's top was laid to rest.

Even in the best of quiet times the Supreme Court and its workings are a mystery not just to the average citizen but also to many of the three thousand journalists covering Washington.

Dealing with many of the most controversial issues of national life, the Justices prefer to work behind the doors of their chambers cut off from daily controversy. They speak largely through the carefully worded Opinions they hand down from the bench.

To get the Court as an institution to address the mounting Watergate speculations was all the harder for confused newspeople, many of whom had never before mounted the broad marble staircase leading into the building. With no better story in town, the journalists, including the one-person bureaus that cover the whole of the Washington news, had to keep trying, had to go on hunting for some new angle.

The newly reorganized Public Information Office was peppered with questions: Has the Chief Justice assigned law clerks to review the procedures he would have to follow as the presiding officer of a senate impeachment trial? Who would chair the Supreme Court while the Chief Justice was at a senate trial? Would the Chief Justice cast votes in cases argued in his absence? What if the Chief Justice were to die? Who would oversee the senate trial and who would preside at the Court?

Far-out hypotheses were heaped on hypotheses in a desperate search for "new leads" on the running story, but reporters were patient when they got few answers. Iffy questions often go unanswered in Washington and, in late 1973, all the inquiries were based on an "if," the question of whether the House of Representatives would seek a presidential impeachment.

Comment of any kind was deemed inappropriate by the Court, yet even the foreign press took a shot at the story. The impeachment-threatened President was the leader of the West, and therefore a "local" story in other countries, friend and foe alike.

French television, through the United States Information Agency, asked for a "three to four minute" interview with Burger to have him explain the rather baffling American Constitution to the puzzled people of France. It sounded like a benign exercise in democratic theory, but what was the news peg? Impeachment, the French confessed. A skillful but ineffective attempt to get Burger to talk, the request for such an interview was denied. The Chief Justice had no intention of prejudging with confused French people or any others what might become his constitutional responsibility.

Lawyers for both the White House and its critics had been sparring for weeks, but finally the latter landed what boxing fans used to call a haymaker. Judge John Sirica in the Washington, D.C., federal District Court agreed with Special Prosecutor Jaworski that tapes of the President's secret conversations had to be turned over for judicial examination for possible use in the defense of Ehrlichman and other Nixon aides.

The President appealed and the Supreme Court agreed to take the case. The Court's role as a bystander was over. It was now at the heart of the story.

CHAPTER 2

THE COURT, THE PRESIDENT AND THE MEDIA

The Justices, sensitive to the division of powers, knew that the unique Nixon case—the head of one governmental branch judged and perhaps ousted by another—would attract extraordinary attention, but it was only on April 19, 1974, that they began to see the true dimensions of what faced them.

The Justices had planned to hear the White House case on the same day they heard *Hazelwood School District v. United States,* a school busing controversy, but early on the nineteeth each Justice was asked to vote "yes" or "no" on two questions. Should the Nixon case be the first order of business at 10 A.M. on the hearing day, and should Hazelwood—slated for the afternoon of the same day—be moved elsewhere on the calendar? Nine Justices with widely different backgrounds and ideas had an eye for even small details, so it was all put to a ballot. By 5 P.M. the votes from the chambers were in, and the "ayes" had it on both counts.

In the earliest years of the two-century-old Court, hearings sometimes lasted for days as Daniel Webster and other great orators performed. In the first decades of the nineteenth century ladies of Washington often took in the proceedings as if they were at a theater; the arguments before the Justices were a social event.

In an ever busier Court that had changed, so that in Earl Warren's time in the 1960s two cases were heard each day in a brisk four-day week of hearings, eight cases in all, in a Monday through Thursday series.

Burger, a judicial innovator ever ready to adapt to a constantly new situation, had tightened the Warren schedule further so that twelve cases were heard in three days, Monday through Wednesday. It meant a 50 percent increase in product, coupled with a day saved for behind-the-scenes debate and the writing of opinions.

Under the Burger arrangement one hour was allotted for hearings on a case, two presentations between 10 A.M. and noon and, after a one-hour lunch break, two more from 1 to 3 P.M. The Burger changes became the enduring Court practice. Lawyers had no time to dawdle. Attorneys had a mere thirty minutes to outline their Supreme Court cases and, worse than that, any questions from the bench came out of a lawyer's time. Many a thirty-minute speech, perhaps carefully rehearsed before a spouse or a bedroom mirror at home, never was heard in court.

For the case of the President there were further modifications. Each side would get triple the usual time, ninety minutes. The hearing would run to 1 P.M. After that, Courtroom business would close for the day. For the thousands of reporters in Washington, the little-loved Nixon before the bar of high justice would be the story of the day. For Congress, the Senate, for all levels of the executive branch, for the thousands of members of the Supreme Court bar and for law students as well as members of the general public, it was clear that the place to be on July 8 would be inside the Supreme Courtroom.

The Court, ever conscious that its work was public business, always saved some dozens of seats for the walk-in public. Some of the seats allowed a full morning or afternoon stay. Others permitted only a five-minute glimpse, too short to understand what was going on but enough to see the nine black-clad figures on the bench, the handsome hearing room and long enough to get the flavor of ultimate justice being done.

Other dozens of seats were reserved for various of the one hundred thousand members of the Court bar.

While anxious to stay as close as possible to routine procedure, the Justices quickly realized that what they had was not just a "sellout," as one of them expressed it in private, but a sellout many times over. It was easy to decide that the walk-in public and the members of the Court bar should receive their customary privileges, but what about the army of Washington political luminaries and the throngs of journalists who would clamor to be admitted? Who would be the lucky sheep and who the goats?

In a city where many pride themselves on being insiders, *The Washington Post* summed up the situation in an eight-column headline: " 'Being in' is being in at all."

Even a blind seat behind a pillar or a curtain would be prized, anything to avoid missing this ultimate debate.

The Post's rival, *The Washington Star-News,* used four columns on page one for a headline making the same point about the Courtroom passes: "The Hottest Ticket in Town."

One Justice announced that he would recuse, taking no part in the case, and that pointed a way to cope with the sellout. He was Rehnquist, the future Chief Justice. As usual in such situations, the jurist provided no explanation of why he was stepping aside. It was assumed that he had sufficient personal reasons that he need not disclose. Justices often recuse, for example, when their old law firms appear for argument, thus avoiding the appearance of a conflict of interest. Rehnquist had been Assistant Attorney General under the indicted John Mitchell, and it was a good guess that that was why he was opting out. A negative effect of the Rehnquist decision was that it opened the possibility of a four-to-four deadlock and an inability to act. On the other hand, an at least small bonus was that Rehnquist, freed from weighing the legal merits, could be the dictator deciding who would get into the hearing.

Rehnquist accepted that distasteful job but split it into two parts. The Court's newly hired Public Information Officer would make all decisions about the media, and the Justice would take care of the rest.

One PIO suggestion quickly was vetoed: How about giving all three hundred seats in the Courtroom to the media as the eyes and ears of the world public? Each journalist, after all, served a broad audience. No others were able to share their impressions so widely, and the fate of the American President and presidency concerned millions.

No, was the answer, the media would have to make do with their usual limited, although usually adequate, Courtroom space. The media had nineteen regular seats on the left side of the Courtroom near the bench. There was a mostly blind corridor behind those seats. A few more reporters could sit there, although they might be unable to see. A loudspeaker would let them hear.

Meanwhile, the rest of the Courtroom was parceled out for other purposes. Fifty places were set aside for the Supreme bar. All lawyer requests would be put in a pile, and the lucky ones would be drawn in random, giving the most recent arrival the same chance as the nation's most famous attorneys and law professors.

Tickets for dozens more of the seats were sent across Capitol Hill to the congressional leadership, leaving to them the thankless business of deciding which legislators would get in and which would not.

And then there were the Justices themselves. How about their wives, their children, their staffs in the chambers, their poker playing and tennis buddies, their doctors and clergymen and their other close friends?

Each Justice was given four tickets—in total, a tenth of the Courtroom space—and that would be all for each of them.

The prime nineteen press seats inside the Courtroom clearly had to go to the reporters who covered on a day-by-day basis, those from The Associated Press (AP), United Press International (UPI), Reuters, *The New York Times, The Washington Post, The Washington Star-News,* the *Los Angeles Times,* the *Chicago Tribune,* National Public Radio (NPR), NBC, CBS, ABC and a few others.

The next media problem concerned artists. The Supreme Court bans still photo and TV coverage and, in the midst of the Nixon crisis, was not going to reconsider that. The artists would provide the only pictorial coverage and, to do it, had to be far enough forward to see. That gave them some priority.

Then what about the one-person news bureaus? Their publishers paid them to be on top of the major stories. How were they going to explain that they pulled so little weight that they could not get in when it counted? Fellow journalists could understand their plight.

And what about the news magazines, the editorial writers, the feature specialists, the columnists, the legal publications? How about authors whose books were part of Court literature? And the foreign press? This was their story too.

The Public Information Office had a new idea. How about piping the hearing into one of the large conference rooms? Hundreds more of the media and the Court's various publics could be served. It was another PIO idea quickly rejected. The Supreme Court, regardless of what the ladies of the early nineteenth century might have thought in Daniel Webster's time, is not a theater. Its hearings occur inside the Courtroom and nowhere else, neither on TV nor radio nor in other rooms of the Court building.

That left the media with the nineteen regular Courtroom seats and the remote corridor behind. Usually there were a dozen or so comfortable upholstered chairs in the latter. How about moving them out and squeezing in eighty folding chairs, quadrupling the usual media allotment? No objections were raised to that and, with the Marshal's help, media seats were expanded to close to one hundred.

Now, to whom would the media "hot tickets" go? To take care of the small bureaus a formula of "one news organization, one seat," seemed like a starting point. There was even a judicial overtone to it. One of the Court's main twentieth-century decisions was "one person, one vote," striking down local electoral laws that disenfranchised African Americans.

But then, what about the news agencies that needed a blow-by-blow running story during the three hours? The rule was bent for them, one seat for the running story, one for a wrap-up, the rounded final summation.

TV networks, too, needed an exception. They had to have both a reporter and an artist; two seats were provided.

The foreign press? This was above all an American story; it was our President even if the man in the White House controlled decisions of high concern to other nations. The foreign journalists *belonged in* but on a sharply reduced basis.

Reuters, with its English background, already had a seat, but the British media were assigned two more. The Germans were given one. These two large national groups were invited to decide among themselves who would get in and for how long.

By then there was a precedent for them on what to do. The PIO was assigning as many as five of the home country correspondents to a single chair on a time-shared and rotating basis. Just over a half hour was given to each, too little for a balanced impression, but long enough for "color."

To let the shortchanged reporters get the two sides of the argument, the outside company that produces the transcripts forty-eight hours or so after hearings agreed to provide them almost simultaneously. Soon the walls of the press area dangled with sheets of transcript.

Tossing the seat assignment ball to the several national groupings of correspondents spared the PIO deciding in cases, such as that of England, how the BBC measured up in importance against the *Times of London,* or how much weight *The Guardian* of Manchester hefted when considered against *The Economist.*

Still more of the overseas press struggled to get in. The PIO allowed glimpses for the Canadian Broadcasting Company, the Japan Broadcasting Corporation, and the Swedish Broadcasting Corporation.

Hard decisions persisted as the formula of one seat or part of a seat for one medium served as a sometimes inadequate guideline. Journalistic celebrities had to be turned away. One such was Eric Sevareid who had done one of the few great Court television interviews with William O. Douglas. Sevareid's network already had double representation.

Other times, to their amazement and amusement, the formula opened the door to the journalistically insignificant. Lou Simons of the minuscule *Beaver County* (Pennsylvania) *Times* applied, presumably for the fun of being turned away. On the basis of at least a peak for every applicant he got the first hour on seat seven. While Lou must have guffawed later in front of his typewriter, he tapped out a story filling half a page in his next issue under a fat four-line headline: "It wasn't easy, but this newsman crashed historic hearings in U.S. Court."

Another borderline applicant was Sally Quinn of *The Washington Post,* a satiric writer who once shared with her readers the information that a celebrity interviewee had an unzipped fly. *The Post* already had a full complement on an outfit-by-outfit basis, but it was clear that Sally's kind of coverage needed direct contact. Sally got an hour from 11 to noon, one-third of the hearing, and, in a suggestion that there had been unfair favoritism, wrote the next day that the PIO had given only a fifth of the time to "those he didn't know." Sally noticed the PIO's complicated seating chart and asked for it. It would have made an entertaining if embarrassing item: the media pecking order according to the Supreme Court. Sally had to do without it.

Theodore "Teddy" White, author of a best-selling series of political books on the "making" of presidents, wanted a seat. He was not a "news organization" but his upcoming book would be in effect "the unmaking of a president," history many would read. Teddy got in.

One who beat the system was Anthony Lewis, a *New York Times* columnist and Pulitzer Prize–winning veteran of the Supreme Court beat. Tony was a well-respected Court watcher, but his successor as resident *Times* reporter already had one of the prized nineteen seats inside the Courtroom.

Tony was turned away but, knowing the Court well, went to the Chief Justice for one of his four seats. Burger, not wanting to upset the media-handling apple cart, requested the PIO's permission, the boss asking his hireling. Tony not only got in, he was the only one who covered from the middle of the Courtroom.

In all, 130 of the media heard all or part of the case, fully one-third as many people as usually hear Court cases.

One feisty woman whose seat was in a rear row in the corridor complained that a lesser journalist sat closer to the Courtroom, but her lamentation was an exception.

On at least one occasion when it counted, the Court and its "secrets" had been displayed fully for many inside the Court fishbowl.

CHAPTER 3

DECISION

Thoughts of many kinds went through the minds of the nine judges on the High Bench as Leon Jaworski pleaded for release of the Nixon tapes, and the fifty-four-year-old James Draper St. Clair, defender of the United States Army in the 1954 Senator McCarthy proceedings, appealed for presidential confidentiality.

Potter Stewart, the suave former editor of the Yale student newspaper, looked down at the New Englander St. Clair and liked what he saw. "A pleasing gentleman," he said. "I never saw him before."

Another of the Justices seconded Stewart's impression: "He handled himself in a very lawyerly manner."

Various lawyers, especially those from the Department of Justice, appear often at the Court, but St. Clair was one of the many to whom a Court pleading might come once in a lifetime.

Ever an administrator as well as a judge, Chief Justice Burger watched not just the arguing lawyers but also the hundreds of persons behind them in the Courtroom. After all the fuss about hot tickets, three rows in the Courtroom were empty. How was that possible?

With an ear to the words of the arguing lawyer, Burger reached for a pad and scribbled a note for retired Airforce Colonel Frank Hepler, the Marshal of the Court, seated at the far right of the bench (as seen by the audience). Twisting around in his chair, Burger handed the paper to a messenger crouched low out of sight behind him. Hepler read it, peered at the audience and sent back a reply:

Those three rows were the ones assigned to Congress. With all the furor about getting into the hearing, what had happened? Had the precious passes gone astray? Had the Hill leadership avoided arguments by giving tickets to no one? Were the legislators busy with other matters, planning to drift in later?

Wait no longer, Burger instructed the Marshal. Give the rows to some of the hundreds outside waiting on line. The first of the anonymous public had lined up in the street forty-eight hours beforehand. By midnight prior to the hearing scores of others had joined them, huddling against the nighttime chill. At least a few more of them could now get in.

Sedate dress is customary for most of those at Court hearings, with formal attire for the Marshal, the Clerk and the advocates from the Department of Justice. The walk-in public come in vacation clothes during the warmer months, but some of those seen from the bench on the Nixon day were clad even more lightheartedly than usual.

"Hippies!" the Chief Justice thought disapprovingly. The counterculture! So he suspected at first but, keeping an occasional eye on them, he changed his mind. There were no chuckles when a Justice lightened the mood with a teasing remark. The young men and women listened intently to the arguments. Not hippies at all, Burger finally concluded. Probably very serious and deserving law students.

Mike Rodak, the Clerk of the Court, sitting at the end of the bench nearest the press area, kept an occasional watch on the record turnout of newspeople, concerned lest they have a negative impact on the proceedings. He heard some rustlings of paper, but it was muted, and the Justices were farther away from the newspeople than he was. He concluded that the immense media invasion had caused no harm.

At 1 P.M., as the Justices filed out through the curtains behind their bench, the consensus was that the first stage of the fateful case had gone off well.

The Burger Court custom in the usual twelve-case week of hearings was to choose up sides on the four Monday cases after the final four were heard on Wednesday. If the Chief was in the majority he would assign himself, or one of those who agreed with him, to write the Court Opinion. If he was voted down, the senior Justice in the majority would choose the decision author. At an all-day conference on Friday the fate of the eight Tuesday and Wednesday cases was determined. By then the die in all but a few cases had been cast, although another half year might go by before the writings and rewritings of opinions and dissents had been completed, and the results were made public.

It is that which creates the bulk of the secrets inside the judicial bowl. Millions, such as in the Nixon case, might be waiting to know the outcome, but only a handful inside the Court building would be privy to what had already happened. Although it is a secret of not more than a few months it is guarded earnestly. Sometimes billions of dollars can change hands on the stock market if speculators learn prematurely what the Justices already have decided.

For newspeople the long wait before publication is tantalizing. Unrevealed facts are news. Tension in Court-media relations is inevitable.

In the Nixon case, while the White House, the Congress, the American public and nations around the world awaited the verdict, the Justices reached their decision faster than usual.

No hearing was scheduled for Tuesday, July 9, so the eight voting Justices assembled that day, only twenty-four hours after the Courtroom session. The decision was quick. Ron Ziegler, President Nixon's press spokesman, had said that the Chief Executive would go along with a "definitive" Supreme Court verdict. His adjective had been disquieting. Was there any doubt in Mr. Nixon's mind that even a one-vote majority was other than the law? With Rehnquist out, would five to three be insufficient?

Richard Kluger in his fine study of the 1954 school desegregation case, *Brown v. the Board of Education,* had told of one occasion when the issue of "definitive" had arisen. Justice Stanley F. Reed, a Kentuckian, could not agree to a mingling of black and white children in a classroom even though his eight brethren wanted to strike down racial segregation. The Chief Justice, fearing any loophole that white racists might exploit, refused to hand down a mere eight to one decision and ordered that the case be reargued a year later. By then Reed gave in, the vote was unanimous and the relatively peaceful integration of American education got underway.

Inside their Conference Room, with hundreds of books of earlier Supreme Court decisions covering the walls around them, the Justices considered the fate of Richard Nixon.

As is customary, none but the Justices was present, but given the way every effort was made to treat the sensational presidential case routinely, one can assume what happened. Presiding at the head of the table and speaking first was Warren Burger, there in the high seat courtesy of the very President who was, in effect, on trial before him. At the opposite end of the table, facing the Chief, was Douglas, who was not at all uncomfortable passing judgments on others in the highest governmental echelons. He had been one of them, not just in the judiciary. He was nosed out narrowly for the

Democratic Party's vice presidential nomination in 1944 by Harry S Truman. Had Douglas been chosen instead, he would have been President in 1945. So far as personalities mattered, and not points of constitutional law, Douglas had made no secret that his word for Richard Nixon was detestation.

Outside the Justices' closed room, politicians and newspeople wondered how the balloting was going. Were the Chief and his fellow Nixon appointees, Blackmun and Powell, siding with the likable St. Clair? Were Douglas and the other liberals, Thurgood Marshall, the first African American on the High Bench, and William Brennan, the son of an Irish-American labor organizer, rejecting the appeal of the Republican President? Could the balance be shifted in the President's favor by the middle-of-the-roaders, White and Stewart? So it would seem, but there were elements in the background of the Chief Justice that pointed in the opposite direction.

At one side of the Conference Room was a door to the Chief's inner office where he did much of his work on Opinions. On its wall was a painting Burger had done years before illustrating the August 1807 Aaron Burr case. That early judgment offered suggestions about how the Nixon matter should be resolved.

Burr had a notorious place in post-colonial history as a dueler who slew Alexander Hamilton. A former Vice President of the country, Burr had been placed on trial for treason before Chief Justice John Marshall, a man revered by Burger and the rest of the Justices as "the great Chief Justice." Burr was charged with having tried to create a new nation of his own inside the Mississippi River valley. President Thomas Jefferson, wrapped in the aura of authorship of the Declaration of Independence, demanded a conviction and offered excerpts of a document to prove Burr's guilt.

No partial text, said Marshall. The whole document or nothing. It was the Court's job to say what was pertinent. A man under so grave a charge deserved to have a complete record spread before his judges. Anyone with evidence, even a President, had to produce it. Jefferson refused and Burr went free. A principle had been established.

Luther Martin was the lawyer with the ungrateful task of defending Burr. Burger had been so impressed with the courage Martin and some other advocates showed in the case, standing up against governmental pressure and public opinion, that he wrote an article extolling them for the law review of the Cleveland State Law School.

In the Nixon case, too, Burger and his brethren were dealing with a President who had just been reelected in a landslide. He had broad public support. There was much sympathy for him, not least among his own Court appointees. Even so, from Burger's point of view, John Marshall's conduct of the Burr trial was not dead history but rather a relevant precedent for deciding the case at hand.

As the Justices chose up sides on 73–1766 the Chief called for surrender of the President's incriminating tapes. At least five others agreed. There was a rumor later that Burger had to pressure one or two holdouts, but Douglas, speaking later about what he recalled, said that by the time all had spoken, there was unanimity. Nixon had lost.

Who should write for the Court? It was the Chief's option and Burger took it.

Outside the Conference Room, reporters, working in the dark, still had to come up with think pieces about what might be transpiring in the running Nixon story. It was no enviable assignment, but one Justice, unsympathetic with the media's instant need to know, could not restrain himself from an ironic comment when he read one story: "The decision will be either divided or unanimous."

"What else is there?" he asked.

Reporters tried to penetrate the Court's secret by making end runs around the Public Information Office to the various chambers, talking to willing Justices or to their law clerks. Some tried Potter Stewart, an old newsman of sorts himself. He shared little of the antipathy for the media that some of his brethren harbored, but he was as anxious as any to protect what he considered basic matters of confidentiality.

Law clerks, all but a few of them in the Courthouse for merely a year, succumbed sometimes to the seduction of being interviewed, but even they were warned in an early-term meeting with the Marshal and the PIO to honor the privacy of decision making. They too could offer little.

As Chief Justice Burger set to work, the chances of learning what he was doing were even fewer than usual. His 1973-term law clerks had gone and a new team had just come aboard. The clerks of the various chambers normally get to know one another, sharing bits of information, but there could be little of that this time. Most of the other chambers were empty except for skeleton forces. Only a handful of the new law clerk generation had arrived. Networking at the clerk level was at a standstill.

Justices, too, had taken off, Douglas to mountain climbing in his home state of Washington, Brennan to Nantucket Island, Stewart to New Hampshire and Powell to the Mayo Clinic for a checkup.

In some cases even the standby staffs in the chambers were cut out of exchanges with the Chief. Douglas, for instance, was kept abreast of the writing of the Nixon Opinion by direct communication in Goose Prairie, Washington, without reference to his aides under the roof.

For forty-two days without a break, often from 8 A.M. to midnight, Burger and his two new, youthful law clerks worked on the President's verdict. It was a relentless grind. For the clerks the initial awe gradually gave way to easier familiarity. The going was hard. Young Timothy Kelly began keeping score of the passing summer days. "Chief," he lamented mildly, "this is the thirty-ninth straight day!"

A picnic basket from Mrs. Burger took care of meals. Some days it was stuffed tomatoes. Chicken others—baked but never fried.

Three particular earlier decisions of the Supreme Court interested Burger especially as binding precedents. For one with so many other Court actions on his mind, it seemed amazing that he was able to cite each of the three in smallest details with never a need to consult the volumes of Court actions.

Then Burger explained. He was the government's lawyer on each of them and had lost all three. Against his best pleading, the Supreme Court had established precedents now dooming the White House occupant. The conclusion to which Burger was coming was that Richard Nixon could not plead "executive privilege" as grounds for withholding the information needed by the Watergate defendants unless he based his refusal on requirements of diplomatic or military secrecy essential to national security. No such claim had been made by the amiable Mr. St. Clair.

As Burger wrote, a page a day, he shared his work with the scattered seven. Some had their usual suggestions, but Douglas, out on his distant mountain, gave the Chief a free hand so long as the basic antipresidential perimeters stayed intact.

Brennan, too, often at odds with the usually conservative Chief, maintained solid support. So did Byron White and Harry Blackmun.

That left Marshall, Stewart and Powell. One rumor had it that Stewart, a fine legal craftsman, was the author of a key section stating why it was appropriate for the Supreme Court to sit in judgment on the head of another governmental branch. But, in fact, the Opinion was Burger's with the exception of manicuring, such as a footnote becoming part of the central opinion.

The Opinion went through two drafts. Ever mindful of history, Burger numbered them for posterity. The Opinion filled thirty-one pages. The vote was eight to nothing. It was "definitive." Announcing it in Court, Burger read an eighteen-minute summary.

Even though the outcome was no longer a secret, there was still no letup in news queries. The autumn 1973 inquiries about impeachment came back in full force. It was still nothing the Chief Justice would discuss, pending action by Congress. Any speculation from him, he felt, would be improper. Assign five hundred FBI agents to find anything I have ever said about that, he remarked, and all five hundred would come up empty-handed.

Nonetheless, the media felt the need to keep trying. Washington's *TV Panorama* program had one idea: a panel discussion among the Chief Justice and others at the Jefferson Memorial on the Potomac River's tidal basin that covered the Constitution and its impeachment clause with "no direct reference to the present situation." There was no explanation of how the program would unscramble an omelet of impeachment talk on the one hand and the President on the other. The Chief declined.

One enterprising reporter took off from the Court's ground floor press area to check how many books on impeachment were in the Court library on an upstairs floor. Only five, he found, too few in his judgment to prepare the Chief Justice. What other books was the Chief Justice ordering? he wanted to know. The librarians provided no answer.

The fact was that preparation for an impeachment trial had been well down the list of the Chief's priorities as he concentrated in the early summer weeks on writing both of the final big judgments of the term, Nixon and the Hazelwood school busing case.

In addition, a stack of administrative matters had piled up. Chief Justices wear many hats, probably far too many. The Chief runs the three-hundred-person Court staff, overseeing hiring and firing. He chairs the Judicial Conference of the United States, a group of twenty-five federal judges who handle the concerns of the federal courts and their hundreds of judges. He presides over Washington's National Gallery of Art and the Smithsonian. He handles all this while taking the lead in acting on five thousand new Supreme Court cases each year.

Behind Burger's desk during his nearly two-decade tenure, more than a dozen manila folders piled on a windowsill, matters to be decided when the needed minutes could be found. At times when there were no marathon days of the Nixon type, Burger would carry home two briefcases of work. Even they finally bulged so much that the Chief shifted to a large suitcase for his nighttime work.

What he needed, the Chief decided, as the Nixon and Hazelwood cases came down, was a three-week vacation. He and Mrs. Burger had not had a long respite in five years. Despite all the news interest, no impeachment trial seemed imminent. If there was to be a rest it would have to be before the semiannual meeting of the Judicial Conference slated for the Supreme Court building in mid-September. Burger would have to be back in his chambers just after Labor Day to prepare for that and to review one thousand new cases that had accumulated as usual during the summer. In late September the Chief would have to take the lead recommending which 950 or so of the appeals would be turned away, either for lack of an important federal question or for sheer inability to find a place for more in a two-hundred-case term.

A question was where to go for twenty-one days or so. Cool New Hampshire sounded good. Potter Stewart always enjoyed his Summers there. But that was the United States. No place in this country was likely to free him from interviews with the Nixon matter unresolved. Europe seemed a better choice.

The American Ambassador in the Netherlands had extended an invitation. From there the Burgers could wander south toward Portugal and Spain. Some last-minute Court business stood in the way: a flight west to attend the annual conference of the judges of the Pacific coast federal circuit, and a stop in Reno to address the National Judicial College, an institution Burger had sponsored in an effort to raise the level of courtroom work. With that behind them, the Burgers set August 4 as the departure date, never suspecting that before a week was out a new President would need the Chief to swear him in.

At the Hague the Chief refused a request from the Ambassador that he give a speech, one more unwelcome opportunity to talk about the American President, but he did agree to a small dinner party with eminent local jurists. The President of the International Court of Justice, a Pole and presumably a Communist, attended, praising Burger for establishing that law governs all people, even chiefs of state. He gave Burger the World Court's silver medal.

It was nice, but Burger felt sick. A viral infection had dogged him through June and July, including the long weeks of work on the Nixon matter. It flared up now. Instead of sightseeing, Burger obeyed a Dutch physician's prescription, bed rest in his hotel.

It was long past time for some repose, but back at 1600 Pennsylvania Avenue in Washington, Richard Nixon was pondering the effects of the Court demand that he hand over his recordings. Should he resign? A stream of phone calls began reaching Burger through the embassy. Move in here for your convalescence, my wife's away, the Ambassador suggested. Washington exchanges would be easier. Burger agreed. By late afternoon on August 8, thirteen days after the decision in 73-1766, the President's resignation was announced, and there was a new deluge of questions for the Court PIO: Where is Burger? Will he swear in Mr. Ford? How could he with the inauguration only a day away?

Reporters were advised not to count out the Chief as the oath-administering officer, but no details were offered. The Chief was still "away on vacation."

It was midnight in Holland, and the bulk of Statesbound commercial flights had departed long hence, but there was an alternative. The incoming President instructed the Airforce in Europe to fly the Chief home.

Still ailing, Burger reached Washington with two hours to spare. President-designate Ford invited the other Justices to attend and it was the PIO's job to reach them. With some as many as four hours away from the nearest airport, none could accept, not even Stewart, who had been Ford's Yale Law School fellow student.

The inauguration over, the Burgers were still determined to get in the European trip, but one aftermath of the White House upheaval remained, the new Chief Executive's address to Congress. It would take place immediately after the weekend then beginning. Supreme Court Justices are always invited to don their robes to take a front-row seat at joint sessions of Congress, and this time the minimum six-person quorum was available.

That over, the Burgers hurried back across the Atlantic, staying two days in Paris with Burnet Anderson, an official of the United States Information Agency, who had been a colleague in the old Minnesota political days.

Unhappily, the virus would not quit. Sick almost all the time, the Chief gave up after a week and the Burgers came home. A few days later, out riding his bicycle for nighttime exercise, the Chief was struck by a hit-and-run driver and went to the hospital.

It was the end of the dramatic Court-versus-President summer. A movie popular some time earlier was *The Lost Weekend.* For him, said Burger, it was rather a "lost summer."

While details of that prolonged Nixon season were harrowing, there were some that were rewarding. A favorite news query after the decision was whether it had been soul-searing for the Nixon four, none of whom backed the President who had placed them on the bench.

"Buncombe," said Burger. It was merely a matter of "taking the case in stride, as any experienced judge would."

Comforting was the way other judges across national lines echoed the words the Chief Justice had heard in the Hague from the President of the International Court of Justice. All over the world, said some, the Supreme Court of the United States had strengthened the role of the courts as the defenders and appliers of law. In dictatorships people could see what they lacked. In free countries the already strong contribution of the judiciary was further solidified. Three or four of the top judges of England sent complimentary notes adding, perhaps ruefully, that what had happened in Washington could never occur in London. There the parliament is sovereign.

✦ CHAPTER 4 ✦
CLOUDBURST

The Justices of the Supreme Court had reason to be pleased that their decision in the Nixon case did not leak prematurely.

They seemed also to have every right to believe that the painful Nixon matter was behind them as they went on to tackle the never-ending myriad of other major national concerns coming to them for the last word.

On neither count, however, were such impressions correct. Far from mere dribbles of awkward news stories, they were about to be soaked in a cloudburst. And the master rainmaker would be none other than the same young reporter of *The Washington Post*, Bob Woodward, whose journalistic exposés brought the President to the Court's judgment. This time it would be the judges who would be judged. The Court had a long-deserved reputation for keeping its limited secrets. Few journalists had managed to thwart that. It was an Everest no specialist in exposés had surmounted. Young Woodward set out to see whether that could be changed.

The youthful reporter by 1977 was a national celebrity. A former writer for the modest *Montgomery County* (Maryland) *Sentinel* and a cub journalist on the much greater *Washington Post*, Woodward had turned coverage of a petty police court case into the unseating of a President.

Helping Woodward and another young colleague, Carl Bernstein, had been an indulgent City Editor, Harry Rosenfeld, who allowed them to keep digging, and a sensation-minded Editor-in-Chief, Benjamin Crowninshield Bradlee, who delighted in "holy shit" copy, news of the most startling nature.

With his Watergate reporting, two books on the subject and a movie about his exploits behind him, there was a question about what Woodward would do for an encore. Decapitating one branch of the tripartite government was one thing. Doing the same to another branch, the judiciary, in the person of the Chief Justice of the United States, would be quite another. The greats of American journalistic muckraking, the Ida Tarbells, the Lincoln Steffenses, the Jack Andersons, would have to move over.

If indeed the defenestration of Chief Justice Burger, his resignation, his impeachment or even his jailing, was a subconscious Woodward goal from the outset, he denied it in a *National Law Journal* interview published after his Court book, *The Brethren*, was in print. Woodward insisted in that interview and others that, at the outset in 1977, a rather sedate, academic topic was what he had in mind, how decisions really are made in the governmental power centers of Washington, including the Supreme Court. Only after immense quantities of private Supreme Court documents began filling file cabinet drawers did his project focus in 1978 on the Court, he said.

Whatever the fact, the reporter did indeed begin history's most massive penetration of Supreme Court privacy by telling the Court PIO in a phone conversation on July 7, 1977, and, over coffee a week later in the Court building's public cafeteria, that he wanted to know how official Washington made decisions, and that he felt sure it was not always "the way people think."

What his comment implied was not clear, but the impression left was that the Supreme Court would play a minor role in the upcoming volume. The Court does indeed make some of the major national decisions, but they are dwarfed by the volume produced each day in the White House and the Congress. Put in the way the inquiring journalist did, it seemed only right that some few pages in his new work should touch on the Court. What the approaching book would not be was "investigative," Woodward added reassuringly.

With Woodward as he sipped his coffee was his new collaborator, Scott Armstrong. He, too, was a veteran of the campaign to bring down the erring President. An investigator for the senate Democratic majority in the impeachment proceedings, his teaming up with Woodward did nothing to reinforce Woodward's "noninvestigative" theme, but the PIO was left to take the visitors' words at face value. Was that an initial calculated attempt at deception?

Without doubt, the talk of government rather than specific Supreme Court decision making, plus assurances that no one would be asked to betray confidences, gave the team an entrée to many former law clerks. Soon, an expanding Woodward-Armstrong team, with that start, fanned across the country seeking information on how Justices hammer out their verdicts in their private Conference Room discussions and in their nine chambers.

Were the informants tricked? *Newsweek* in a long discussion of the Woodward-Armstrong product, quoted a "top level source" at the publishers, Simon and Schuster, as saying that talk of Washington decision making was a "cover" and that the sole intent from the outset was to do a book on the Court. The $350,000 publisher's advance and the leave with pay from *The Post* for the two writers surely was not for a scholastic enterprise. Subsequent publicity for the book described the Court as a "sitting target."

Are "exposés" worthwhile for their own sake regardless of harm to major national interests? The visitors hinted at their own answer when Woodward asked the PIO archly: "How do you like your work here?"

Implied seemed to be that instant total revelation, in or out of context, is an overriding social good. Wouldn't a veteran newsman agree?

The questioner listened expressionless to the answer: "These Justices have appallingly great responsibilities. I am happy to help."

Whatever their initial intentions, the team followed the coffee with a twenty-month effort to penetrate the marble walls, showing no concern for any privacy the nine needed as they struggled with such national issues as abortion, the death penalty, pornography and also press freedom. One of the team's first requests came from a new Aide, Benjamin Weiser: the names of every law clerk who had served in the first years of the Burger Court, the late 1960s and the early 1970s. It was a starter, Weiser said. He would be back for more. Eventually the team sought out every clerk of the first seven Burger years.

Law clerks are asked to preserve the confidences of the chambers during the year or so each serves, and to be discreet after that. Each Justice and their clerks operate as a little law firm, each coping separately with the thousands of new cases flooding into the Court each year. Usually a tight family relationship develops, an alumni association is formed and many Justices dine each year in reunions with their old clerks.

With that background it was up to each Justice to decide whether to give Weiser the requested list. Some agreed. The clerks were paid by public funds and thus were part of the public record. Others refused. The clerks were part of the process of justice and not to be interviewed. Weiser picked up the proffered lists, and soon scores of former law clerks were approached by the inquiring team.

Some clerks turned off the inquirers with no ado. Justices in their Opinions state what and why they decide, or why they dissent. The public record spread through hundreds of volumes of Supreme Court decisions, is copious. Nothing more could be said appropriately.

Others slipped into the visitors' trap. Armstrong, in a candid interview later with Tamar Lewin of the *National Law Journal*, told how it was done: "My usual scenario is to get some idea of the situation and then go around asking people if my version of things is right.

"But on this book, we used Bob's method more. We asked people a lot of broad questions, and they gave very general answers. Then we'd say, 'Prove it to me! Show me what you mean!' And they would begin to give us specific stories and examples."

Armstrong added that various of those interviewed had "different ideas about what was confidential." Some, he said, felt that "as long as they did not tell what the Justice said to them, it was all right." Putting two and two together after that enabled the inquirers to come up with their impression of what might have happened.

Several of the Justices consented to talk to the team. In their view the Court has no great secret, the end product placed on the public record is detailed.

Others thought it inappropriate. One such was the Chief Justice. Woodward asked for "five minutes to five hours" with him. He got no interview.

Many of the scores of persons approached by Woodward could not resist seeing him. Thanks to his presidential exposé, he was himself a personality portrayed glamorously in the movies by the ruggedly handsome Robert Redford. It was often a question of who was interviewing whom.

Four months into their effort the "noninvestigators" had documents to induce reluctant witnesses to speak up. Some ex-clerks reported seeing in the hands of the callers a variety of internal Court papers, including an early draft of a Byron White Opinion on the return of the long-suspended death penalty. With evidence that others had surrendered so much, and perhaps with concern that a clerk's own Justice be portrayed in a favorable light, more testimony and documents flowed to the inquisitors. By the time the book was written, Court papers in the hands of the team filled several file drawers. Included was the jackpot, Justice Brennan's private diaries on the back-and-forth among Justices as decisions were made.

It was not just the law clerks and some Justices who interested the interrogators. No fry were too small. When Joey Waddy drove Burger to a downtown hotel meeting, Woodward asked him for an interview.

One woman on the Court staff who had served along with Armstrong as a consultant on a government project was asked, friend to friend, for a list of the Justices' social contacts. To her, Armstrong was hardly a friend, rather a mere casual acquaintance. Was it her caller's idea that Justices' friends influence Court decisions? she wondered. She provided no names.

A former Secretary of Justice Douglas was phoned in New York. How were relations of the ailing, aged Justice with his young fourth wife, Cathy? How about dinner, she and her husband, with an "unlimited expense account" available to grab the tab? Shocked, the woman declined.

One year into the investigation there were no remaining illusions about what the team was up to. A former high Central Intelligence Agency official, sharing a TV program with Woodward, was appalled at what he heard the writer say. What had been called an exploration into Washington decision making was zeroing in on the Court alone.

"You have trouble coming up on your left bow," the former officer warned a Court friend.

With mounting evidence that a flood of internal Court documentation was flowing to the writers, the Court faced a problem. Ought the FBI be called in? There was no agreement. Justice Stewart, for one, held strongly to the principle that although government had no constitutional requirement to surrender internal documents, the media in the spirit of the First Amendment had the right to seek what they could find. The FBI stayed out.

Twenty months into the project, the sarcastically titled *The Brethren* was published. Far from loving brothers, the Justices were depicted variously as lazy, overly aggressive or otherwise unattractive gossips and backbiters. But nothing said about the eight Associates compared with the vituperation heaped on the head of the government's third branch, the privacy-minded Chief Justice who may have been from the beginning the designated victim. He appeared as a conceited fool.

The Book of the Month Club took *The Brethren* as its choice for December 1979 at the height of the Christmas book sales. Six hundred thousand copies of the book were soon in print. *The New York Times* listed the volume as a best seller for the next half year. Hundreds of newspapers ran excerpts. The Court PIO was deluged with requests for comment, but the Court said nothing. Woodward said later that the silence was a disappointment. He had hoped the Chief Justice would attempt to block publication by Court action. The Court sitting in judgment on its own case! The spectacle could well have found a place in the history books. The big first press run would have been only a beginning.

Others interested in magnifying the scandal may have been thinking along the same line. A man in New York phoned the office of Mark Cannon, the Chief Justice's Administrative Assistant, and dictated for the Chief Justice:

> If the facts in *The Brethren* are untrue or open to serious question, it respectfully behooves you to file a defense or designate a responsible advocate to speak for you and the Court.
>
> The sanctity of this bedrock institution must not be allowed to tarnish or crumble. Your silence may cast a shadow to give consent or acquiesce to the facts contained in the book.

It was an interesting gambit, however disguised may have been the caller's motivation, but whatever "facts"—and not mere character assassination—and whichever preliminary Court documents were contained in the volume, there is a judicial tradition against responding to criticism. The caller's suggestion was ignored.

Lawyers instead, responding to a legal tradition, spoke for the pilloried Justices. Leonard S. Janofsky, president of the American Bar Association, was one. He made a point repeated in a dozen law review articles and in book reviews that the team had found no smoking gun, no evidence that the Chief Justice or any other member of the High Bench had done anything wrong or even unusual. There would be no jail terms for Justices, no impeachments, no resignations. The ballyhooed sequel to the White House's Watergate revelations, however roughly it handled the persons of the Justices, had ended up, curiously, even as a tribute to the Court's integrity.

Janofsky asked the two writers what Court changes they would recommend on the basis of their unprecedented study. None, they said.

Woodward went even further in the *National Law Journal* interview: "You could certainly argue that what we found out was that the Court works, that it comes to the right conclusions. The votes are not for sale. In the one lobbying incident, the lobbyist was thrown out."

Armstrong seconded that in another interview: "Had there been Presidents intervening in the Court, had there been lawyers up there lobbying and passing envelopes with money, there's no question in my mind that we would have found it. It just doesn't happen."

How then should such a project be judged?

D. Grier Stephenson Jr., an Associate Professor of Law at Franklin and Marshall College, offered an answer in the *Brooklyn Law Review: "The Brethren* is to the Supreme Court what pornography is to love; it excludes some vital aspects."

The inquest proved that, with sufficient resources, energy, nerve and guile, the Supreme Court's security could be breached, but it left unaddressed why the Court should not be allowed some reticence as it serves the cause of justice.

❧ CHAPTER 5 ❧
DRIBLETS

While the Niagara of *The Brethren* washed over the Court, producing little more than the embarrassing picture of tired jurists passing occasional harsh judgments on one another, it was the small leaks across the years that much troubled the security-minded Justices. These were the premature announcements of Court decisions.

Conscious that when there is, for example, an *IBM v. Telex* case, billions of dollars can go to speculators with early information, the Justices through history have guarded knowledge of their decisions until the moment when everyone was informed at the same time.

From 1891 to 1946 a midtown Washington printer, Clarence E. Bright, was a keeper of the secrets. It was in the olden days of printing when the man in charge wore a derby as his insignia of office, a sign that he was special, that "he could read." Bright would divide up the Court Opinions, their decisions, among several printers, so that no one could get a coherent idea of just what Oliver Wendell Holmes, Charles Evans Hughes, Louis D. Brandeis, ex-President William Howard Taft, Benjamin N. Cardozo, Hugo L. Black, Felix Frankfurter, William O. Douglas and their confreres had to say. For extra insurance Bright would set type himself for the concluding and crucial part of each Opinion. Only he had a rounded idea of what was to come down in the Courtroom, then inside the Capitol Building. And he would never say.

The Justices were so appreciative of Bright's half century of custodianship of the confidences that Chief Justice Frederick M. Vinson thanked him from the bench at the conclusion of his labors. The Chief's words are inscribed for all history to see on page ix, volume 329 of the *United States Reports.*

For a century and a half, back to 1845, the Bright shop and its predecessors had the Court's business but, as World War II ended, Bright closed down the enterprise and the Justices decided to open their own print shop in their then new temple on Capitol Hill. Bright had done well, but presumably even greater security could be assured inside a building guarded by the Court's own scores of police officers.

Linotype hot-metal machines were moved into the basement to set type in the equivalent of a small-town newspaper shop. Presses capable of turning out eight thousand pages an hour were installed. As Justices drafted and redrafted Opinions, a seven-man team, recruited from the Government Printing Office, turned out Bench Opinions (the initial run intended for distribution to reporters and others on decision days), and Slip Opinions (for use by lawyers for a year or so until issuance of additions to the *United States Reports,* the series of books carrying Court actions). All three, including the *United States Reports,* were struck from the same type except for occasional nit-picking of typos and similar small errors.

The effort to keep the secrets was so intense that the concept of "need to know" not only excluded the PIO until the very morning of decision when he received seventy sets of the bench Opinions an hour before release, but it also cut out the Reporter of Decisions, the lawyer on the Court staff who writes a three- or four-page summary of each decision for inclusion in the bound volumes.

The Reporter of Decisions's summary, known as the *syllabus,* or head notes, was a godsend to attorneys looking years later for quick analyses of old cases, but was un-available to journalists with their instant deadlines.

One of the first reforms in media relations placed in effect by the press-conscious Burger when he took over at the end of the 1960s, was to take the Reporter of Decisions into the inner circle, letting him see the decisions a day or two beforehand, so that the syllabus could appear on the Bench Opinions.

Some old-timers on the bench questioned the new Chief about help for what they considered the pestiferous media, but Burger had an answer for them. The change was made not for the benefit of the reporters, he insisted, but rather for the good of the Court and the public's understanding of Court decisions. Horrendous mistakes had been made on occasion as reporters attempted split-second interpretations of hundreds of simultaneously released pages.

Few could argue effectively against the change, but it meant one more group of potential leakers. Now there were more than two score people in the know, the Reporter's staff as well as the twenty or thirty young law clerks, the dozen secretaries of the Justices, the half dozen printers in the basement and the Justices themselves. All were deserving of trust and few ever failed in that, but periodically, to the consternation of Justices, there were premature disclosures.

David Beckwith, then of *Time* magazine and later the Press Officer for Vice President Dan Quayle, scored a scoop on the nation-shaking 1973 *Roe v. Wade* abortion decision. Little was made of the exclusive, however, for the decision came down just a few hours after Dave's weekly hit the newsstands. Scoops need a period of exclusivity if they are to ring award-winning bells. It was still enough, however, to attract pained, although brief, attention from the bench.

A scoop that never happened did get wide publicity, however. On June 6, 1981, Fred Barbash, then *The Washington Post* man on the Supreme Court beat, published a seven-inch-long story under a two-column headline: "Supreme Court Apparently Springs a Leak."

Fred's account was that young Betsy Olsen, the recently arrived Chief of the United Press International bureau, had information on the Court's unannounced decision in *County of Washington v. Alberto Gunther.* Four former jail matrons in Oregon had sued on the basis of the 1964 Civil Rights Act saying that it was unfair that their male colleagues got more pay for guarding men than the women took home for supervising female convicts.

Was Betsy's information right? How did she get it? What would UPI do with the scoop? These were the questions.

There was scant doubt about the accuracy of Betsy's information. It was a secret beginning to surface. The decision had been in type in the basement print shop for fifteen days or so. Copy for the syllabus had reached the printers June 4 and, as well as the printers could recollect, the headnote was in print twenty-four hours later, the day Barbash went to his typewriter to report what Betsy had.

There had been a party in the building that day with reporters attending. Had Betsy by some accident stumbled on the syllabus? Was that the explanation rather than it being a tip from a Court employee? More important, would UPI, a beneficiary of a transmission booth in the Court press area, a privilege shared only by the AP, choose to beat the Justices on their own story?

Betsy had assured Barbash she would "file" her beat, but Grant Dillman, the UPI Vice President in charge of Washington coverage, decided otherwise—to the PIO's relief. It was Betsy's job to offer material to the wire; it was his to determine what went out to clients, Dillman said. UPI's policy, he added, was to have two sources on a scoop; what Betsy had was one, however impressive.

Betty Wells's portrait of Barrett McGurn handing out decisions to the press corps. On a typical decision day, a half dozen case verdicts would be released in a thirty-minute period. McGurn would have stacks of each decision facedown on his desk, awaiting a call relayed from the bench that the Chief Justice had announced a release; within seconds, the decisions were distributed. Rarely was there a last-minute change of mind, but when that happened it was up to McGurn to make sure that none of the prepared copies was leaked. Also in the illustration are Tim O'Brien of ABC (second from left in the foreground), *Carl Stern of NBC* (to Tim's right, with his right arm outstretched) *and Charlotte Moulton of UPI, one of the pioneer women in the Court's press corps* (speed reading opinion in the middle right foreground.) Betty Wells.

For the news community it raised a peculiar question and UPI, to its discomfort, found itself center stage in a different story. If a news agency has information of public interest should it not publish it? Is not that some sort of corollary to constitutional freedom of the press? Now interrogated instead of interrogating, UPI put a terse advisory to editors on its wires: "There will be no story at this time."

The agency held back, the weekend passed, the decision came down, everyone got the same story at the same time and there was no scoop.

In addition to the question of whether it was worthwhile to frustrate the Court's efforts to preserve confidentiality, there was also the fact that a news organization that scoops the Court has to tell the story a second time when the decision comes down. There is nothing new—there is no news—in a twice-told tale.

If that was UPI's reasoning, it was a view not shared by some others in the media. National Public Radio's Nina Totenberg and American Broadcasting Company's Tim O'Brien provided examples.

NPR opened its airwaves to Nina, an assiduous cultivator of friendships with Court secretaries and even an occasional Justice, when she came up with a one-day scoop in 1977 on the Court's refusal to hear appeals from the jail-threatened Watergate defendants, former Attorney General John N. Mitchell and Presidential Aide H. R. Haldeman.

Far more scalding was a series of leaks poured from the hot transmitters of ABC in spring 1979. They were the work of thirty-five-year-old O'Brien, a personable product of New Orleans television, a newcomer to the ABC network, and a more recent addition to the Court's press corps.

Tim went before the ABC cameras on April 16 with the startling announcement that Byron White, over some opposition from Justice John Paul Stevens, would rule for the Court that journalists could be interrogated about their mind set when sued for libel. It was the case of *Herbert v. Lando.*

Tim said that emotions had run so high as the Justices hammered out their decision that shouts were heard coming from their closed Conference Room. The detail added plausibility but was unlikely. Two oaken doors separate the Justices' discussion room from a corridor, and a police officer stands guard there, allowing no loitering. Were there such outcries in that or any other case?

Not in the memory of at least one Justice. "All you ever hear around that table," he said, "is someone asking, 'Will you please speak up!' "

Thirty-six hours after Tim climbed out on his limb with his forecast, the decision came down. Stevens was on White's side, not against him, but the core of the verdict was exactly what Tim had foretold. His source was good.

A day after the first scoop Tim had another. He said that Chief Justice Burger had written a decision for the Court limiting prisoner rights in parole hearings. It was the case of *Greenholtz v. Nebraska Inmates.* This time Tim had no immediate confirmation. *Greenholtz* did not come down. Tim's listeners would have to wait to see how close he was to the truth.

There was no Court comment of what might have delayed *Greenholtz,* but it was the Chief's option, as it was that of each of the Associates, to postpone a release as long as he wished. Tim had to wait on that one, but soon he was on the air with a total of six exclusive predictions, generally correct. Five came in April and May of 1979. The first, with limited Court notice, had been at the end of the previous term. It was in the case of the *University of California Regents v. Bakke.*

Allan Bakke, a white, had sued, charging reverse racial discrimination, because he had been turned down for admission to medical school to make room, he said, for a less qualified black.

Colleges and universities were alarmed, fearing riots either by whites or blacks, whichever group lost. It was the colleges' hope that the Justices would not announce a decision before the final late spring days of the term when campuses would be relatively empty. Tim brought good news to the worried officials of academia, *Bakke* would be delayed until the end of June. He was on target. The decision was announced on June 28. Tim alone had known.

What attracted the Justices' appalled attention was the string of O'Brien exclusives as the 1978 term wound down. No longer a mere question of dates for release, content was involved. The first in Tim's series was an action by William H. Rehnquist, the future Chief Justice. He granted a stay in an Alabama death case. Tim was the only one to know.

Next, with the media especially interested in *Gannett v. De Pasquale,* Tim alone told his watchers what the Court would do. The public, including the media, could be excluded from pretrial hearings in criminal cases to avoid prejudicing the future trial. Potter Stewart would be the author of the Opinion. On July 2 *Gannett* was handed down precisely in the way Tim had foretold.

Justices and reporters alike were astonished. How was Tim doing it? What should be done?

Morton Mintz, *The Washington Post*'s prize–winning Court correspondent, challenged the PIO: Protect your secrets. We have all we can do to study five thousand cases a year, and to report on two hundred decisions. If the leaks keep up, we will have to try to match them. Our job is already all but impossible and will be twice as difficult.

Justices were even more upset. Chief Justice Burger estimated that Tim's enterprises cost him in May "not less than twenty hours on my personal schedule." Those May hours, he lamented, were "worth twice as much as hours in any other month." It was the end of the term crunch when all the toughest cases came down and all the hardest-fought backs-and-forths took place.

What was Tim's secret as he breached the Court's privacy? One of the Court police remembered seeing Tim late one evening in the upper floor Court library; it was three hours after the official closing of the building. During regular work hours a half dozen reporters a week were accustomed to ask for permission to use the library for research, and the PIO routinely granted that. Late hour use of the library was different. Barriers on the lower floors kept unescorted reporters as well as the general public out of sensitive areas such as the corridors of the Justices' chambers, but the library was a security sieve: side exits led to otherwise closed areas. Should the press henceforth be allowed into the library only under escort? Would that be overreaction?

At least one of the middle-of-the-road Justices did indeed feel that the escort idea was excessive. He pointed out that the one hundred thousand lawyers who were members of the Supreme Court bar had free use of the library and remarked: "I could name some members of our bar whom I think are far less trustworthy than the regular reporters here.

"To be sure, they are not as frequently in the building, but when they elect to come apparently we presume that they are less likely to breach confidentiality than the members of the media whom we accredit."

The Justice's calming counsel was accepted. Draconian limitations on the media use of the library were headed off, but then the question was whether to cut down the hours during which reporters could occupy the press area. The resident correspondents appealed against any limitations. They cited the White House where the press area is open twenty-four hours a day. Some reporters of AP, UPI, *The New York Times,* the then *Washington Star* and the *Chicago Tribune* were accustomed to work well into the evenings and also on Saturdays and Sundays when the building was closed to the public. Shortened hours would involve a severe handicap for them as they read deep piles of briefs and took notes on issues awaiting decision. Sharply reduced press access hours were pondered but then set aside for a token change: The press area was closed merely in the wee hours after 10 P.M. and, when needed, exceptions would be granted even for that. Weekends remained open.

Still undetermined was how Tim had done it. He had been seen chatting with one of the printers, John Tucci, an amiable extrovert who seemed to enjoy all human contacts, including those with reporters and such celebrities as TV correspondents. Could the printing operation, after an almost uniformly successful century of confidentiality, have become a leaky faucet?

Chief Justice Burger, whose duties included oversight of the Court staff and building, called Tucci to his chambers. Had he been talking to newspeople? Tucci, a former printer for the breezy *Washington Daily News,* later filled in Lyle Denniston of the *Star* on what occurred: "I told the Chief Justice that I had done that all of my life. But there is no proof, there is no particular way, he can prove that (I) was the leak." Tucci was returned to the Government Printing Office with no further action. Did this leave a cloud over the print shop?

Not obviously nor immediately, but within the next few years the Court found an alternate way to print its Opinions. The print shop was closed and law clerks, secretaries and Justices did preliminary work on computer terminals in the chambers with a high-tech "publications unit" completing the process.

Extensive computerization had been a Burger innovation. When he took over from Earl Warren he had been amazed to find that carbon paper in the tradition-minded Court was still the duplication system of choice. The unlucky Justice who received the eighth copy needed good eyesight.

The Court's entrance into the age of the computer was cautious and deliberate but sustained. Four years into the Burger period, in 1973, a Wang computer was moved into the Clerk's office to handle form letters; young Linda Blandford was in charge. When Linda moved to the Powell chambers as a Secretary three years later she made a place for herself in Court history by preaching the computer gospel. She convinced her Justice to try a terminal for the drafting of Opinions.

By 1983, and a million dollars later, the Court had seventy-one terminals. Two of the Justices—White and Stevens—had their own. The print shop vanished. The circle of those in the know about Court intentions was reduced.

That left the question of the rights and wrongs of Tim's scoops. Not just the Court, but many in the media debated that. The Court's view was that no public purpose is served by allowing penetration of the decisional process. The reason for secrecy in financial cases where speculators could profit was easiest to understand. If one type of information could leak so could others. This had been taken for granted since the Court's first years. Examples were provided by the cases of *Gibbons v. Ogden* in 1824 and *Charles River Bridge v. the Warren Bridge* in 1837. *Gibbons v. Ogden* in the judgment of Justice Arthur Goldberg (1952–1965), was the foundation for America's prosperous common market, a monumental John Marshall achievement. It would also have been a gold mine for traders had they been able to divine Marshall's intentions beforehand.

At the heart of the case was the fact that New York State, euphoric about Robert Fulton's invention of the steamboat, had given him a monopoly on navigable waters including bustling New York Harbor. When Fulton's rights passed to Aaron Ogden, a suit for equal access was brought by a rival steamshipper, Thomas Gibbons, who wisely hired the eloquent Daniel Webster as his Attorney. Marshall's Court gave Webster the nod and the flourishing New York bay was opened to all steamers. Gibbons's backers could have cut losses, and shareholders in rival steamship ventures could have hiked their investments if either could have known the upshot in advance. None did either. No one had pried into Marshall's secret.

Charles River Bridge v. the Warren Bridge, the first great Taney Court decision, struck another blow at trade-limiting monopolies and was also a potential fortune-builder for those who could get advance information.

In Massachusetts a 1,503-foot toll bridge had been built in 1789 across the Charles River, linking Boston's Prince Street with Charlestown. Fat fees poured in for years until the Taney Court allowed construction of a second span nearby. Holders of Charles River Bridge stock could have dumped shares on unwary buyers had they been tipped off in time.

While the Court was upset by leaks so were some in the media. PIO staffers were surprised one day to hear angry voices raised in the adjacent press room, a place normally as quiet as a library as writers pondered lawyers' briefs. A scoop-seeker was in a heated exchange with one of the reporters who felt that coverage should be limited to what the Justices released.

"Don't talk behind my back!" demanded the would-be scooper.

"Then I'll tell it to your face," was the answer.

"You're the Justices' pet!"

"I'm no one's pet!"

It was a nose-to-nose exchange just short of violence, and it reflected what some elder members of the media were saying in print in more measured phrases.

An example was provided by James "Scotty" Reston of *The New York Times* who used his column to decry the O'Brien exclusives as "obviously (serving) no public interest and (as) a drop of poison in the whole democratic process."

Carl Stern of NBC-TV, a competitor scooped by Tim, protested in the May 7, 1979, issue of *Broadcasting Magazine* that "the journalistically unprincipled use of unverified, peripheral sources to claim knowledge of the Court's deliberations ... was valueless and degrading conduct of a type long resisted by most news agencies."

In the *Columbia Journalism Review,* David M. Rubin, a New York University journalism teacher, agreed with Stern:

> Admittedly it would have been a difficult decision for [George] Watson [the ABC Washington bureau chief] and O'Brien and [Dick] Wald [the ABC vice president for news] to add their Court stories to the pile of excluded material, given the penchant for the "scoop."
>
> But this would have been a decision in the best interests of the profession and the Court. The stories are unworthy of ABC's efforts to improve its image as a respected source of television news.

Wald and Watson backed up O'Brien and rejected the criticisms. Said Wald: "The Court is composed of men who have great power over our lives. ... That such power has gone unexamined except on the Court's terms is not in the best interests of the public."

Watson took a similar line in a letter to *The Times* objecting to Reston's piece. He wrote:

> What is the public harm, and where is the poison? ... I hope that publishers and broadcasters alike regard their basic responsibility to be reporting the news not gauging the public interest.
>
> I am very uncomfortable with the notion that the press and the courts should work together in common pursuit. We do not shrink from an adversary relationship with other branches of government. If Mr. Reston believes that the Supreme Court is entitled to a privileged position, the burden is on him to explain why one journalistic standard should apply to its proceedings while a different one applies everywhere else.

It has been true that in the waning years of the twentieth century there has been an adversary relationship between much of the media on the one hand and the White House and Congress on the other. The Supreme Court has missed much of that, but there have been enough pinpricks of many different kinds to maintain a fairly high level of irritation among the Justices.

CHAPTER 6

ADVERSARIES

In news rooms there was a saying among cub reporters that they had a twofold mission: to comfort the afflicted and afflict the comfortable. At the Supreme Court, as Justices studied the media, the flip side of that point of view was expressed this way: A whisper here is a shout! Each translated into a Court-media relationship that is often adversarial.

One reason is that news can be described with a mathematical formula: If the perpetrator is otherwise insignificant, it is still news if the offense is sufficiently horrendous. Conversely, if the person or institution is eminent, it is news if a toe is stubbed or even if it appears to be stubbed.

The three-room press area on the northwest corner of the ground floor of the Court building is usually tranquil as reporters pore over briefs, but it is a false calm, for three powerful elements of the American democracy collide there; the Court, the media and public opinion. For the Court's Public Information Officer, it means that a cautious choice of words is crucial.

This was borne out in the 1970s when the Court's new PIO was asked about an unpublicized rejection of an application for membership in the one-hundred-thousand-member Court bar, the corps of lawyers who may bring cases to the high tribunal. A state Judge had resigned at a time when impeachment seemed possible. The Justices refused him entry into their bar, but the Court spared him renewed embarrassment by treating the matter as just one of the flood of details that are handled each day without publicity. Then news of the incident leaked, and the PIO was asked to explain the "cover-up." In an indiscreet moment there was a clumsy, generalized reply: "Not everything that goes on here is made public. It is public business, but that doesn't mean it will become public knowledge."

Thousands of small details are worked on each day with all the main conclusions ultimately published, but The Associated Press jumped at the ungraceful quote, giving it nationwide publicity. It earned a scorching letter from Tucson, Arizona:

> Your appallingly arrogant remark ... is an outrageous attitude to take in our democracy which is dying because of men like you and men like the justices. ...
>
> There is hardly a shred of respect for or confidence in the judiciary left in this country, and then you have to go and make a snotty crack like that to the Sovereign American People, whose servants you and the justices all are.

It was a PIO shout when it should have been a whisper.

The Court's media clients run a gamut as broad as that of the media itself, some scrupulously accurate and fair, some sensational, others muckraking and what might be called simply fun-loving twisters of the judicial tail.

Cartoonists were among those who enjoyed themselves at the expense of the Court, often distorting grotesquely what were really only slight modifications of the national law.

An example was offered by a series of cartoons in 1979 commenting on several tightly limited rulings on malicious libel and on privacy for early-stage court hearings. The Washington Post's brilliant but acerbic Pulitzer Prize–winning cartoonist,

Herblock, published two sketches, one on April 20, labeled "breaking and entering," showing a black-garbed Justice stealing off with the Bill of Rights, and another on July 6 depicting a snarling Burger and his accomplice and successor, Rehnquist, stripping a shirtless citizen of an array of rights including protection against false imprisonment and secret trials, and defense against "search and snoop operations."

In the *Chicago Sun-Times,* John Fischetti limned a scowling Justice tipping the scales of justice against the "citizens' right to know," portrayed as a dismayed young couple locked in a bird cage.

The same daily on May 24 ran a Bill Mauldin cartoon showing a sinister but delighted Richard Nixon gloating over a headline: "U.S. Supreme Court hits media malice; Nixon appointees unanimous as usual."

Exaggeration for effect is a traditional right of cartoonists, but reporters, too, were sometimes tempted to emphasize the negative for the sake of readability. Errors and controversy in high places make news, and one reporter who covered the Court off and on explained one day how he went about his coverage of a decision: "First, I read the summary. Then I go to the dissents."

In the making was one more negative story playing up the objectors: Look what that Court has done now!

One provocative and perhaps tongue-in-cheek view of how the Supreme Court should be covered was expressed by Lyle Denniston, of the *Baltimore Sun,* the senior member of the Court press corps in the 1990s. In a telecast, he said, "As a journalist I have only one responsibility, and that is to get a story and print it." Lyle was asked how he went about gathering information. Would he steal it?

"Exactly," was the blithe reply. "And hopefully without [the possessor of the information] knowing it," he added.

"It isn't a question of justifying it in terms of the law. It's a question of justifying it in terms of the commercial sale of information to interested customers. That's my business. That's the only thing I do in life is to sell information, hopefully for a profit."

Many newspapers such as *The New York Times,* the *Los Angeles Times* and the *Chicago Tribune* covered the Court in sober detail, trying to explain Court actions methodically inside space limitations, while others swooped in with an occasional crusade. One such single issue campaign was conducted at a one-thousand-mile range by the *Des Moines Register and Tribune* in 1980. On June 11 the paper ran a large headline: "U. S. Supreme Court and the Stock Market: Injudicious Investments." Other headlines followed: September 12, "Justice Powell's Promise." September 13, "Cloud Over High Court." December 3, "Silence by the Court."

What had triggered the paper was an antitrust lawsuit brought by a local Nebraska manufacturer of disposable plastic gloves, Handguards, Inc. Target of the suit was Ethicon, Inc. A local federal District Court found for Handguards, awarding the company $2,073,000, but the regional United States Court of Appeals overruled, ordering a retrial.

Handguards appealed to the Supreme Court, but there were not the required four votes needed to accept the matter as one of the two hundred main national issues to be decided that year. Handguards and Ethicon went on the Court's "dead list," and Des Moines's hope for an infusion of two million Ethicon dollars faded.

What would normally be the end of the matter was just a beginning. Gil Cranberg, the *Register's* editorial writer, did not take the hometown defeat lightly. He started an investigation.

Ethicon, it turned out, was a wholly owned subsidiary of Johnson & Johnson, Inc. Two of the wealthier members of the Supreme Court, Potter Stewart and Lewis Powell and the wives of the two, had large diversified portfolios including some shares of Johnson & Johnson. The editorial writer had a blizzard of questions and suggestions for the Court PIO and for the readers of his page: Did the two Justices realize that Ethicon was owned by Johnson & Johnson? Did they "recuse," refusing to vote on the case since their own financial fortunes were benefited in no matter how insignificant a way by the Handguards turndown? In effect, were there three votes to hear the case, a controlling number with only seven voting?

Inquiries and recommendations went on: Why don't the Justices announce it when they recuse? Why don't they explain recusals? Why don't they and their spouses get out of the stock market altogether?

A short answer to the questions was that the nine Justices were close to the limits of human possibilities just deciding 150 to 200 cases a year and explaining themselves in Opinions. There was no time to go into the details of why each of the thousands of rejected cases were shunted aside each year.

As for family investments, most of the Justices lived middle-class lives. A handful had small fortunes, some of it inherited, some earned in earlier private practice. Each year each Justice made a public disclosure of his assets and income. Should further penalties be exacted as the price for public service?

Although few could have believed that a Justice would decide a case based on the fact that he owned a few shares of a company that might indirectly be affected, one Burger Court Justice did respond to the *Des Moines Register* campaign by going to further lengths to fend off suspicions. He had little knowledge of what was in the family portfolio and even less about what companies were subsidiaries. Before mounting the bench he had sold every stock in firms under governmental regulation. Now he obtained a list of every stock and subsidiary. He gave it to his clerks and secretaries, instructing them to flag to him every case concerning anyone on the list. However remote they might be, he would have no conflict of interest.

Unsatisfied, the *Register* editorial writer took his campaign to the pages of the bible of American lawyers, the *American Bar Association Journal*, decrying in the headline: "A Supreme Court of Secrecy." Not all the *Journal's* readers went along with him. P. Rowland Greenwade, for one, in a letter to the editor expressed it: "Cranberg sums up his article in one sentence:

" 'In the absence of disclosure of reasons for recusal, the public can only speculate ... .' " Greenwade commented:

> I would not discount the value to our society of an inquiring press; however, that does not relieve it of certain responsibilities not only for those it writes for, but also those it writes about. Cranberg's article is just one more sordid example of a style of journalism that espouses the theory that any officer of the government is out to deceive and defraud the public for his own private advantage. I reject that logic and repudiate the conclusion.

While Cranberg might be faulted for concluding too much from too little, he was not alone in arguing that it was in the public interest to have more information about the Court. The usually thoughtful columnist Ellen Goodman did a piece on that: "The Court Needs a Much Closer Look."

She wrote: "If the sort of massive social issues raised in Court cases were to be decided in one of the other top levels of government—Congress or the White House—there would be a full, elaborate public investigation of the process of decision making and the lives of the decision makers."

Instead, Ms. Goodman protested, "The robed justices are rarely even defrocked in photographs." The reference was to the often stiff group photo of the black-clad jurists taken when membership changed.

While Ms. Goodman said she did not favor combing through Justices' garbage or bugging their Conference, she did think that a "bit of demythologizing was in order." The country did not need awe of the Court bred by ignorance but rather respect induced by understanding. Justices made no reply, but one objected privately that the Court's Opinions, concurrences and dissents tell far more about what the nine do and why than any legislation reflects Congress's inner workings.

Despite exceptions, most of the regulars on the Court beat maintained an amiable although usually distant and infrequent relationship with the Justices. Occasionally there were social receptions. Some members of the bench would receive journalists in their chambers explaining such things as reasons for recusals, which typically were previous association with litigants.

Always out of bounds was discussion of issues facing judgment. That went not just for reporters but with all acquaintances. Chief Justice Burger, for one, had a ready ploy when conversations drifted into white-capped waters. "Oh, by the way," he would interrupt. "Have you seen the new exhibits we have at the Court ? You must see them!" Few missed the point. They did not attempt to return to the previous topic.

Rarely did the inherent adversarial relationship provoke an incident, but there was one early in the Burger period. At the end of a hearing, as the Justices and audience stood up, a news wire reporter kept his seat. One of the police on regular duty in the Courtroom demanded that the journalist show respect by getting to his feet, and he did.

Had the reporter meant a subtle reminder to the Justices that they, too, were mere citizens? Or was he oblivious, engrossed in his note taking, as he told the officer? Neither was clear, but as the Courtroom police watched the reporter for any repetition there was none.

Among the most persistent of the Court's "adversaries" was Jack Anderson with his one thousand subscribing newspapers and his American Broadcasting Company newscasts. For many across the land, at least until the proliferation of TV newscasts, Jack was a main source of impressions on how the national government worked or failed to function. Jack was a specialist in exposing governmental mischief and seemed fascinated by the Court. His ear was to the ground for whispers that could be shouts. His staff of reporters kept the PIO busy.

One query concerned whether Justice Stewart had misused government personnel and property. A Court policeman on the night shift had been dispatched on some sort of midnight mission. What was that about? The Justice's son had fallen ill and was arriving at that hour, three blocks away, at the Union railroad station. Using one of the few Court cars, the officer gave the ailing youth a lift home.

No "shout." The column lost interest.

On another occasion Anderson did come up with a column. This concerned Ed Douglas, the Court's gifted and dedicated full-time Carpenter and Cabinetmaker. The columnist found Ed guilty of using what the Cabinetmaker insisted was scrap lumber on a dock he was building at his Colonial Beach, Virginia, home. Anderson had other particulars. He said that when Justice Brennan put in wall-to-wall carpeting Ed shaved the bottom of doors that could no longer close.

Other Justices, the columnist said, had bookshelves installed in their apartments. It smacked, the columnist seemed to feel, like some sort of scandal. Justices did, on occasion, pay staff handymen for off-hour chores at their homes, and there was a century-old tradition of helping Justices with household law libraries, but the Court went into no details with the columnist. With what he had, Anderson made a piece of it.

The principal Court object of Anderson's interest and scorn was Warren Burger, whom he saw as a foe of news gathering and one who was "rigidly conservative, obsessively secretive, pompous, condescending, manipulative and possessed of a hair trigger temper." Hours of time went into coping with the columnist's queries, and he was not always happy with the answers. Extracting what he wanted from the Court's PIO, he complained to his readers, was like "pulling teeth from a rhinoceros."

The oddest example of the adversarial relationship was when Mike Wallace, the investigative reporter for CBS's *60 Minutes,* was himself in the Supreme Court dock. It was the same case of *Herbert v. Lando,* on which Tim O'Brien scored his clamorous scoop. Mike, as narrator, and his producer, Barry Lando, were sued for $44 million for defamation by ex-Colonel Anthony Herbert who had been the target of an eighteen-minute *60 Minutes* segment on February 3, 1973. Herbert had attracted wide publicity, charging his superiors in the American forces in Vietnam with concealment of atrocities. The telecast gave the former officer the lie.

Also in the Court pipeline awaiting decision were two other CBS cases: *Broadcast Music Inc. v. CBS* and *American Society of Composers, Authors and Publishers v. CBS,* the latter a multimillion dollar issue with Ira Gershwin, Gian Carlo Menotti, Virgil Thomson, Sammy Cahn and Eubie Blake among the petitioners.

Investigator Mike was more accustomed to judge than to be judged, and he saw no reason to treat this new situation differently. Nine days before his lawyers appeared in the well before the Justices to plead his case, Mike phoned the Court PIO to invite the Chief Justice to step before his cameras to air his views on freedom of the press. Mike's tone was smooth and pleasant, but the answer was no. The outer limits of press freedom was at the heart of the case the nine Justices would be weighing.

Mike was undeterred. A month after the Court hearing, with Justices busy on their Opinions in his case, Mike tried again, this time in a letter to Burger. "Specific matters" before the Court (such as his own case, one could presume), would not be raised, he assured the Chief Justice, but why, he went on, should not the American people get to know more about the man who presided over the highest Court? Mike could not deliver all the American people, but he could come close; his audience was forty-four million.

The Justices compared notes over lunch. Each had received a similar letter, and one of the nine agreed to talk to Mike. A gentleman of gracious manner, he found it difficult not to engage in civil conversation with anyone with a claim on his time.

Another had an opposite view. He remembered what had happened to Justice Brennan when an uninvited visitor had raised with him the case of the *Utah Public Service Commission v. the El Paso Natural Gas Company.* Although Brennan's own involvement was only momentary and wholly innocent, his scruples were such that he gave up his vote in the case. The remembering Justice was determined not to compromise his own vote in the CBS matter.

If most of the Justices would not talk, others would. The Wallace team fanned across the country. Even the Chief Justice's Messenger, Alvin Wright, met a blizzard of questions: Which Chief Justice did you find better, Earl Warren or Warren Burger? What does Burger have for breakfast? Does he ever fuss with his wife? Is he rude with secretaries? What are his moods?

Wright, new to national TV attention, assured the inquirers that his regard for his employer was high, that as a matter of fact, he was especially grateful after years of messenger service that Burger gave him a new title, Secretary of the Justices' Conference, a recognition of one of his various chores.

Two months into the Wallace team process, on January 4, the Court PIO dropped the telecaster a line: "Several persons—judges, former law clerks and so on—have had the impression after talking with your representatives that the Chief Justice will be appearing on your program. ... Basing themselves on that impression, some have considered joining the Chief Justice. ... As I feel sure that you know, the Chief Justice will not take part. ... It would be most improper for him to do so; as you know, a case involving your program ... is currently before the Justices awaiting their judgment."

In March, *60 Minutes* ran its show. To Edwin Yoder, who wrote in *The Washington Star* that the program struck him as a "hatchet job" on Burger, the segment's producer, Marion F. Goldin responded coolly that some others saw it as a whitewash. It was in the eye of the beholder.

On April 18 it was the other way around, this time the Justices judging their media judges. CBS lost. Byron White wrote for the Court, supported by the Chief Justice, and by Justices Blackmun, Powell and Rehnquist. Justice Brennan dissented in part. Opposing were Stewart and Marshall. White cited the Court's unanimous 1964 ruling, written by Brennan, in *New York Times v. Sullivan*, saying that the media cannot be sued for libel when they publish "robust" criticisms of public figures so long as there is no "malice," so long as the media do not know that their accusations are false and so long as there is no reckless disregard of whether they are true or false.

CHAPTER 7

A CHIEF JUSTICE'S VIEW

Few editors could surpass the Justices of the Supreme Court in their tributes to the First Amendment and to freedom of the press as an essential fourth leg of the American democratic structure. But it is one thing to applaud the idea in principle and another to live with it.

Burger smiled, admitting some truth in it, when a newsman friend, Hugh Sidey of *Time* magazine, said on Martin Agronsky's television show, "The Chief Justice loves the First Amendment; it's just reporters he dislikes."

Valuing in theory the free flow of information makes it no easier to labor for the public welfare while suffering the fleabites of captious criticism.

That a number of other Justices had a similar reaction Burger found early in his tenure when he tried to get his brethren to agree to include summaries with the Court's Opinions. As the nine Justices assembled around the long table in their closed Conference Room at the back of the Court building, there was a recurring theme, lamentations, especially from the Justice who had written the Court Opinion, that cartoonists, headline writers and reporters made hash out of carefully crafted decisions.

With decisiveness and a willingness to try something new, Burger made a suggestion: Since summaries, called *syllabi,* are included when the Court decisions go into the bound volumes a year after the decision, why not publish them with the Opinions so that fast-working news wire, radio and TV reporters and writers for the early deadline afternoon newspapers, would have a better chance of understanding the Court ruling?

There was an immediate argument against the idea, sufficient to kill it so far as some of the veterans were concerned: It had never been done in the previous seventeen decades of the Court's existence. In a legal world of *stare decisis,* a community that believes that what has been done before generally should be left unaltered, why change?

Justices around the table had other weapons with which to shoot down the proposal. The Reporter of Decisions, Henry Putzel, was one of the army of people who were denied access to the Court secrets as judgments are hammered out. Henry would have to be cut into the know a day or two before the announcement of the Court verdict. Why widen the circle of the informed? Could Henry be trusted?

Burger tried a quick answer: "If Henry can't, then no one around here can be." That still did not satisfy the dubious.

"Why do anything for those reporters?" asked one Justice who had painful memories of past headlines.

"I feel the same as you do," the Chief assured him, "but this is not for the reporters, it is for the Court."

Media and Court interests were dovetailed in this case, Neither wanted false reports.

Resistance persisted. Ailing John Harlan could look back over fourteen years during which the Court had no such practice. Hugo Black had an even longer vision into the Court past, thirty-two years. How could Putzel in a day or so, or even in a year for that matter, boil fifty pages of closely argued text into two or three? Burger gave up. Try again some other day, he decided.

Months later the newly minted Chief Justice saw his chance. Hand-wringing about news coverage resumed at the table. Burger returned to his proposal. "Let's just do this on a provisional basis," he suggested. The syllabus would be included with the Court's decision only if the author of the Opinion consented.

One or two of the Justices never agreed, but retirements gradually changed the Court. Within two years both Harlan and Black were gone. Soon everyone signed on to the new system. Some Justices glanced over Putzel's summary, suggesting changes. Others made a point of never looking; it was Henry's responsibility. Burger took a middle course. He had his senior Clerk read summaries of his Opinions. Where the Clerk detected problems he invited Burger to do his own review.

An irony in the reform was that one of the regulars in the Court press room objected that there was no need for the summaries. The Chief Justice took wry note that the reporter who had that reaction worked for a morning newspaper. With decisions coming down at ten in the morning, he had all day to study them. His main rival had an afternoon newspaper with an instant deadline. How much better it was for the morning paper reporter if his opposite number stumbled in his haste.

Sensitive to news needs, Burger acted sometimes as one who "used to be a newsman himself" to use an expression reporters often hear from those in other pursuits. Burger's news role had been a modest one but enough to give him some feel for the requirements of the journalistic craft. A poor boy in the Minnesota twin cities, he had earned petty cash while in school, serving as a "stringer" for the *St. Paul Post-Dispatch*. He was paid by the number of column inches he filled in the paper; a string run the length of his stories measured what he was paid. Reminiscing in his chambers one day, Burger recalled how he would seek ways to spread his accounts through several issues, greater distances for the strings to stretch.

As Chief Justice, Burger used a version of the spread-out technique, not to get more space in the papers, although it had that effect, but rather in the hope that what did see print would be closer to the truth.

The change came from annual talks Burger had with the reporters who were regularly assigned to the Court. The meetings, Burger would explain with a laugh, were limited to "wages, hours and working conditions," no discussion of pending cases. So far as the first two were concerned, wages and hours, there was no way he could help, Burger would remark. As for the third something might be possible. Did the reporters have suggestions?

They did. For decades it had been the custom to release all decisions and orders as the first business on Monday mornings. With that done, the Justices would proceed to the hearing of cases. It was a custom honored by tradition, but for reporters it was a nightmare. There was an enormous news glut. A dozen decisions sometimes were released at once. On top of that the Justices' Orders List usually included one hundred cases the Justices were turning away and a half dozen they were agreeing to hear. Stories of every kind were in the Orders List. Even the cases turned down were news. It was the end of the road for them, a climactic development for the litigants and perhaps major news locally or regionally, or perhaps even for the whole country.

In the meantime, the Justices were proceeding to hear the first case of the week. That, too, might make a story. Carl Stern of NBC had a horror story. One day reporters were handed enough rulings to fill an entire one-thousand-page volume of the *United States Reports*. In the batch were a half dozen landmark decisions, each of them worthy of a broadcast by itself. In a two-minute radio broadcast one of the decisions had to be handled in a subordinate clause; there was no time to give it a sentence of its own.

To understand what the Court was doing while faced with instant deadlines was all but impossible. There was no wonder mistakes were made.

Meanwhile, major news went ill-reported. Editors could not give all their space to the Court; there were other claimants for news attention. By the next day untold stories were already "old news" and hard to recapitulate. It was all a news disaster.

Burger listened, and another change was made. Release of orders at the start on Mondays was continued, but most decisions were handed down thereafter on Tuesdays and Wednesdays, the other bench days. Reporting became more accurate to the satisfaction of the Justices, but there was a downside. The Court now hit page one and the TV newscasts three times as often.

For the Justices that was no gain. Newbold Noyes, the Editor of *The Washington Star,* thought mistakenly that Burger was pulling his leg when the Chief told him that if the Court could have its way it would have no news coverage at all. Justices quietly, without headlines and political cartoons, would make rulings that would go into the books along with all others since the eighteenth century, creating precedents for the lower courts to follow. While that could be the Court's dream, it was not part of the real world, so Burger accepted the greater publicity in exchange for truer reports.

The addition of the *syllabi* to the Opinions and the spacing out of announcements were not the only Burger changes affecting the media. Another was physical. When Burger took over, he found a bench that was straight across with a half dozen desks in front of it for a few favored newspapers and wire services. A Justice at one end of the bench could not see or hear one at the other. From what Burger understood, the reporters out of the Justices' sight would sometimes laugh and pass notes as lawyers behind them made their arguments. Burger set out to correct that and, in the process, reaped what proved to be a stream of bad news reports.

Burger ordered Ed Douglas, the Court Cabinetmaker, to slice the Justices' bench into three parts, swinging the ends forward so that the nine could see one another. The invisible news desks under the bench were removed and a new expanded press area was created off to the Justices' right. Instead of a half dozen places for reporters there were now nineteen, with Justices and newspeople able to see one another. News organizations that had started Court coverage early no longer had a monopoly. There was space now for radio and TV representatives with their pads and pencils but minus their recorders and cameras. It was a gain for many in the media, but it produced one of many negative stories that soon beset the new Chief.

Perhaps because he was seen as an aloof law-and-order man replacing the liberal Earl Warren, some press sniping began. Why had Burger redesigned the bench? For vanity's sake, said one story, so that he could preside vaingloriously in the middle. Other potshots from the media followed so that one day Burger told a friend that he was wondering whether there might be a media agreement never to "publish anything favorable about me."

There was, for example, Burger's problem of a work desk. Earl Warren had been using a large one. It filled a good share of the Chief Justice's main office. "With that in here it was as crowded as the office of an English solicitor," Burger said. "Papers were piled high." All that flat surface was just too tempting. Move the big desk out of here into the Justices' conference room next door, the new Chief ordered, "and get me an ordinary lawyer's desk!"

The all-purpose Ed Douglas made the changes, the previous Chief Justice desk was preserved as a part of Court history, and all seemed well until the repercussions began.

First, Earl Warren, who had retirement chambers in the building, let on that he still wanted something like his old big desk. The talented Douglas built him a duplicate.

Then came the stories: Burger has taken over the Justices' Conference Room as part of his suite. The Justices would have to meet somewhere else! There was a second version: Burger plans from now on to sit apart when the Justices have their Conference. The eight Associates as usual will be at the table where all nine have sat until now. Burger will be across the room presiding imperially from behind his vast desk. The upshot, went this version, is still not clear, for aged Hugo Black says that he will refuse to go to Conference until Burger agrees, like all his predecessors of recent decades, to share the table with the eight.

Had Black or some other Justice of the old Warren team, frustrated by the brusque, quick manner of the new Chief and longing for the previous easygoing ways, jumped to wrong conclusions? Was he the source?

And had reporters taken it a step further?

Burger was satisfied that it had all come from one person whom he chose not to identify. It was bad reporting in any case, he said. Impressions from one source should not have been enough: "My journalism teacher always told me you have two sources."

Faithful to one Washington maxim that it is wiser "never to correct and never to complain," Burger let the stories go unanswered, but he did chide the reporter who had made the most of the rumors: "Move the conference?" he asked. "Where?" There was no other convenient room.

It was frustrating and, to make it worse, the reduced flat surface of the smaller "lawyer's desk" proved inadequate to cope with all the judicial and administrative details of the Chief's office. Soon there was a foot-high pile of nearly a score of manila folders of current problems on the window sill behind the Chief's chair.

The historic Chief Justice Warren desk, preserved for posterity, sat unused in a corner of the Conference Room and Burger, as he had always intended, shared the common table. Still, mocking stories continued. One was that Burger was so carried away by his sudden propulsion into the upper echelons of the nation that he had carpeted in gold the Justices' walkway onto the bench. A new yellow floor covering had been installed, but overarching pride was not the reason, the Chief explained to a visitor: "[John Marshall] Harlan was very old and Black was frail. After a session, Black would stretch his legs. He could hardly move. Coming off the bench it is uneven and hard to see. I was afraid Black would fall and break his hip."

It was for them, not for himself, that he had acted, the Chief emphasized: "I was twenty-five years younger. I told Ed Douglas to get some carpet that was visible. He found some remnants in the old Abe Fortas chambers."

There were more stories suggesting foolish Burger pride. One was that he had arranged for silver goblets for use at the Conference, hardly the sort of thing for a simple democracy. Wrong again, Burger protested to friends: "Black came to me one day to say that the drinking water was tepid after an hour or so. He missed that good Alabama water. I got aluminum cups with a pewter finish, inscribed with the name of each Justice." Far from an overweening thirst for luxury, the new drinking-water system was actually a step down from what the Justices had before, Burger said. The glasses of the Warren Court had rested on a tray of silver. Burger used the facts to chide the reporter who wrote the silver cup story: "He looked embarrassed, but he never retracted."

Despite his early days as a newspaper stringer, Burger's disenchantment with the way the Fourth Estate uses its constitutionally protected freedoms had begun long before he reached the Capitol Hill Courthouse. As Assistant Attorney General of the United States, he one day told his superior, Herbert Brownell, that he could never hope to get a good press: "Too often you will have to say, 'No comment.'" That could only frustrate relationships.

With Burger on the Brownell staff was another Assistant Attorney General, William P. Rogers, who was later Secretary of State. He did somehow seem to get along well with newsfolk, belying Burger's jaundiced vision. But, Burger decided, Rogers's willingness to chat was deceptive. His pleasant manner did not mean he was surrendering sensitive information. Skillfully, he was managing to get more out of the newspeople than they out of him.

A remark one day from James A. Farley, President Franklin Roosevelt's artful Campaign Manager, strengthened Burger's caution. Farley told him: "Write very little and save all the letters you get!" Touched with cynicism, it was hard-bitten counsel from a veteran of the political and media wars.

A tangle of reasons seemed to explain the Burger-media impasse, not only the Chief's inability to converse easily with reporters but also his intimidating, godlike appearance at the center of the bench, an Old Testament mane of white hair above his features. Even the latter provoked a teasing query for the PIO: To get it so silvery, does he use a beer rinse?"

The PIO theory was that there was no such thing as an indiscreet question, only indiscreet answers. Most questions were checked out for a reply, but an inquiry about rinses was too far afield from judicial matters to merit a response.

Most important as a reason for Court-media tensions at the start of the Burger period may have been the widespread belief among reporters and editors that the "Nixon Court," as the Burger team was called, would indulge itself in a wholesale rollback of citizens' rights, including those of the Fourth Estate. When it became apparent that the Court that helped oust Nixon might refuse to put new limitations on police in addition to the Miranda advisory against self-incrimination, but would not cancel the bulk of the Warren Court's liberal concessions, media fears seemed to subside, but Burger's diffidence remained.

An example occurred one day when Burger stood at the door to his chambers chatting with another Justice. Such discussions often touched on the deciding of cases, the Court's great secret. Glancing to his right, Burger was appalled to see a television reporter loitering within earshot. The newsman had been in to see Potter Stewart in the adjoining chambers. Stewart, an editor in college days, was at ease with men and women of the media, often receiving them in his suite.

It was an incident that never was repeated; the Chief saw to that. The Justices' Conference Room was between the Burger and Stewart quarters. Burger posted one of the Court police at the Conference Room door, had barriers installed closing off the whole of the Justices' area and required escorts thereafter for anyone calling upon a Justice.

As Burger's one and one-half decades on the High Bench went on, the longest tenure of any Chief Justice in the twentieth century, the country's lead jurist glanced through a half dozen newspapers each day, coming to the conclusion that reporters become jaded if they stay too long on the Court beat, and that the struggle to make page one tempts them to exaggerate the importance of decisions where only slight, if any, modifications are made to the law. Were he the Editor, he told friends one day, his instructions to his Court reporter would be plain: "Don't write anything if nothing happens."

The 1977 case of *General Electric v. Gilbert,* reported in the 429th volume of the *United States Reports*, illustrated what Burger had in mind as misleading reporting. Justice Rehnquist, with Burger's support, wrote for the majority. General Electric had a contract with its employees providing disability benefits for various ailments. Pregnancy was not listed. The company was sued on the grounds that the contract violated the 1964 Civil Rights Act, which banned sex discrimination. Rehnquist rejected the claim. The contract, he pointed out, provided for women the same benefits it afforded men for identical injuries. The liberal Brennan was in the minority, contending that women needed special protections. Many a headline followed Brennan's lead, blasting the all-male Court for chauvinism. It was one case when Burger's irritation with news reports led him to break his rule about debating decisions apart from the texts of Opinions. He recalled later: "A woman came up to me at a party and said, 'I support your views generally, but that General Electric pregnancy decision was terrible!'

"I said, 'You have mentioned the subject of pregnancy, so may I ask you: Is pregnancy a disease?' She said, 'No, under proper circumstances it can be a woman's proudest moment.'

"I told her I agreed: 'All that was said in the decision was that pregnancy was not a disease. The union contract in that case said that it covered diseases. All the union had to do, if feeling was strong enough, was to get a clause in the next negotiation saying that pregnancy, for contract purposes, would be considered a disease.'"

Apropos of that, the Chief Justice went on: "I am doing an Opinion and I asked Justice Powell today to do a short concurrence highlighting the point of the decision. We are terribly rushed here. It's an assembly line. What we needed in that [General Electric] case was a concurring opinion saying that the point of the decision was that the contract covered diseases, and pregnancy was not a disease."

Another example of frustration with news coverage was a *Time* headline in the year of Justice Douglas's long and fatal illness speaking of "justice delayed."

For Justices it was an especially galling charge, for it is gospel in the legal world that "justice delayed is justice denied."

"The fact," Burger observed, "was that we finished that term on July 5, only a week later than usual." He added: "The article said that Blackmun, Marshall and I were behind in writing Opinions, that Marshall was lazy and that Blackmun was making too many speeches. The fact was that, when that appeared, I had handed down seventeen Opinions, more than any other Justice. The next had only fourteen. Blackmun was above the average of twelve." In passing, the Chief conceded that, in any case, "The number of Opinions is not important." Some are vastly more difficult to write than are others.

Burger smarted under charges in the media that although he deserved some credit for being a competent administrator he was not a very good lawyer. He drew some comfort from his avid reading of Court history.

"Just think of the attacks that were made on John Marshall," he remarked one day, thinking back to the "great Chief Justice." Marshall, the jurist who established the Court as the last word in judicial matters, was a foe of his popular contemporary, Thomas Jefferson, and was known to some as a wrong-headed fellow distinguished largely by the sloppiness of his dress.

"And," Burger added, "the attacks on Taft as a poor lawyer! He was not a poor lawyer. And Charles Evans Hughes!" Taft, President of the United States from 1909 to 1913, was Chief Justice from 1921 to 1930, the only person to serve at the head of both the executive and judicial branches. Hughes, a former Governor of New York State, also came close to duplicating the Taft feat when he ran as the Republican candidate for President in 1916, but he was bested by his Democratic opponent, Woodrow Wilson. Hughes was Chief Justice from 1930 to 1941, crossing political swords with another popular president, FDR, thwarting the latter's attempt to change the Supreme Court complexion by packing it with up to six of his own nominees.

While Burger could wish that the media would just go away, leaving the Justices to fine points of the law and the *United States Reports,* a glance from the bench to the new part of the Courtroom to which he had moved the reporters was a constant reminder to him that the media were still there. Sometimes what he observed drew his attention for a moment away from what the Lawyer before him was saying. On one such occasion he scribbled a note, handing it to the Messenger behind him for immediate delivery to the PIO on the floor below. It read: "We seem to have a cluster of 'strangers' in the press box today. Four, and not one of them taking notes! One was asleep!"

It was the PIO's job to issue passes to the press area, so a prompt explanation was in order. Back went a reply.

The four were from the *New Orleans Times-Picayune & States Item,* Kiplinger News Service, the *Ottaway Register* and the States News Service, none of them regulars but all of them bona fide newsmen, bearers of White House or congressional credentials.

Using the Courtroom as a place of repose could not, of course, be condoned, but absence of note taking could be explained by the way the issues had been spelled out in fulsome detail in briefs the lawyers had provided.

All was well in the press section, the Chief was assured.

CHAPTER 8

ROPE-A-DOPE

Justices for decades have felt that one of the Court's best secrets often goes unrevealed: What it was that the Court actually ruled in a case.

As Justice Antonin Scalia has explained it, a ruling may be merely the upholding of an important principle of the law. It may be the application of a clause in the Constitution. It could be dictated by an act of Congress or a state law. Laws often are the result of bargaining among legislators with sometimes unforeseen and undesired consequences. Applying such laws may be a case of garbage in, garbage out. The remedy, in the minds of many Justices, is a constitutional amendment or revised laws.

Absent either, Justices winced from time to time as headlines damned them for outrageous decisions.

An example in the 1970s was the Court order forbidding a Western dam to be put into use after scores of millions of dollars had been spent bringing it close to completion. There was no question about the value of the dam for water control and usage, but Congress, properly alarmed at depredations of the environment, had passed a law forbidding the destruction of any more species, however seemingly insignificant. Behind the dam lived an obscure little fish called the snail darter. It appeared to be unique to that stream.

Which was more important, the great dam, or the tiny fish? Garbage in, garbage out, was the Court decision. Until Congress rephrased its draconian law the dam could not function.

The snail darter was then found elsewhere, and the controversy was resolved, but not until the Justices had taken a drubbing.

The fact, one Justice mused, is that the media focus on results. Did the good guys win? In doing that, he conceded, the media give the public what they want to know: How did it come out? But, the Justice, a conservative, insisted what results in a specific case is not what is important. What matters is that correct legal procedure be followed. He offered an example: A serial killer is brought into court and the prosecutor rushes to judgment with insufficient evidence. The jury acquits. Then conclusive proof is found. The court refuses to grant a rehearing and the killer roams free. The bad guy wins, society is imperiled, but the constitutional ban on double jeopardy, a protection of the innocent against malicious, repeated prosecutions, is preserved to the longer-range social benefit.

Headline writers, and even most space-short reporters, could not be expected to explain all this, the Justice conceded. But that, he added, is why "no news is good news." If the media just stopped covering the Court he, for one, would be happier.

Another of the Justices, known also as a conservative, was of a similar view. He said: "I think I surprise old friends. If I were a Congressman making the laws I might well vote another way. But I am not a Congressman. They make the laws. I don't. I apply their laws."

At issue was whether the day of the old common-law judge was over, the jurist who detected new consensuses in public opinion, applying them as belatedly perceived inherent laws. Was there still a place for an Oliver Wendell Holmes or a Benjamin Cardozo? In the view of at least one conservative on the bench in the 1990s, the answer was no; social attitudes were now far too complex for judge-made laws.

Both liberals and conservatives on the Court across the decades have smarted at what the media have said about their decisions, but tradition calls on judges to suffer in silence. It is a "rope-a-dope" situation, as one Justice put it. His reference was to a famous but questionable tactic Muhammed Ali invented when he was the heavyweight boxing champion of the world. It was a potentially disastrous alternative to dancing and weaving, going into clinches, and trading haymakers in the middle of the ring.

As the Justice explained it with some bitterness: "You just lay back against the ropes and let your opponent beat the bejabbers out of you until he gets tired." It has the small satisfying aspect of frustrating an unjust attacker who cannot establish a dialogue, but it takes a toll on the human punch-

Justice Antonin Scalia. Collection of the Supreme Court of the United States.

ing bag. The revered John Marshall was one who tried to find a substitute for rope-a-dope, but common judgment since then has been that he provided no helpful precedent.

In 1819, in the case of *McCulloch v. Maryland,* Marshall made a crucial choice, affirming the superior claims of the nation over the narrower interests of the states. His wisdom has been honored since, but he was blasted at the time.

An article in the Richmond, Virginia, papers by the now all-but-forgotten Spencer Roane nettled Marshall so much he decided to fight journalistic fire with his own editorial flame. With "A Friend of the Union" as his byline, he came up with a prolix, unconvincing, five-part series that led friends to believe he would have been far better off just standing on his Opinion.

Even the rope-a-dope tactic, however, involved a problem, as Justice Brennan, the acclaimed "saint of the First Amendment," found out when the Court struck down state laws that had permitted public school devotional exercises such as Bible readings and the reciting of the Lord's Prayer. Rope-a-dope requires a thick skin. Brennan's was not tough enough for what followed the issuance of *Engel v. Vitale.* The protests were so vehement Brennan felt forced to speak out.

Informed criticism is one thing, he said, but what if naysayers sound off without reading the reasons set forth in the Opinions? In the prayer case, he protested, he and Justices Clark, Douglas and Arthur Goldberg had provided one hundred printed pages to explain why they decided as they did.

Getting copies and working through the long texts would have taken time yet "within two or three hours," far too soon to have given the Court logic a hearing, "distinguished American public figures and clergymen" were on the air and in print decrying the Court action and, in some cases, "stating flatly and unequivocally that the Court was wrong in its interpretation of the First Amendment."

Himself a devout, mass-attending Catholic, Brennan was stung by the negative reports. Coming from Brennan, the excoriation of what went on the public record in the school devotions case had special significance. Few Justices were stronger in defending not just the right of the media to publish what it learns, but even the tools the press needs to uncover information.

How vigorously Brennan felt about the principle, if not the application, of broad press freedoms, was spelled out a few months later when he struck down a libel suit in the case of *New York Times Co. v. Sullivan*. L. B. Sullivan, the Commissioner of Public Affairs of the city of Montgomery, Alabama, had objected that *The Times* had defamed him. Writing for a majority of six, Brennan ruled: "The First Amendment requires that debate on public issues should be uninhibited, robust and wide-open, and such debate may well include vehement, caustic and sometimes unpleasantly sharp attacks on government and public officials." That, of course, included the Justices no matter how much they rued what they saw in print or on television.

Across the years, loyal to the concept of rope-a-dope, Justices rarely complained, but Brennan, for one, recalled how "petulant" Oliver Wendell Holmes could be when the subject of press coverage came up.

A more recent Justice, when one reporter's coverage was mentioned, changed the subject. "Don't get me started," he begged.

Hugo Black, an "absolutist" in the defense of a free press, saw one limit—the doorsill of his chambers. A former member of the repressive, bigoted Ku Klux Klan, and a later convert to broadest Bill of Rights freedoms, Black was "hounded" by the press during his first Court years as his widow, Elizabeth Black, wrote in her memoirs. Black's first Law Clerk, Jerome A. Cooper, described in his privately printed *Confessions of the Law Clerks* how the Justice handled efforts of journalists to enter his quarters: "An unconditional embargo was placed on all newspapermen. The judge felt ... a complete dedication to the freedoms of the Bill of Rights including, of course, freedom of the press, but that freedom did not include personal entry into a certain office of the Supreme Court Building."

Cooper indicated that he urged Black often to answer articles that both of them felt were irresponsible and wrong, "But, with consummate patience, the judge simply said, 'No, time is on my side.' It was." In Black's case, rope-a-dope worked.

Among those Justices least nervous about journalists was Potter Stewart. He seemed to have no concerns when scandal-focused reporters lunched with members of his staff. Yet he, too, saw limits to how much help the press should receive. He spelled out his ideas at the 150th anniversary of Yale Law School of which he and Byron White were alumni.

Mentioning that the conservative White did not always agree with him, Stewart summed up his own view of the media: Was President Nixon "hounded out of office by an arrogant and irresponsible press that outrageously usurped dictatorial power?" No, quite the contrary. In Stewart's view, the media (Bob Woodward and *The Washington Post*) "performed precisely the function it was intended to perform by those who wrote the First Amendment"; in a system of checks and balances the three branches of the government were flanked by a fourth institution, the press. Friction among the four was inevitable, but it was necessary "to save the people from autocracy."

Were press rights limitless? No, again. In this Justice's opinion, "So far as the Constitution goes, the autonomous press may publish what it knows, and may seek to learn what it can"; it can "do battle against secrecy and deception in government, but it cannot expect from the Constitution any guarantee that it will succeed."

Translated into terms of the Court's own battle with the media, the Stewart position seemed clear. The media were constitutionally free to do what they could to push aside the heavy drapes behind the Justices' High Bench in quest of premature news of coming decisions, but the Justices were just as much at liberty to thwart them if they could.

Stewart saw rights and wrongs on both sides. Though basically a friend of wide press freedoms including coverage of the Court, he conceded in his Yale talk that any review of the way the media operate would show that "newspapers, television networks and magazines have sometimes been outrageously abusive, arrogant and hypocritical."

That said, he added: "It hardly follows that an elimination of a strong and independent press is the way to eliminate abusiveness, untruth, arrogance or hypocrisy from government itself."

Although he saw limits, Stewart tilted more toward press freedom than most of his colleagues. In the test case of *Branzburg v. Hayes* (1972), the majority of five with White as their spokesman held that reporters, despite their professed need to protect news sources, had no right to refuse information to a grand jury in a criminal investigation. Stewart and the three other dissenters, Douglas, Brennan and Marshall, lost that one, but the Justice told his Yale audience that maybe they had not. Half in jest, he pointed out that the moderate Lewis Powell had hedged his concurrence with the majority so significantly that perhaps the vote should have been seen as four and a half to four and a half, a wash!

At issue in *Branzburg* was whether reporters needed to shield confidential sources so that they could serve the "people's right to know."

On that subject Stewart's colleague, the future Chief Justice Rehnquist, took a far more restrictive view. Rehnquist told a group at Washburn University that what really mattered was "the public good."

The public, "in the sense of the electorate at large, may have a 'right to know' with respect to virtually every activity of the government," said Rehnquist. But, he added, the public, acting through its representatives, might choose not to exercise that right. The key to the door of total disclosure of public business, in the Rehnquist view, was in the hands of the public's delegates, the Congress and the courts, and not in those operating under First Amendment strictures against the abridgment of press freedom. Rehnquist added: "No Court decision with which I am familiar has ever held that the First Amendment to the Constitution authorizes the media to force their way into governmental deliberations that the deliberators choose to keep private, in the absence of positive law to that effect."

Though rope-a-dope silence on Court decisions is the rule, the gracious Lewis Powell was sufficiently stung by media coverage of the Court that he unburdened himself publicly on at least one occasion. When he, Burger, Rehnquist and Blackmun were added to the Court by Richard Nixon, he protested, the media trumpeted a "woeful expectation" that the "Nixon bloc" would vote consistently as a near majority to "dismantle the great decisions of the Warren Court." It was, he objected, a dire forecast that was never fulfilled.

Undeterred, he said, media critics shifted gears to the reverse charge: The unconservative Burger Court suffered from being "leaderless." For that, the courteous Powell had an uncharacteristically harsh word: it was "nonsense." Those who wrote in that fashion, he said, "simply do not understand the responsibilities either of the Supreme Court or of the Chief Justice; they seem to want a Court that would take every opportunity to advance some preferred moral, philosophical or political viewpoint." Were that evil to befall the country, Powell protested, the High Bench "would not be a court of law; it would be a supreme legislature appointed for life."

From the moment they take the oath all nine Justices have a vote of equal weight, but seniors on occasion offer advice to newcomers. Not always is it accepted.

Don't give any interviews until the Senate confirms you, one Justice advised a nominee.

"But that's my window on the world," objected the elated, until then obscure, nominee. It was his chance to be known.

The senior did not persist but, still bruised from his own encounters with interviewers, he was convinced that he had counseled wisely. "A window, yes," he said. "A window to fall through."

❧ CHAPTER 9 ❧

"SLEAZY TV"

A few months into the job, the Court's new PIO faced a media problem. William O. Douglas was about to break the record for longest service as a Justice of the United States Supreme Court, thirty-four years and a few months.

Douglas had already been on the bench twenty weeks longer than the departed Hugo Black, and a month more than the nonpareil, Chief Justice John Marshall. He was about to surpass the longevity record-holder, the bearded, balding Stephen Johnson Field who had stepped down at age eighty-one in 1897 after being a member of the Courts of Melville W. Fuller, Morrison R. Waite, Salmon P. Chase and the Roger B. Taney of the *Dred Scott* decision.

The event was a candidate for the TV evening news. What the fledgling PIO did not yet understand was that there was a vigorous tradition limiting cameras, still as well as TV, anywhere inside the Supreme Court building. Nor was any Douglas love lost with regard to trouble-seeking reporters. Have a TV press conference, the PIO suggested.

No, was the instant answer. Douglas had been "scorched and hanged" so often in the media, even—in his view—with tapes manipulated to have him say the opposite of what he intended, that he wanted no part of it. Not all newsmen were so bad, he said, "but my trouble is that I can't tell one kind from another."

Days later, the PIO was back: "You'll be traveling the day you break the record. When you change planes in the airports you may face cameras, getting questions on the fly. Patched together, who knows what will come out of it. Give me thirty minutes here and you can say what you want to say." Having had the intervening days to think it over, Douglas consented.

"Then," the freshman PIO interjected, "keep in mind that they will try to get you to attack the Court."

Douglas, until the arrival of the "Nixon-Burger Court" had been in Earl Warren's liberal majority. Now, in the closed conference discussions, Warren Burger's initial, conservative recommendations often were challenged by Douglas who spoke second as the senior Associate. There had been many opportunities to disagree, but there was one matter on which all nine Justices concurred, a defense of the revered Court itself as a crucial American institution. Douglas listened quizzically and responded curtly: "I've been around longer than you have." That the media would seek a negative was to him a truism.

Douglas had, indeed, been around. When Franklin Roosevelt tried to water down the anti–New Deal conservatism of the Charles Evans Hughes Court of the depression years, the whiz kid Douglas, still in his early forties, was one of FDR's first Court appointees. Then when Roosevelt ran for his final term, Douglas was on the short list to be Vice President, narrowly nosed out by the little known Senator from Missouri, Harry S Truman. Had the political chips fallen another way it would have been Douglas to make the atomic bomb decision and to fight the Cold War.

Seventeen television cameras showed up for the unprecedented conference. The questioning went as expected: "What do you think of the other Justices with whom you are serving?"

"I've been here more than thirty-four years and, in all that time, I have never been with a man I did not like."

It was a sweeping statement encompassing Warren Burger and all the sitting Justices, but also a wide range of other judicial luminaries and characters from the crotchety James Clark McReynolds to Chief Justice Hughes, Felix Frankfurter and James F. Byrnes, Truman's Secretary of State at the post–World War II Versailles peace conference.

No luck with the first question, reporters tried again: "Don't you agree that Presidents always choose Justices in their own image?"

"Yes, and if I were President it is exactly what I would do."

That sounded more like it, but the Justice continued: "I would do it but, you know, every President tries and every President fails. He chooses Justices for issues that are already behind us as a nation and he is as incapable as any of the rest of us of foreseeing the actual issues the Justice will vote on in the future."

In brief, Nixon could seek law-and-order Justices instead of Bill of Rights devotees, but when the Court's real cases came along, each new appointee would be on his own, acting in unpredictable ways and tied to no White House apron strings.

Nothing doing, the camera crews packed up and left. The Court as an institution had suffered no wounds.

Days later, William Rehnquist stopped the PIO in a corridor with a remark: "Something new around here. Justices' press conferences! Yes, but after they have been here thirty-four years!"

Rehnquist himself had just finished two years. You could look for his appearance before the cameras in 2005! Brennan, second in seniority, had served only since 1956, the last surviving of the four Eisenhower appointments. By the Rehnquist count, the PIO had another seventeen years to wait before calling back the TV and then only if Brennan consented! In short, forget it!

Two years later, however, the TV was back, Douglas again on camera, this time in his small chambers. He had suffered a devastating stroke but was struggling to stay on as a Justice. From the PIO point of view, the Justice had to reassure the country of his competence if he were to remain. A brief, successful, TV interview could provide that.

The ailing Douglas again agreed but the interview was a disaster. Douglas peered at his questioners and labored to form words. Months later, his condition getting worse, Douglas, in a wheelchair, informed Burger during the noon break on a day of four hearings that he was quitting the bench. He had served thirty-six years.

That ended TV in the Courthouse until six years later when Potter Stewart left the Court and Sandra Day O'Connor joined. It was one thing to exclude TV conferences while a Justice was still sitting on cases, but how about when he or she was off the bench, no longer taking part in decisions? To the TV and to the PIO there was a difference. Stewart, a friend of newspeople whom he saw as the ears and voice of the democratic public, consented. A press conference with little controversy was held in one of the building's large reception rooms, and a new Court tradition was established. The Court hesitates to create precedents but is loyal to them once they exist. After Stewart's departure, farewell TV conferences became routine.

The arrival of Justice O'Connor forced another TV first. She was the first woman Justice in the Court's two-century history, and the President, Ronald Reagan, wanted to see her installed.

It was a major story for TV news and a political plus for the President, a claim on the potentially decisive women's vote.

The White House was all for maximum TV coverage, but the Court was determined to keep the cameras out of the hearing room where the new Justice was sworn in. There was a compromise. If the White House could arrange to install a temporary mini-grandstand in one of the open-air courtyards on the building's second floor, thirty still and TV cameras could be accommodated at a "photo opportunity" with three principals in the picture: Mrs. O'Connor, the President and the Chief Justice.

There would be no questions. That is, the ground rules would exclude them, but what if someone like the loud and aggressive Sam Donaldson, then a member of the White House press corps, ignored the request and bellowed some inquiry?

No problem, the White House emissaries were sure. Neither Burger nor Mrs. O'Connor would be the questioner's target, just the President. A rope fifteen feet from Reagan would keep the shouter at a distance. If the Chief Executive liked the query, he could reply. If he did not, he "would not hear."

Sam and his peers arrived. Perhaps there was some reverence for the Court, some respect, some awe. Perhaps it was just unfamiliar turf. There were no questions and the cameras quietly rolled.

Such timid, step-by-step admission of TV cameras into the country's premier Courthouse may seem odd, but the fact was that cameras in courtrooms were a frequently bruited issue as TV news gradually became an ever more important source of national information. In the middle of the last decade of the twentieth century, the Supreme Court, concerned about the dignity and decorum of its grave proceedings, continued to ban all cameras from its hearings, both TV and still. On top of that, it even forbade all note taking except by newspeople, and refused to let the journalists supplement their written notes with tape recordings.

Pictorial representations of Court proceedings, except for the work of news artists who were freely admitted, remained one of the Court's big secrets.

Was there a public "right to know" what the Court was doing? Yes, at least in part, it was conceded. To meet some of that need, a few rows of seats during hearings were always left open to the walk-in public if only for a three-minute glimpse of the nine on the bench. Others, who signed up for it, could stay for two hours, but, except for the texts of Opinions, that was the extent of public exposure.

The ban on still photos did not mean, however, that no photographs were taken. Secrets cry out to be revealed. Perhaps it should have been no surprise, therefore when, in 1935, a New York City newspaper rotogravure section came out with a shot of the Charles Evans Hughes Court hearing a case. In the 1970s, a quarter of a century later, an elderly gentleman dropped by the PIO one day to unburden himself about how that picture was taken:

> A German photographer, Dr. Eric Solomon, had it in for Chief Justice Hughes. He asked me to help him take a photo of the Court in session. He came to the Court with a huge box-shaped hearing aid on his chest.
>
> His hearing was fine but inside the box was a camera. He took some shots but they did not come out. The box slanted down too far and all the heads were cut off.
>
> "Then he tried again. This time his arm was "broken." Inside a cast was the camera. It worked. All the heads were on and he had the picture.

The ban on still photos during hearings did not go so far as to bar all group shots of the nine. For a century and a half, going back to the Matthew Brady period in the

Civil War, the black-robed Justices have sat for the same stiff shot when a member is added, the Chief seated in the middle flanked by the senior Associate on his right, the next senior on his left, the following two on the flanks, and the four juniors standing in the rear, the latest comer on the far right as seen by the camera. It is one occasion when the men with seniority sit while freshly arrived women stand.

Group photos of the nine, apart from the traditional pose, and the Justices in street clothes, have been rare, but Burger allowed one when the Smithsonian Institution, of which he was *ex officio* chancellor, asked him to give their magazine an inside look at life at the Court.

Yoichi "Oke" Okamoto, who had been President Johnson's White House photographer, was assigned to do the pictures. He asked for an informal group pose to be used as a wraparound for the front and back of the magazine. It was something new and, by that fact, unappealing, but Burger agreed and the Associates went along.

Eager on the one hand to preserve Court traditions, Burger, on the other, was an innovator in the face of new situations. A part-time painter in oils, he was also picture-minded.

For his unprecedented study of the ungowned Justices, Oke chose one of the Court's handsome reception rooms with a painting of John Marshall on the wall behind. He had two heavy tables shoved together end to end as a prop against which to shoot the nine and posed the PIO in all nine planned positions, adjusting his camera each time.

Four junior Justices would be assigned to positions on the left, respecting seniority, a space would stay open in the middle "so that the staples in the spine of the magazine will not go through Thurgood Marshall," and the Chief Justice and the three longest-serving Associates would be placed on the right.

Oke planned it even further: John Paul Stevens and Lewis Powell would chat. Blackmun, one of the shortest, would sit on the table, his feet dangling, as the tall Rehnquist glanced down, Marshall and Brennan would confer, and Burger, Stewart and White would be on the far right. That would put the five seniors on the front cover and the four juniors on the back.

Accustomed to individual command when they voted on the nation's gravest issues, but also adjusted to the idea of accepting group decisions, the nine members of the Court took the photographer's directives with docility. Burger was posed chatting collegially with Stewart and White, something with which he was comfortable. Although he had extra duties and distinctions, the Chief did not forget that he had only one of the nine votes in Conference. The camera clicked. Then Oke called out: "Chief Justice!" All eight Associates stayed frozen in their assigned poses but Burger, startled, looked up. The camera flashed again. Oke had his wraparound. Burger alone, the Chief, staring at the viewer. It was nothing the politically sensitive chairman of the Court would have approved, but it gave the newsman-photographer what he saw as the truth, the Chief as the first among equals. The first shot, the Chief in conversation with two colleagues, was the one Burger chose for his chambers walls. The second, Oke's preference, ran on the magazine's cover. That was not the last use that was made of the second pose. Woodward's and Armstrong's editors got it for the cover of the mocking volume, *The Brethren:* An imperious Burger alone peering into the camera while good-natured colleagues chatted among themselves.

Can pictures lie? Would it have been better to stay with the stiff, old, robed photo?

These were unanswered PIO questions. Larger and more pressing was whether cameras should be in courtrooms, any courtrooms, as the awesome work of justice is done. Most state courts allowed TV by the mid-1990s, but those in the federal system, the United States District Courts and Circuit Courts of Appeal, tried the experiment for three years in the early 1990s and then pulled back.

To all TV appeals and, from the 1970s on, they came constantly from the networks and from public television, the Supreme Court refusal was adamant, there would be no filming of hearings.

TV officials argued in vain that a concealed, silent pool camera could do the work with film shared among the various competitors. Justices could summarize their Opinions in their own words as they already do for the few hundred Courtroom witnesses, but now for the TV millions.

Part of the background of the Court refusal was a 1969 luncheon meeting in the chambers of retired Chief Justice Warren. With him at table was his successor. The TV question came up, and Warren wondered what Burger would do about it. His own attitude was clear. He had never admitted the cameras, and he felt strongly that it would be a sad day when they did get in, destroying, in his view, an important aspect of Court practice.

To his relief, the otherwise liberal Warren found that his sermon to Burger had been preached to one who was already a convert. Days before, Burger had told Senator Eastland as his confirmation hearing was being arranged that he would not appear if TV covered it. He added that he had "not asked for the [Chief Justice] job." Eastland told him he could not be confirmed if he did not appear but that, in any case, the TV problem would not arise—his committee never permitted cameras.

A straitlaced gentleman of the old school, Burger was appalled by the large amount of sex and violence on commercial TV. He made a partial exception for public television. He liked some of its educational material such as wildlife documentaries and, in the 1970s, even wrote part of the script for a public TV series on early Supreme Court Justices.

As for the high Courtroom, however, Burger wanted no cameras there, neither commercial nor public.

An insight into how strongly Burger felt on the subject was offered one day when Pat Oster, a former reporter for the *U.S. News & World Report,* said that, in one of his back-and-forth off-the-record and on-the-record remarks to that magazine's editors, Burger had said that "only over his dead body" would TV get respectability for its "sleazy" programming by getting in to cover Supreme Court hearings.

Burger's custom in the *U.S. News* interviews was to state his gut feelings bluntly, then edit the transcript for publication. It was the same way he wrote his Opinions, his basic instincts first, then a careful rephrasing in a final draft.

None of the colorful quotes about the general level of commercial TV appeared in the text cleared for publication, but Walter Cronkite, mid-century TV's distinguished father figure, took Pat's word for it and aired the salty judgments. Presumably the veteran telecaster was mildly shocked.

By an irony, both Cronkite and Burger in that period made the top ten in the annual *U.S. News* opinion poll about who were the most influential Americans. Cronkite was rated just ahead of Burger.

The Chief Justice never confirmed Oster's quotes, but in a pile of papers he kept in his chambers there was an issue of *Newsweek* decrying TV pornography.

No great watcher of TV himself, Burger did make use of free moments in a 1979 trip to Florida to watch coverage of a state court murder trial. He saw nothing to change his negative opinions. The defendant seemed well on his way to conviction for killing a man with a shotgun blast through a door into the victim's abdomen, but the undejected accused "preened" and his lawyer "postured."

If indeed, as it appeared, the two were playing shamelessly and unpardonably to the television audience, Burger did make use of one small concession to the propriety of the filming. The Judge, to his credit, did appear to ignore the camera.

What did all this say about TV's hopes for Court coverage? Morton Mintz, who covered the Court for three years, had a piece in the *Chicago Tribune* in February 1980 saying that he put that question to the nine. Burger made no reply, but the consensus among the Associates was that the "conference," the Justices speaking among themselves, would have to grant approval if it were to be done.

Rehnquist told Mintz he would be "guided by the views of the majority, after hearing what everyone had to say, before making up my mind."

White wanted, too, to hear "what others have to say."

Marshall saw "a whole lot of problems" but had "an open mind on it."

Powell chose not to "express a personal view."

Stevens stood on his policy of never giving interviews.

Brennan remarked merely that it was "a Conference matter."

There is solemn dignity as the nine take their seats at the bench to weigh some of the nation's gravest problems such as a woman's right to abortion or the carrying out of death sentences.

Would TV impinge negatively on that? Was that Earl Warren's concern? One Justice, musing about the problem, had other questions: Would the Chief Justice have to send notes reminding his brethren to wear blue shirts and dark suits? Would the Chief have to counsel his colleagues not to ham it up? ("We all have some ham in us," he said.) How about the lawyers; would they be tempted to perform for the broader audience? Would the nine, asking questions, have to be given equal time? And what useful spectacle would it be if there were a revival of the way Justice Frankfurter sometimes ranted on the bench against his brethren?

There was no likelihood that any of the Burger Justices would emulate Frankfurter in that, but why open a door even on the possibility?

Congress had authority to tell the Court what it must do on such matters as when to begin the annual term, and might even be able to legislate TV into the Supreme Court hearings but, short of that, there was no hint in the mid-1990s that the Court itself would decide in Conference to bring in the cameras.

Three things were in play during the eighteen years of the Burger Court, as the TV question persisted: the Court's traditional caution about comments on or off the bench, the Court's decisions in First Amendment cases including those directly affecting the audiovisual media and Chief Justice Burger's periodic encounters with microphones and cameras away from the Courthouse.

On the subject of caution in statements apart from Opinions there had long been a consensus. What a Justice needs, said Frankfurter, is "judicial lockjaw." Louis Brandeis made no public comments apart from his Opinions from the first moment after he was inducted into the William Howard Taft Court.

Cardozo refused to discuss matters past, present or future because all of them might impinge on Court decisions. Even when a cousin appealed to him to speak to a women's forum, Cardozo begged off, explaining plaintively that "You have no idea of the inhibitions that hedge the soul—the pure, undefiled soul—of a Justice of the Supreme Court."

A few Justices responded to the petitions of TV, consenting to be interviewed. Black, Douglas and even Earl Warren did so, but they were rare exceptions.

Among Court decisions on TV one notable one was handed down June 7, 1965, in the matter of *Billie Sol Estes v. the State of Texas*. Estes, a financier, was charged with swindling and was convicted. Over his objection, TV was allowed in the Courtroom. Tom Clark wrote the Court decision, canceling the conviction on grounds that constitutional due process had been denied the camera-shy defendant.

Earl Warren, Douglas, Goldberg and Harlan made up the rest of the majority in the *Estes* case with Stewart, Black, Brennan and White dissenting.

Warren explained his vote: It is a violation of the Sixth Amendment guarantee of a fair trial to allow TV to cover a criminal trial in a state court. Douglas and Goldberg took the same view. Harlan hedged. He agreed that criminal trials of great notoriety should not be televised, but he would not ban TV coverage at more or less routine hearings.

White, joined by Brennan, said that it was premature to ban all TV courtroom coverage, and Brennan added that the qualifications laid down by Harlan meant, in effect, that only a minority had outlawed all criminal court TV.

The issue was back in the Supreme Court fifteen years later in the case of *Chandler v. Florida*. Again it was a question of whether TV in court had denied the defendant a fair trial. No, the Court said this time. Burger wrote the Opinion, agreeing with Stewart that Harlan's limited consent in the "four and one half to four and one half" *Estes* decision was the key. Was Burger softening on TV? Not in his mind. For him, *Chandler* was a state rights question, not a matter of the Constitution.

Justices are expected to decide matters on the basis of the Constitution, applicable judicial precedents and the laws, not on personal feelings, but during the long Burger tenure—longest of any Chief Justice in the twentieth century—few of TV's encounters with Burger did anything to enchant him with that medium.

Sharing the Brandeis, Cardozo and Frankfurter views, Burger believed strongly that many subjects should never be discussed by a Judge in off-the-cuff spot interviews. Where a Judge is concerned, the most interesting subjects are those that are litigated before him and, Burger was sure, they should be addressed only in Opinions handed down after hearings and consultations with colleagues.

Months after the fact, Burger still seethed over the tactic one network reporter used to invite comments that the Chief Justice deemed to be improper. The man's secreted microphone peeked out from an armpit. On another occasion, a camera crew crowded into an elevator car with the Chief. The crew complained later that the nation's heavyset top jurist, a multiletter athlete in his school days, lowered his shoulder, crashing into them with a soccer shot.

Congress never asked Burger to supplement the President's annual State of the Union address with his own report on the needs of the judiciary, but the American Bar Association did offer such a platform at its annual convention. Burger seized the opportunity to plump for a range of judicial reforms, he welcomed pencil coverage, but against TV he drew a line. He listed several objections: Bright TV lights blinded him and, in any case, he wanted no TV on occasions when TV normally would be absent.

All that led to a clash with NBC's Carl Stern. At a 1978 ABA convention a notice was posted for the media saying that Burger would confer with bar association presidents at a non-ABA function. A small room had been reserved. The topic was unexciting, whether to merge the Institute for Court Management with the Judicial College in Reno, both schools for improved court practices. In terms of the nightly news the meeting promised little. But footage of Burger was so scanty in TV files that any occasion for getting some was a good one.

All went sedately at the little session until Stern and his crew walked in. The *National Law Journal* of February 28, 1978, described what happened: "Either you leave, or I do," said the Chief Justice. The NBC team saw no need to depart, so next followed the spectacle of the Chief Justice of the United States "ducking" out through a pantry, and slamming a door in the face of the pursuing camera, the *Journal* reported. Other public officials meet TV needs, why not the Chief Justice, the weekly wanted to know. The paper added with full sympathy for Stern: "Burger's point of view is due a measure of respect and honor [but] we sincerely hope that if he again blusters, 'Either you leave or I do,' that he will politely be shown the door."

ABA feelings were mixed. The lawyers' organization valued the Chief's talk as a major item of interest and as a source of valuable publicity, but it also saw TV as a premier instrument for reaching the public.

A compromise was attempted. Let the Chief speak undisturbed to the convention while reading five or ten minutes of his address to the cameras in a separate session. It was tried, but when reporters fired questions after the reading, there was little appetite for repeating the experiment soon again.

The Burger TV problem never was resolved. Sometimes the Chief Justice tried whimsy even when he was not the target of the moment. In 1978 when the cameras were on Douglas at a civil rights forum, the Chief strolled over to the camera crews with a quip that very likely bewildered them: "I'm glad you are here. I've always wanted to be on television!"

A gambit of a different sort was used in February 1977 in Seattle, when a microphone was thrust in Burger's face, and he was asked about a group of black students who were picketing against the Supreme Court hearing the *Bakke* reverse discrimination case. Like a page in "Alice in Wonderland," the exchange went: "What do you think about those pickets?"

"What pickets?"

"Those students. They don't want the Court to take the *Bakke* case."

"Oh, what is it? Is it in our Court? If it comes, we will decide it."

It was footage of sorts, but nothing usable for the nightcast.

A Sunday morning talk show promised Burger that if he would come on he would not be subjected to "bulldog techniques," and that house correspondents would quiz him, not "outside tigers from the newspapers." Even so, the Chief's answer was no. Too many questions would have to be answered with a "No comment."

Of all Burger's brushes with the TV the one that probably nettled most was one in which no camera focused on him. John Dean, Nixon's legal counsel, had just been released from prison after serving one of the Watergate sentences. He had testified copiously, but it was Carl Stern once again who was sent to Los Angeles by his network to see what further could be extracted from him. Burger was on the bench hearing a case when Stern phoned with the results: "Dean says that he talked with Charles Colson in prison and that Colson said that Nixon, on one occasion, remarked that we need not worry, Nixon had talked that very day with Chief Justice Burger."

Colson was another of the jailed Nixon assistants. The implications were horrendous: The Chief Justice of the United States, in disregard of his sworn responsibilities, had advised the beleaguered occupant of the White House that the fix was in, the

Supreme Court, whatever the evidence, would give the President a pass if the tapes case reached it! Second- or third-hand hearsay and suspicions in direct contrast with what Burger had ruled on behalf of a unanimous Court, the PIO protested. No matter, was the answer. How does the Chief reply?

It was like grasping the tar baby. By answering the Chief Justice would be validating the preposterous. It would dignify what was not even an assertion, merely a half-formed question.

The reporter suggested that he would be reasonable. It was 8 A.M. in California, 11 A.M. at the Court. Stern knew from the Court schedule that the Chief had just finished hearing the first case of the day, and that he would be off the bench and at lunch in another hour after the morning's second case. Get the Chief's answer during the lunch break, the reporter demanded. By 3 P.M. at the latest, after the day's fourth case, he would have to receive an answer.

It was time to talk to Stern's network chiefs. The felons' half-formed wonderings were outrageous. Though Burger had been appointed by Nixon, the two never had been cronies or even more than the most casual of acquaintances. Burger had seen the President only a handful of times and then in fleeting fashion. The story was a baseless slander and should not be aired.

No, was the network answer. Put the Chief Justice on camera and let him make his denials. What a great story that would make, a Chief Justice pleading his innocence in the face of two convicts' imaginings. There was no statement from the Court and the story ran. There was an announcement that Court sources were dubious.

It was one of the last Nixon case "scoops" but a very limited one. Good exclusives last briefly until others confirm and republish them. This was a one-shotter. No one picked it up.

Sleazy or not, TV was still absent from Supreme Court hearings a decade after Burger took his retirement.

There was no question but that television in the Courtroom could have some informational value, and even an entertainment potential but, so far as the latter went, the Justices were content to let TV seek it elsewhere.

As for still cameras inside boxes for the hard of hearing or casts for those with "broken bones" no repetition of the 1935 Solomon feat was likely. Metal detectors now in place at the Courtroom door would pry beneath such shields.

❦ PART II ❧

INSIDE THE
GOLDFISH BOWL

CHAPTER 10

TWO CHIEFS

Earl Warren, as a retired Justice, had chambers, a suite of rooms, in the Court Building for the remaining half decade of his life.

A Californian who never in spirit left his home state, he loved flowers so it was a happy surprise one day at his window to see a bed of bright blossoms on the lawn below him. Warren's successor, Warren Earl Burger, at a May 27, 1975, Courtroom memorial service for the deceased Chief, told how the buds got there: "Knowing that ... he was accustomed to very colorful flowers most of the year, I ... asked the gardener to put masses of color in that particular bed. "In some way he became aware of this. He jokingly asked how I 'found time to worry about flowers.'"

It was his custom, Burger told Warren, to walk around the outside of the Court building almost every day "to relax and relieve my frustrations." On one such swing he noticed the drab flower bed. Just as Earl Warren liked to cheer the Washington Redskins at football games or to hunt ducks on other occasions, the walk was his release, Burger explained. Warren's response was a laugh.

"You better find a bigger place to walk," he told Burger. "This place is not large enough to work off the frustrations of a Chief Justice." The episode was a sequel to handing over the Chief Justiceship in June 1969.

The contrast between the two Chiefs scarcely could have been greater: Earl Warren with his concern for the rights of individuals including criminal suspects, and Burger's insistence that swift justice be done to wrongdoers.

Each agreed that freedom and order were essential to American society, but where each placed his emphasis was as separate as the two sides of a coin.

One of the points on which the two holders of the Chief Justiceship reached a quick agreement, however, was an aspect of life behind the Court's marble walls that astonished them both, Warren when he took over from Fred Vinson in 1953, and Burger now. The list of tasks assigned to a Chief Justice of the United States is as long as Goliath's arm, but the personal staff with which he was expected to meet the responsibilities was less than a corporal's guard.

Your own staff is six, said Warren: a messenger to handle odds and ends, two secretaries and three law clerks, the latter young recent law school graduates. Warren in his time had been bewildered by the discovery. As a three-time Governor of California he had enjoyed the help of hundreds at his direct command. When laws needed drafting a general idea was sufficient from him. Others worked out the language. Burger, too, earlier in his career had come from a post as Assistant Attorney General in charge of civil and international litigation where a couple of hundred lawyers were at his service.

Making it all the more amazing was the list of tasks imposed on the Chief Justice by law, tradition and his own personal vision of what the leader of the Third Branch of the government should do. On the long list were these:

- It was the Chief's job to screen four or five thousand new cases each year, creating a "dead list," the nineteen out of twenty cases that the Court would turn away without a hearing. What the Chief decreed was final unless one of the Associates found any of the close-to-death thousands to be worth a second look.

Chief Justice Earl Warren. Collection of the Supreme Court of the United States.

- The Chief presided over the Court as one hundred to two hundred cases were argued each year.
- In the closed conference at which the Justices choose up sides on how to decide cases, the Chief spoke first, setting the tone.
- After Justices expressed themselves on how a case should be decided, the Chief voted last. Regardless of the views he had expressed at the outset, he was free to declare himself part of the majority and then had the right to choose which of the Justices, including himself, would speak for the Court. Where nuances are important, the influence on the course of national law thus granted to the Chief was significant.
- The Chief did his share of writing the Opinions deciding cases, some fifteen or twenty a year, more than one a month on an annual basis.

For much of this the Chief and the Associates shared equally, all of them tirelessly busy, but for the Chief there was more. It was his job to oversee the three hundred employees, hiring and firing.

Then there were chores for the Chief beyond the Courthouse walls:

- By law, the Chief Justice is chair of the Judicial Conference of the United States, a score of federal judges who meet twice a year in the Supreme Court building to govern the affairs of the nation's seven hundred federal judges.
- The Chief chairs the Federal Judicial Center, the think tank and training center for the federal judiciary, an institution housed in Burger's time along with the White House in Washington's Lafayette Park.
- Apart from direct judicial functions, the Chief Justice is, by law, a trustee and, by tradition, Chancellor of Washington's Smithsonian Institution, one of the world's greatest concentrations of historical, scientific and cultural collections.
- He is Chairman of the Board of Washington's magnificent National Gallery of Art.
- He is a trustee of the National Geographic Society.

As if all this was not enough for the new Chief and his personal staff of six, Burger was arriving with a huge additional agenda of his own. He had spelled it out two years earlier in a commencement address at Wisconsin's small Ripon College. It was a talk that had caught President Nixon's eye, boosting Appeals Court Judge Burger high on the White House list of successors to Earl Warren.

Not just that era's Vietnam, but another war had to be fought, Burger had told the graduates, a war against inadequate justice at home. Crime, he said, had to be punished surely and swiftly, but, once jailed, the convicts should not go into "warehouses" as idle, useless humans, but rather into prisons that were "factories and schools," places where convicts could learn and practice trades useful after release.

It called for a crusade, and who better could lead it than a Chief Justice? How a Chief could go about that had been suggested to Burger sixteen years earlier by a friend at the Department of Justice, Deputy Attorney General Bill Rogers. He had urged that Earl Warren, as the newly installed Chief Justice should give an annual State of the Judiciary address to a joint session of Congress. The President as the head of the executive branch had his annual input to Congress in his heavily publicized State of the Union talk. Why should the leader of the judicial branch not do the same?

Unfortunately for the idea, the Eisenhower White House showed little enthusiasm for sharing the high congressional platform, and the Rogers proposal got nowhere. Yet Burger did not forget it. If a State of the Judiciary address to Congress was out of the question, why not something similar at the annual convention of the American Bar Association, a focal meeting for the hundreds of thousands of American lawyers, and an association in which Burger already had been active?

Preparing the annual addresses would be another strain on his little team of aides but, thought Burger, bursting with ideas from a lifetime as a Lawyer and Judge, it could be worth it. He gave it a try.

Within two months of his initial chats with Earl Warren, Burger was in touch with the ABA with one of the ideas that might be promoted in annual ABA addresses. This one, he felt, was too important to wait even for that. It was, in part, a way to add to his own tiny staff of six. What he and other judges needed, he said, was help from appropriately trained nonjudicial administrative assistants, people who could take care of the myriad of Courthouse details not involved in the deciding of cases.

Would the ABA assist him in getting that? The officials of the lawyers' association agreed. Then, said Burger, what we must create is an Institute of Court Management (ICM). On vacation a month later, the new Chief roughed out an ICM blueprint. As Burger recalled later: "We had the first meeting on it in October. On December 7, 1969, we had the final meeting, approving the structure, selecting a Director and setting up the plan of operation."

By June 15, 1970, with the help of a $750,000 Ford Foundation grant, the ICM opened its doors on the campus of the University of Denver, offering a six-month course. It was just one year from the time Burger had taken over from Warren.

The swift pace did not diminish. By December 1970 the first twenty-one graduates were at the Supreme Court Building in Washington, receiving their certificates from Burger. By March 1977 seven of the circuit executives of ten federal judicial circuits were ICM alumni.

Burger was not the least of the presiding judges to benefit. A star student in the first ICM class was Mark Cannon, a Utah Mormon, holder of several Harvard degrees, and a former missionary in Latin America. Burger in the meantime had been trying to get Congress to give the Court a tenth Justice to handle administrative matters. The idea got nowhere, but Congress had agreed to expand Burger's staff to seven, assigning him an Administrative Assistant. Cannon was tapped for the job.

The Chief's Administrative Assistant, first in Court history, had ideas of his own. Seven were far too few to do all that Burger wanted to do. The White House had

Chief Justice Burger (right), Dr. Mark Cannon (left), and McGurn conferring on press matters in Burger's chambers at the Court. Burger wanted Cannon to be the tenth Justice, in charge of administration, but with no vote on the cases. Unable to get congressional consent, Burger settled for the post of Chief Justice's Administrative Asssistant, a then novel, but now traditional, Court office. Barrett McGurn.

"fellows," bright young people who helped out the presidency for a year or so, bringing their young energies and their recently honed academic skills: Why could not the Supreme Court have the same? There was nothing in the judicial tradition to allow for any such thing, but Burger and Cannon arranged for it just the same.

Young holders of doctorates and college professorships from the various academic specialties were brought to widen the mental horizons of Justices focused narrowly on the law. In return, in addition to modest salaries, the judicial fellows had a chance to peer beneath the legal tent, expanding their own visions.

One of Cannon's fellow Mormons, the genial Dr. Elwood Gordon Gee, signed on as the first Judicial Fellow, contributing so well that he was kept on for a second year, becoming the Court's first Personnel Officer and lightening that aspect of the Chief's burdens. With the brief Court years behind him, Gee went on to become, in succession, the president of West Virginia University, of the University of Colorado and of Ohio State University.

Gee's successors as judicial fellows soon were major helps to Burger, assisting among other tasks with early drafts of ABA speeches.

With the judicial fellowships working so well, and the need for helping hands still great, Cannon urged another device, unpaid interns, college undergraduates and young people to give talks to tourists and to take care of other small tasks Congress was reluctant to finance. That, too, was a Court novelty.

No longer cramped with the tiny staff of the Warren era, the new Chief hurried on with his long agenda. In a talk in colonial Williamsburg, Virginia, in 1971 at a national conference on the judiciary, Burger said that the twenty thousand state court judges needed a mutual clearing center. By March 1978 such an institution, the National Center for

State Courts, was in existence following the expenditure of $3.5 million, a place where the fifty separate state court systems could compare notes, learning from one another.

While the new Chief acted the whirlwind, making changes in legal and judicial procedures inside and outside the Court building, and refusing on the bench to expand on the liberal Warren Court policies, the two Chief Justices under the one roof continued to see one another from time to time.

On at least one litigated issue the two, even before the changing of the Court guard, had had an opportunity to compare views and to disagree. It concerned police conduct while making arrests.

In June 1966, over the objections of Justices Clark, Harlan, Stewart and White, a Court majority of five had thrown out evidence against Ernesto Miranda, an accused kidnapper and rapist, on the grounds that the arresting officers had not advised him that he had a right to say nothing until a lawyer could advise him. Thus was born the reading of "Miranda Rights," which have been part of police procedure ever since.

Warren had been assigned a plane for a trip to Florida. Hearing that Judge Burger had the same destination, he offered him a ride. They chatted for two and a half hours and the Miranda case came up. It was no way to change police rules, the Appeals Court judge told the author of Miranda. There should have been "a broad investigation," he said, not a Court ruling on "the narrow record of a particular case." Two basic visions of individual rights and law and order were in collision.

Despite their differences, the two Chiefs under one roof managed to work out something better than a mere *modus vivendi*. The peace between them began with Burger's swearing in. As he recalled at the Warren memorial service, he asked his predecessor to administer the oath to him inside the Courtroom "to emphasize the continuity of the Court as an institution, at a time when there was too much loose talk about prospective changes."

Warren, said Burger, seemed emotional moments later in one of the Courthouse reception rooms, when he expressed the hope that all future turnovers of the Chief Justiceship would follow a similar pattern. Burger said that Warren's "wise counsel" was always provided whenever requested after that but never was volunteered. "He leaned over backward," the new Chief said, "sometimes, I thought, unnecessarily so, to avoid the slightest appearance of wanting to participate in dealing with the particular administrative problems that crossed my desk."

Goodwill from one side was reciprocated from the other. Burger was outraged when he heard that an officer on duty at one of Washington's military hospitals told Earl Warren that, as a retiree, he could no longer be treated there. Warren had been nonplussed.

Burger got in touch with the Service Secretary, demanding an apology for Warren. As Burger saw it, a Supreme Court Justice never "retires" in one sense of that word. He remains eligible to serve on federal Courts of Appeals as some did. He gets the same pay and many of the same benefits as those still active. As dust settled on the incident, Warren was placed back on the hospital's approved list.

On another matter Burger was upset for months. The great hallway leading to the Courtroom houses the marble busts of former Chief Justices. Burger wanted his predecessor to see himself so immortalized just as Burger surely hoped for the same for himself. Warren had many conservative foes. Whether for that reason or another, despite repeated fund appeals from Burger to Congress, it was only after Warren's death that financing, carving and the installation of the bust took place. Burger's earnest efforts had failed but, in his own case, he had better luck. He lived to see his own bust in place on a pedestal just outside the Courtroom doors.

CHAPTER 11

FIFTEENTH CHIEF JUSTICE

Chief Justice Burger gave his PIO a two-sentence handwritten note one day summing up his philosophy as the successor of John Marshall and the Chairman of the Supreme Court of the United States. It read: "We are not here because we are unique. We are unique because we are here."

Introducing Lewis Powell to the bench in 1971, Burger expressed the same thought even more forcefully with a word change: "We are infallible! Because we are here. But we are not here because we are infallible."

We are the last word. God help us all if we are wrong.

Every Justice felt the strain, some more than others. Early in the same decade of the 1960s in which Burger joined the Court, Charles Evans Whittaker surrendered his seat on the bench after only a five-year tenure. He had suffered the pain of decision in an especially acute way. Scrupulously dedicated, he saw many sides to questions, agonizing over choices even after making them.

It was true even of his personal correspondence. Days after dictating a letter he would tell his Secretary he should never have sent it. The change of mind seldom came as a surprise to her so often she was able to reassure him: "It's all right, Justice. It's still here in my drawer. I didn't send it."

Exhausted, Whittaker resigned in 1962, dying eleven years later at seventy-two.

Burger handled the challenges differently. "I decide," he remarked, "and then at night I sleep."

The buck had to stop and Justices are not gods, they can only do their best.

That, at least, was Burger's self-appraisal although he may not have been as far removed from the Whittaker tensions as he thought. At night he maintained a rack of a half dozen books beside his bed. He would read one volume for an hour or so, then a second for thirty more minutes, a glass of water in one hand. Sometimes sleep came a bit quicker than expected such as one evening when the glass rotated slowly, finally drenching him.

Other nights it was different. Sleep would not come. At 2:30 A.M. one morning, unable to doze, Burger began dictating memoranda to his recorder. There were so many that the Chief later that day told a staffer that he had no idea when his Secretary would be able to get to the last of them.

Warren Burger was born in 1907 on the wrong side of the tracks, starting life on a small family farm in Minnesota. A good student and husky, he won letters in high school in hockey, swimming, track and football. Although he got the emblems of participation, he gave himself in later years only a mixed review on his playing field accomplishments. He summed it up: "I was good only in track, in long distance running. I was fair in swimming, but I was left-footed in hockey and football."

In the latter sport, the future Chief Justice was "too slow for the backfield and too small for the line." Up against those shortcomings, the coach put the young Burger in the line "and I had my brains beat out."

What Burger lacked in bulk and speed he made up in self-confidence, self-reliance and drive. A fellow classmate from the fourth grade in St. Paul who kept in touch through the years, not always approving his energetic and aggressive old acquaintance, summed

The McGurn Family with Chief Justice Burger at the Supreme Court. Left to right: *son Lachie and his wife, Sharman née Wallace, son Martin, Janice Ann McGurn, Burger, Barrett McGurn, son Bill and his wife, Catherine née Roche and son Mark.* Barrett McGurn.

up the ten-year-old Burger and the later Chief Justice as an unchanged personality: "He is a very domineering person and he gets away with it most of the time." However that may be, there is no doubt that the future chairman of the Supreme Court started life with a forcefulness and daring that never slackened.

At home on the farm were several grandparents. Even as Chief Justice, Burger took a central pride in the fact that his paternal grandfather was one of the very few hundreds of Americans who have won the Congressional Medal of Honor. A fourteen-year-old immigrant from the German part of Switzerland, the elder Burger enlisted in the Union Army and was badly wounded at Nolansville, Tennessee, losing an arm, and suffering a severe leg injury and the crippling of the surviving hand. He received a battlefield commission.

After the interstate conflict, the Chief's grandfather made his living as a Lawyer handling veteran benefit cases, and hiring himself out, giving speeches for pay, in behalf of political candidates. Never, however, the latter-day Burger insisted, for candidates of whom he disapproved.

The maternal grandparents immigrated in 1880 from Germany. Perhaps from them the future Chief Justice learned a German proverb that comforted him when, as Chief Justice, he provoked firestorms of criticism with his attempts at unprecedented and sometimes painful reforms of the judiciary and the legal profession, and as he tried to face down liberty-minded fellow Justices inside the closed Judicial conference: "They don't shake a tree that bears no fruit."

His opposition might have no taste for his apples but, at least, they were fruit. Another down-home saying that guided him during his later efforts to stem the flood of litigation engulfing the nation's twenty-five thousand judges, was to set a reform in motion and then let it take its course for a while without interference. Burger, one day in his chambers, cited the applicable maxim: "You don't pull up the radishes every three or four days to see how they grow."

Most important of all was one thing his mother told him: "Don't fret. Worry is a tax from which you draw no profit."

These early views of reality were supplemented later by others picked up in reading. One came from Justice Felix Frankfurter's remark about the value of each moment: "Anyone not carrying a book in his pocket is making an enormous mistake; he doesn't realize the value of time."

A further pithy observation went to the heart of Burger's law and order conference room debates with Bill of Rights brethren. It was from Lord Acton: "The American Constitution is all sail and no anchor."

Finally, as a guide to the way to calm down a negative controversy, there was Wellington's counsel to a flustered Disraeli: "An attack is a nine-day wonder. An answer adds another nine days."

The young Burger's successful high school effort to win four athletic letters was accompanied by a parallel drive to excel in the classroom and in nonathletic extracurricular activities while, at the same time, supplementing the family's sparse financial resources.

Burger edited the school newspaper and, with typical courage and a lively sense of propriety acquired in Sunday School and in the Boy Scouts of America, had the nerve in that capacity to launch what turned out to be a very short-lived campaign against a faculty member as a Peeping Tom. At the same time Burger doubled as President of the student council.

The future jurist's entry into the workforce was at the age of ten. Out of bed at 4 A.M., he carried copies of the *St. Paul Dispatch and Pioneer Press* to 265 customers. The limit now, Burger remarked, was one hundred thanks to "the child labor laws."

Later, in his teens, there was additional work for the newspaper. The Sunday edition had extra sections and "fillers" were needed to insert them. Work as a filler kept the teenaged Burger occupied far into some nights, even until 3 A.M. Up again at dawn for the paper deliveries made it a short rest indeed.

There were further spare jobs. On a visit to his hometown of St. Paul in the late 1970s, Burger stood at a Radisson Hotel window pointing down at a Mississippi River bridge. "I built it," he said. Not quite all of it. He was one of the laborers. It was one more way to add a few dollars.

At graduation from high school Burger won a scholarship to Princeton University, free tuition and books. It was a rare chance to take the high road to national success, but the youth had to turn it down. Room and board would be at his expense and his family could not afford that. Deepening the disappointment was that one of Burger's closest childhood and early manhood companions, Harry Blackmun, was heading for Harvard.

Besides sharing the same Boy Scout troop and Sunday School class, the two had often faced one another across tennis court nets, and Harry had been at Warren Burger's side as best man when the future Chief married Elvera Stromberg, the bilingual Swedish-speaking daughter of immigrants from Gothenburg, Sweden.

Not much more affluent, Harry had to work his way through Harvard College and Law School, but he did come out with two Harvard degrees.

Though they had once been so close, the two saw one another after college only sporadically for several decades until they wound up as often ill-at-ease brethren on the Supreme Court.

With his high school diploma in hand and no further hope of an Ivy League education, Burger went to work full-time for the Mutual Life Insurance Company, but he also signed up for night classes at the University of Minnesota.

Still selling insurance, Burger enrolled in a second night school, this one the St. Paul College of Law. The dark-hour scholars were admittedly second class, their degrees worth less than those of the daytime fledgling lawyers.

Burger became Vice President of the nighttime student council, and Chief Justice of the Honor Society. With him joining in, there was clamor for equal status with the daytimers. It was granted, but only after Burger was already out practicing law and serving on the same law school's faculty; he had done so well that the moment he got his diploma he was taken back to teach contracts in his off-hours.

As a lawyer Burger needed only four years to make partner in the firm of Farley, Burger, Moore & Costello. The practice was profitable, but Burger found time for feeless *pro bono* work and for politics. He was a Republican but not a member of the hard-right Nixon wing. He and some others in their twenties who were known as the diaper brigade got behind a country lawyer of their own generation, Harold Stassen, helping elect him governor of Minnesota at thirty-one, reportedly the youngest governor in the country's history.

At thirty-two Burger was President of the St. Paul Junior Chamber of Commerce. The Mississippi valley city had a sinister reputation as the hangout of master criminals such as John Dillinger, a stellar member of the "most wanted list" of the Federal Bureau of Investigation. To clean up the hometown, Burger assisted in reorganizing the police department.

A St. Paul Council on Human Relations was formed to protect Mexican sugar beet laborers and other victims of racial and ethnic mistreatment, and Burger became its first President. He gave hours of time to helping members of unpopular minorities.

When an African-American university student, an alleged Communist, was sentenced to jail for a year on a charge that he had exposed himself in a dormitory window, Burger, working without a fee, took the youth's appeal to the state Supreme Court and won it.

When, at the outset of World War II, Japanese-Americans were exiled from their West Coast homes, Burger worked in the St. Paul area to find them shelter and jobs, and took one couple and their baby into his own home. Thirty-five years later the infant, by then a mother herself, called on the Chief Justice to show him her own small child and to thank him.

Piecemeal efforts to solve social problems satisfied the energetic Burger only partially so, in 1944, at thirty-seven, he and some others proposed Stassen, absent in the war, as a candidate for the Republican nomination for the presidency.

This time the maturing diaper brigade failed of their purpose. Governor Thomas E. Dewey of New York got the 1944 and 1948 Republican nominations. Still, the dogged Burger kept at it, convention after convention, until 1952 when, as Stassen's Campaign Manager, he read the handwriting on the wall, saw that his candidate would miss once again, and threw his support to Dwight Eisenhower, thus ending Earl Warren's

Chief Justice Burger at his desk. Collection of the Supreme Court of the United States.

own bid for the high prize and paving the way for the eight-year Eisenhower presidency.

Ike's manager, Herbert Brownell, did not forget. One of the first moves of the new administration was to call Burger out of Midwest obscurity to take over the post of Assistant Attorney General handling the government's civil and international cases.

One strong card in Burger's hand, as he mused about it later, was that he did not get a quick case of "Potomac fever," the passion to stay on in the national capital at whatever cost, a Washington phenomenon.

That gave him room to be his own man. In speeches and law review articles, with confident self-assurance, he began attracting attention with protests against what he saw as excesses of liberalism, too much emphasis on personal rights and too little on society's defense against criminals. His own early liberalism, it was clear, had limits.

With the Republicans still in command in 1955 Burger was offered a seat on what is called the Little Supreme Court, the strategically placed federal Court of Appeals for the Washington, D.C., circuit. There Burger did battle with some of the country's leading judicial friends of freedom. Later as Chief Justice, Burger would refer to it sometimes as "that other court" and would describe himself as a practitioner of two arts, the law and psychology, the latter cultivated in "the main psychiatric institution," the other court.

One Court of Appeals episode stuck in Burger's mind: "We had a Chief Judge who was an agnostic, probably an atheist. One day he said that he thought we should eliminate the cry, 'God save this Court.'

"One of the other judges answered him: 'Do that! And after the cry, before sitting, I will stand and say "God save this Court!" ' "

"That ended it."

As Chief Justice, Burger refused a TV request that the nine Justices take turns before the cameras, spelling out their various "philosophies." In Burger's view as the nation's chief judicial officer, few exercises could be more detrimental. A Judge's job, as he saw it, was to consider one case at a time, weighing the particular facts and not seeking to impose his personal perceptions on the country.

Even so, Burger had his own general guidelines, which he scribbled down on a bookmark 2 inches wide and 8 inches long on a plane ride to Europe, either to England in 1964 or to Portugal in 1969, he could not recall which:

The timid make few mistakes but they finish near where they begin. If their condition at the start was good, perhaps they can rest on their oars and let tides or currents carry them.

But if, at a given time, all is not well, or if it is bad, things will get worse for the timid. The static condition timidity produces, assuming anything in life ever stands still, results from fear of failure.

But we ought to take heart from what Lord Acton pointed out in cataloging the failures of famous men. He reminded us that "No error is so monstrous that does not find defenders among the ablest men."

He then drew attention to the terrible mistakes made by men such as Thomas More, Francis Bacon, Cromwell, Napoleon and Jefferson.

But we can remember Napoleon's lasting contribution as a lawgiver whose code survives the error of his march on Moscow. We remember Bacon's wisdom and brilliance, and More's magnificent nobility of mind and spirit.

Great values are not preserved or advanced by small measures or timid men fearful of making a mistake. We can use such mentalities to guard bank vaults and libraries but those are not the spirits to build banks or fill our libraries or nations with good things.

It was with that willingness to dare and even to err that Warren Burger, the student of the dark hours, took his place in the awesome judicial line running from John Marshall through Roger B. Taney to Oliver Wendell Holmes, William Howard Taft, Charles Evans Hughes, Louis Brandeis, Hugo Black, Felix Frankfurter and his immediate predecessor, Earl Warren.

CHAPTER 12

OTHER CHIEFS

Sherman Minton, who was a member of the Supreme Court from 1949 to 1956, told the story of what happened when, on a quiet Sunday afternoon, he showed his ten-year-old grandson the Court's hearing room.

Minton shared the account with his colleague, Tom Clark, who repeated it later: "The lights were a little subdued; they never turn those lights out. They sat in what we call the Justices' pews, up beside the bench. Justice Minton explained about the lawgivers up there in the friezes and, over the bench, the Ten Commandments, and the fasces in the carpet that came from Rome and all this.

"And the young man, after listening, looked around and said: 'Granddaddy! Where's God?' "

The Courtroom does give you that "reverent feeling, and it takes a little time to get acclimated to it," Clark added. Ever natty, with a trademark bow tie, Clark served as a Justice from 1949 to 1967.

The lawgivers in the friezes to which Minton called the child's attention were Menes, Hammurabi, Moses, Solomon, Lycurgis, Solon, Draco, Confucius and Augustus from antiquity, and Napoleon, the Court's own John Marshall, Blackstone, Grotius, Saint Louis, King John, Charlemagne, Mohammed and Justinian from the modern era.

The Minton child did not find God, but not a few visitors who saw the impressive, bearded Charles Evans Hughes or the white-maned Warren Burger presiding over hearings surely felt that someone more than human loomed above them.

As Clark told the story, he added that even newly arrived members of the Court have a similar sense of awe. He said that one day on the High Bench he turned to the Justice beside him, Robert Jackson, asking how long it had taken him to "get acclimated."

Jackson answered with a story: "I asked Chief Justice Hughes that! He said, 'About three years, what do you think?' "

Jackson's estimate was five.

Warren Burger's reaction to the High Court was mixed. Preparing for a trip to Washington as a young Lawyer, he was urged to pay a call on Justice Harold Burton, the former Mayor of Cleveland and a Justice from 1945 to 1958. "He'll give you a cup of tea!"

Burger was too shy to venture it and Burton, when they encountered one another years later, chided him for his early timidity.

In July 1976 when the cast of *The Magnificent Yankee*, an Oliver-Wendell-Holmes-based show, visited Burger in the Court's Conference Room, he explained his reaction. "Burton was a big man," Burger told the troupe. "In fact, except for one or two, they were all big." Playing on the word, he went on with a smile, "Bigger than some people think we are now."

His reference was to liberal critics including even some of the Court's own staffers. As one of the latter, Court Librarian Ed Hudon expressed it with disapproval: "This is not a philosophical Court like those of Holmes, Brandeis and Frankfurter. This is a practical lawyers' Court."

Before coming to the High Bench, Burger had his own ideas about justicial propriety and was shocked when Chief Justice Fred M. Vinson, the Chief from 1946 to 1953, went counter to it.

Burger, at the time, was Assistant Attorney General, a position he considered fairly low on the official totem pole. On a visit to the Department of Justice, Vinson took Burger aside to speak about a historic case awaiting Supreme Court judgment, *Brown v. the Board of Education,* the watershed case reversing centuries of discrimination against African Americans.

"I have told only a few people about this," Burger reminisced in his chambers in April 1977. "I was so surprised."

The Vinson Court had already heard the case. "Chief Justice Vinson practically told me how they would decide it—to me, a young Assistant Attorney General!" It was a time of change of administrations, Truman leaving, Eisenhower arriving. "He told me they wanted to keep politics out of it."

Evidently, Vinson feared that the Department of Justice, shifting from Democrats to Republicans, might seek to pressure the Court against desegregation. The newly arriving and discreet Earl Warren, Burger felt sure, would never have spoken in the Vinson fashion. "He kept everything to himself," Burger said approvingly of his immediate predecessor. "He told no one what went on inside." But Vinson, he added, "came from a political background and was accustomed to work that way."

Vinson, a Kentucky Congressman in his early years, had held top government positions during the 1930s and 1940s, including service as Secretary of the Treasury.

In any case, the outgoing Chief had nothing to fear from the new Department of Justice. Burger said that around the third level down in justice there were some staffers worried about how various of the Southern Senators would react against school desegregation but, at the top, where he was, there was never a question but to support black rights. It was time for the Court to reject the logic of Chief Justice Taney's 1857 *Dred Scott* decision and the Melville Fuller Court's 1896 "separate but equal" ruling in *Plessy v. Ferguson.*

Taney, the immediate successor of John Marshall, and the only Catholic to be Chief Justice, was among the predecessors to whom Burger gave some thought. In Burger's view there was more to him than just the appalling seven to two *Scott v. Sandford (Dred Scott)* decision that declared blacks ineligible for American citizenship and rights. Taney, in fact, was much like Earl Warren, a populist, Burger remarked.

Were it possible to put *Sandford* aside, there were numerous constructive contributions during the twenty-eight year Taney tenure, he felt. Burger weighed for a while the idea of a Taney exhibit at the Court, but there was no follow-through on that.

To a visitor in April 1976, Burger shared a lesson he drew from his predecessor Taney: "He said blacks were things, not people. He thought he was averting a civil war, but he contributed to causing it. New England and the abolitionists went wild. It showed that a judge should not make political decisions."

CHAPTER 13

FIXING CRACKS

The timidity Warren Burger showed when it came to calling upon Justice Burton was long since gone by the time he took over from Earl Warren.

In his mind was his mother's old counsel: Fix the cracks before you get used to them. The "cracks," in his mind, were things he saw wrong in legal and judicial practices. Burger spoke of it five years into his Chief Justiceship when he was visited by his opposite number from Australia. He had come with a reform agenda, Burger said, and up to that point had accomplished about a third of it.

Along with his many projects, Burger brought his own style, an abrupt take-charge manner that reached into what some subordinates considered petty details.

The Marshal of the Court traditionally took care of housekeeping, but the new Chief Justice plunged into those matters with the same enthusiasm he brought to the deciding of cases. Marshal T. Perry Lippitt, a twenty-year veteran, left amid some bitterness, and retired Marine Colonel Frank Hepler, a professional Court Administrator, who succeeded him, was no happier.

In a typical incident, while treating aides to coffee in the Court's public cafeteria, the Chief Justice noticed a wandering bug. "Cockroach!" he gasped. "They are only supposed to come out at night. Get the cafeteria cleaners on this."

Burger was aware that he was accused of energy-wasting micromanagement but, he said, "If I do not do it, it won't get done."

On a daily walk inside the building to get exercise and to combat a weight problem, Burger was on an unremitting inspection tour. He noticed that the ground floor was cold, empty and forbidding, all marble: "Not a stick of wood!" As an amateur painter and sculptor, his artist's eye was offended. "It's like a mausoleum," he said. It was true that the stark, antiseptic walls looked as if niches for cremation urns would not be out of place.

The Court has a half million tourist visitors each year. They should have something to see, something to explain the Court's role in national history and life, Burger decided. The ground floor needed exhibits. As a first step in that direction, the Court needed a Curator, someone to preserve the artifacts, the documents of historical value, portraits of the one hundred Justices of two centuries, busts of the Chief Justices, showcases. Unself-conscious lawyers, the Justices of other generations had never bothered with such things. How was it to be done?

Congress clings tightly to the Court's purse strings. An artsy-sounding "Curator" would not go well with economy-minded members of the Appropriations Committee so how about a "Property Custodian?" That looked better on a budget line, and soon young Cathe Hetos was on the Court staff. A year or two later when Congress relented and gave Cathe the title of Curator, she was so pleased that no pay raise was needed.

Cathe charged into the work with enthusiasm, spending freely where she felt there was need. Soon she became aware of constraints. She was "Assistant Curator," Burger made clear, he was Curator! He would have to sign off on all main decisions.

In one sense not even the Chief was Curator, the nine Justices were. If as many as two raised objections in the Justices' conference, no project of the Curator or any other staffer could go forward. For the hard-charging, action-oriented new Chief Justice it was an important fact of life inside the Court walls that he could not discount. Cathe and he would have to move slowly. They did, but soon the ground floor was alive with exhibits, including a small, free movie theater with a film in which Burger and other Justices explained the Court's workings.

A history buff with the Court and the United States central to his interests, Burger saw triumphant proof of the wisdom of having a Curator when Cathe's successor, Gail Galloway, found in the Court Library a handwritten letter by John Jay, the first Chief Justice, explaining with pain why he could never forgive his brother for siding with the British against the 1776 Revolutionaries.

Even the High Bench Burger inherited from Earl Warren received a sharp second look from the incoming Chief. Seen from the audience, the tops of the Justices'

Chief Justice John Jay, the Court's first Chief Justice. C. Gregory Stapko, Collection of the Supreme Court of the United States.

chairs had a ragged appearance, some high, some low, like the skyline of a city with no building protocols. Why was it that way? Burger wanted to know. Might there be some venerable tradition?

There was none. Ed Douglas, the Court's all-purpose Carpenter and furniture builder, explained that whenever a new Justice came on board, he would ask whether the newcomer had any preferences in a chair. If he had none, Ed would put something together from whatever he had on hand in his shop.

One of the peaks on the back-of-the-bench skyline had been ordered by Byron White. His years as an all-American and pro football player had damaged his back. The high rise gave him welcome support. Suffering himself from childhood polio, Burger told Douglas to copy White's chair for him.

As for the jagged skyline, if new arrivals had no preferences, all future chairs should duplicate White's. Chair styles proved to be far down the list of new Justices' concerns, so soon a nice high, smooth line reigned above the Justices' heads.

A new chair was needed each time the Court changed personnel because it was the custom of the remaining eight to chip in personal funds to buy the chair of the departing one to give it to him or his family as a souvenir of the years at the bench. Built in the basement carpenter shop, the chairs were the property of the United States Government. Checking the government second-hand property rate, the eight would pay that into the Treasury, no great sum, the cost of a few restaurant meals.

In every direction, including Courtroom procedures, Burger found need for plastering. Instead of hearing two cases a day in a total of four hours, Burger made it four,

South wall and bench of the Supreme Court Courtroom. A side view of the Courtroom showing two of Chief Justice Burger's innovations. The old ragged skyline of Justices' chairs, caused by the Carpenter's practice of putting together whatever was on hand in the basement, had been replaced by creating an identical height for all chairs. Burger ordered that, absent other preferences by newcomers, all future chairs, including his own, should be modeled after that of the old footballer Byron White—good back support for everyone. Also shown is another Burger innovation. Through the time of Chief Justice Warren, the bench was so straight that junior Justices at the end could not see, and often could hardly hear, various of their colleagues. Burger told the Court Carpenter to slice the bench in three, with the ends pulled forward, so that all the Justices were in one another's view. Often a target of media gibes, Burger was accused of vainglory, making sure that he would be all the more evident in the middle. Franz Jantzen, Collection of the Supreme Court of the United States.

one hour per case. Instead of eight cases in four days he changed it to twelve in three, with Thursdays and Fridays free to debate issues and write Opinions.

Some Justices had the habit of reading from the bench the text of the Opinions they wrote, many of them forty pages long. There were days when nothing else was accomplished, no hearings. It was a time-wasting luxury no longer affordable, the new Chief objected. Hold it to a summary of no more than five minutes, he urged his colleagues, and he would go the extra mile. All he would do with his as a rule would be to announce the bottom line; who won, who lost. It would be the end of a custom that had given Justices many special moments on the bench, but the change was accepted. Soon the hearing of cases was starting within ten minutes of the time the reading of Opinion summaries began. Some theater was lost, but for those interested in the decisions, there was no problem. Complete printed texts were released immediately.

Next died another practice many had enjoyed. Membership in the Supreme Court bar, the body of lawyers authorized to practice before the High Bench, is not as exclusive as a layperson might expect. Unlike England, where courtroom practice is limited to specially trained barristers, or France, where high court pleading is reserved to a corps of ninety members, the Supreme Court bar is open to any Lawyer who is already admitted to practice before his or her state's upper court.

Until Burger's arrival, there was one significant limitation. The aspiring member of the Court bar had to appear before the Justices to be sworn in, a problem, particularly in the pre-airplane era, for busy attorneys living far from the national capital. No other American court required the personal appearance. The old Court practice had one compensation. The swearing in could be a family high point with the thrilled spouse and children looking on. It was great for them, but Burger fretted at the lost time. He remembered later: "One day Senator [Ted] Kennedy read the names of a group from Boston. We twiddled our thumbs, talking to one another, waiting for the Courtroom to be cleared to let in another group."

New applicants for the Court bar sometimes arrived by busload. Burger recalled one dismaying occasion when 604 lawyers showed up to be admitted.

Let applicants for our bar sign in by mail, Burger ruled. Those wanting the Courtroom ceremony could still have it. The latter number fell off and mail admissions soared. Soon five thousand new members were joining the Court bar each year, swelling the total to one hundred thousand, a fourth of all the American lawyers.

Signing the certificates of admission became a significant chore for the Court's amiable Clerk, Mike Rodak. A friend urged him to get a machine enabling him to sign a batch at a time, but Mike insisted on doing each one individually. The certificate would mean a lot to the recipient, claiming a prize place on his studio wall, Mike argued. It deserved a one-at-a-time handling.

Burger's changes in the Courthouse and throughout the country's legal and judicial practice were all the more remarkable in the light of the way the mentality of *stare decisis,* the idea of "let well enough alone," governs the world of the law. Swimming against the inertia tide, Burger marveled at how much unreviewed procedure had endured through the generations. He expressed it several times in conversation: "We have a court system basically the same as it was in Jamestown and Plymouth. ... If Thomas Jefferson, Aaron Burr and John Adams were to walk into court, they could get some overnight briefing and be able to function. ... It is not a bad system, but the question after two hundred or three hundred years is whether it is the best possible."

It was not just a matter of procedures, but even physical accoutrements that resisted evolution. Beside each Justice when Burger mounted the bench was a spittoon. Any of the nine could have whiled away the time during hearings gnawing at a tobacco plug, releasing the noxious juice into his own personal container. There were no tobacco spitters among Burger's brethren and, indeed, by the word of Justice Oliver Wendell Holmes, there had been none since the last of the lot stepped down in 1911. He was the first of the two Justice John Marshall Harlanses, with whom Holmes served, starting in 1902. When Burger took his seat, and the second of the John Marshall Harlanses as his brother Justice, the spittoons were still there, but serving by that time just as wastebaskets.

Another remnant of antiquity was the goose quill pens laid out for the pleading lawyers. They had served to inscribe the Declaration of Independence and the Constitution, and they were still there for any Lawyer who cared to use them to take notes. Retired FBI agent Louis D. Wine of Sacramento, California, remembered that it was one of his chores as a Court Page at the time of World War I to set out the pens.

Until World War II the Court imported the quills from England. The arrival of ballpoint pens or some other influence of the advancing decades wiped out the English supply and temporarily interrupted the custom but, in the 1950s, it was revived. Marshal Lippitt found an elderly Virginian handy with a penknife, Lewis Glaser, who could turn out pens from the plumes of Embden geese at the rate of four a minute. Glaser received a multiyear contract for one hundred pens a month, and an antique practice was brought back to life.

Spectators, however, would have to wait before seeing any lawyer use the pens. The Court provided no inkwell. The pens went home with the attorneys as souvenirs. Burger did not interfere with the nostalgic quill pens, but he kept finding other cracks in need of repair. His law clerks recognized his handwriting on signs in his chambers telling everyone to turn out unnecessary lights. The Chief Justice, fiscal-minded, had better uses for congressionally provided funds rather than waste them on electricity bills.

One budget item that interested the fifteenth Chief Justice was one he never had to face. Aware that the government sometimes charges the judiciary rent for the use of courthouses, he was happy no federal auditor had ever thought of billing the High Court for its monumental structure.

Crack plastering reached out of the Court building to all corners of legal and judicial practice. Some slits proved too deep for repair, but a remarkable number succumbed to the Burger trowel.

First was the way lawyers handled cases in court. Always happy to compare notes with fellow judges, Burger heard from several how inept they considered many of the attorneys who appeared before them. A quarter of them were incompetent, some judges told Burger. We'd say three-quarters, others grumped.

In a speech at the Fordham University Law School in New York City, Burger split the difference, saying that half the courtroom lawyers knew too little about what they were doing. An admirer of the English system limiting courtroom appearances to the specially trained barristers, Burger doubted even his own effectiveness as a pleader. He had argued three Supreme Court cases, learning how it is to lose.

Presenting a case in court requires a special skill and when "a real trial lawyer" goes by, Burger said, "I take my hat off to him."

Be that as it may, this effort at Courtroom improvements broke open the crack in earthquake fashion, giving the Court PIO, for one, many busy days. Speakers at bar associations cried out that Burger had slandered thousands, not just the 10 percent who appear in courtrooms but, by inference, the other nine-tenths whose work is confined to law offices.

Burger's aides did a check and came up with only 8 percent as the number of trial lawyers failing to meet a tolerable standard, but Burger refused to back down. Even 8 percent, he insisted, was too much. It was with relief and satisfaction that Burger learned after a few months that Harvard's eminent law school had agreed to supplement theoretical instruction with a nuts-and-bolts course in the art of courtroom practice.

Another item on the long Burger agenda was the question of juries. Is juror time wasted? Many persons summoned for jury duty had lamented to the Chief that they had been required to waste two or three days, only to be dismissed without sitting on a case. Ever mindful of his immediate predecessor, Burger told his aides that "I am sure Earl Warren heard the same thing." In the Chief's view, it was no way to win friends for the judicial system. Beside that, millions of dollars were being paid out in the small juror fees for services never required, a vast waste of money. Federal courts were calling up twelve hundred prospective jurors at a time and could only process seventy-five in a day. Burger arranged to cut the federal juror call by a third.

Next question: Why was there a need for twelve men and women in jury boxes? How about just six? Or even five?

And why not eliminate juries altogether in civil cases? England, a country Burger tried to visit each summer, had abandoned juries in civil cases years earlier. "I know a large share of the barristers in England and none of them would want to go back to juries in civil cases," Burger noted.

Was all this far afield from the Supreme Court's mission of weighing crucial national questions? Not in Burger's view. If a Chief Justice did not lead the way to needed courtroom reforms, who could?

Burger took at least a small step in the direction of a jury solution. A grade school chum, Ed Devitt, was the Chief Federal District Judge in Minnesota. The two had stayed close through the years. When Ed had run for Congress, Burger managed his campaign. Ed agreed to try six-person juries in civil cases and was able to report that it worked well. It was at least a start.

As Burger saw it, there were still more fissures in the walls of justice. One set of them threatened even to bring down the walls. These were the free of charge petitions from convicts. Prisoners who were able to read and write were hard at work in many jailhouse libraries, combing the law books, looking up old cases, and trying to find some grounds to be set free. As Burger drafted the Court's weekly "dead lists," cases the Justices would turn away without ado, fully a third of them had come in forma pauperis, pauper-fashion, meaning that the often cell-bound litigant had no court costs to pay.

The logic of the IFP cases, as they are called at the Court, is that every person, penniless or not, has a right to justice, but the free ride into the High Court meant that one out of three of the cases each Justice had to weigh was, in the Court's word for them, a "frivolous," baseless appeal, lacking merit. Hours of Court time were consumed brushing pointless IFPs aside. The rest of the federal courts were inundated in like fashion.

One pauper case caught Burger's eye as a clamorous example of what was wrong. Three dollars worth of cigarettes were confiscated from a prisoner. He felt that it was unjustified and raised the question in court. For months the matter ricocheted through the federal court system, bouncing from one federal Judge to another, until a dozen had handled one aspect or another. Before a solution was found, one of the twelve judges, wholly exasperated, said he would be happy to settle the thing by digging down into his own pocket to refund the $3.

One could not deny, said Burger, that the cigarettes may well have meant a lot to the man in confinement, but surely one had to admit that there had to be a better solution. Burger appealed to the federal prisons to stem the IFP tide by putting in a system for hearing complaints inside the walls. The reform was made.

As Burger's years on the High Bench went by, his mother's fear that he would get used to the remaining cracks was not borne out.

Judges as well as trial lawyers needed ongoing training. Some years earlier, other reformers had made a start on that, and in 1968 retired but tireless former Justice Tom Clark expanded the effort at the Federal Judicial Center. A close confidante of Burger, Clark won the Chief's support for an even broader attempt. Burger became an enthusiastic advocate for the National Judicial College in Reno, Nevada.

Special training for judges seemed to go well, but Burger decided that more was needed, some guarantee that those on the bench followed up on what they had been taught. The answer, Burger decided, was a "single" calendar for the federal judiciary, no more "master calendar."

The master calendar meant that a case might go through the hands of many judges. Burger found one bit of litigation that had called for the attention of fourteen judges, each of whom must have used at least half an hour becoming familiar with the matter. Besides wasting bench time, it was a system wide open to judge-shopping by manipulative lawyers. There was a further problem. It provided great cover for judges who were "dogging it," taking in ballgames, going fishing or just drifting into the courthouse at 2:00 in the afternoon.

The single calendar took care of all that. One Judge saw the case all the way through and had to make reports every thirty, sixty and ninety days and then six months on how the matter was proceeding toward a resolution. Burger kept an eye on these progress reports. Within a half decade of his intervention, "productivity," the number of cases settled, was up by a third. There was one less judicial crack.

Still the Chief found more. One was the way the nation's two court systems were getting along with one another. Besides the seven hundred federal judges there were twenty-three thousand judges in state courts. Thanks to the doctrine of *habeas corpus,* literally in Latin, "you shall have the body," many a person convicted in state courts was appealing successfully to the federal courts for a new trial and sometimes an acquittal. The Supreme Court itself was not least in this process of overturning decisions of courts below. Many state court judges, Burger found, "were so mad they couldn't see straight." Some refused to speak to a federal judge.

Making it worse the state courts were all reinventing the wheel. Cut off from one another, they had no way of learning from the successes of some and the failures of others.

To close that crack Burger campaigned successfully for periodic state-federal judicial conferences. Further, he got behind the creation of a National Center for State Courts. It was established at Williamsburg, Virginia, a clearinghouse for ideas from the fifty separate state court systems.

Not everything Burger saw as a repairable crack looked that way to others. Burger was willing to think the unthinkable. One such pondering touched even on the all-but-sacred doctrine of *habeas corpus,* the old thorn in the side of state-federal judicial relations. We were taught to look down on European courts because they do not have *habeas corpus,*" he mused in his chambers, "the idea that prisoners were locked away in the slammer." But, he said, "In Europe they do have review boards of psychiatrists and others who go into the jails to review cases." That seemed to him to work adequately as a substitute.

Even a good share of the legal adversary system could be considered for history's dustbin, Burger believed. He had a story to illustrate it: "A lawyer in a small town was starving. Then another moved in. After that they both prospered." Lawsuits filled the air of the little town.

Suits were better than duels with pistols and swords, the Chief conceded, but even more helpful, he urged, would be neighborhood citizen arbitration boards to handle minor quarrels over matters like bad roofing jobs. America, in Burger's view, was far too litigious, and "the courts too popular."

To one visitor he pointed to a case the Court recently had judged. A social activist was bumped from an airplane fight. Well accustomed to bringing lawsuits, he went to court over the missed flight and got as far as the final Court.

Consumer rights needed a defense, Burger said, but taking an incident of that sort to the Supreme Court was like using "a train to pull a wheelbarrow."

Though he had applied to Presidents before world TV audiences the oath to uphold and defend the Constitution, Burger was willing even to take a second look at that basic national compact, not to scrap it, but to reconsider how it should be applied after two centuries to a much different nation.

As the two hundredth anniversary of the Constitution approached in 1987, Burger's dream was to inspire a three-year discussion of it in colleges and elsewhere, one year devoted to each of the three branches of the national government. Are we, for instance, demanding too much of the President, expecting him to be a universal answer man at press conferences?

Our lesser generation, Burger told friends, could not hope to come up with such a brilliant explanation of the meaning of the Constitution as the Founding Fathers provided in the Federalist Papers, but even a more modest consensus on how to apply the constitutional principles could help.

Most ambitious of all his efforts, this one did not work, but Burger did step down from the Court at age seventy-nine in 1986 in time to lead a three-year celebration of the constitutional bicentennial. At least, he felt, he could make better known the document on which the Supreme Court draws to make crucial national choices. Burger handed out thousands of copies of the 1787 pact.

Seventeen years after taking over from Earl Warren, the fifteenth Chief Justice still left unplastered some cracks in the judicial and legal walls, but his mother could have been proud that he had never grown used to any of them.

CHAPTER 14

ONLY HUMAN

"Remember, you are only human." Elvera's voice was earnest as she counseled her seventy-five-year-old Chief Justice husband.

"No," was the answer. "If I were, I would not have lived this long." The reply was typical of the longest serving Chief Justice of the twentieth century, a driven, complex man of humble origins, an endless worker who demanded much the same of his subordinates, a man willing to sign off on prisoners' death warrants yet also a sentimentalist with a playful side, a moderate Republican, a horseman, a bicyclist, an antique fancier, an omnivorous reader, a gardener, a cook and a lover of the practice of law. He was all that while at the same time suffering from the effects of childhood polio, from a bicycle accident soon after he became Chief Justice and from accumulating fatigue.

An example of what concerned Mrs. Burger was the Chief's acceptance of an invitation to address the annual convention of the National Association of Newspaper Editors. The Burgers had an agreement between them to accept no invitations on Court days, and four cases had been argued that day. Yet Burger consented. When she heard of it, said Mrs. Burger, "I thought he had lost his marbles."

It was not that Burger had not had enough for one day, it was rather that he felt that he should seize the opportunity to tell journalists, who saw him as a foe of some of their freedoms, that the media and the courts basically are allies. Both needed independence. Each ought to support the other. Both would go down if democracy were to fail.

That his wife eventually would go along, Burger did not doubt. Asked about his bruisingly long work weeks, clocked by his Court Secretary at up to eighty hours, Burger said of his evening meal: "Often it is at eleven. My wife's used to it. I did the same when I practiced law."

Presiding solemnly with godlike authority over Courtroom debates, or seen on television administering the oath of office to Presidents, the "only human" side of Warren Burger was not visible.

His responsibilities were daunting, so much so that he was asked whether he and his brethren were themselves in awe as they went about their grave tasks. No, he responded, the nine are so engulfed in work that there is no time for such considerations. "We are on a treadmill," he said. "We are like the Volga boatmen." Ever straining at the oars, no end of the river ever was in sight.

His questioner persisted. Justices are solemn on the bench. Is that not evidence of the gravity they sense?

"No," the Chief repeated. "We are just trying to concentrate."

A typical Burger day began at his small nineteenth-century Virginia farmhouse with the arrival of a Court limousine bearing District of Columbia tag number ten. The Chief alone among the Justices had an assigned car. Most of his brethren arrived at work behind the wheels of their own modest family cars. In his first Supreme Court years, Burger would climb into the back seat hefting two briefcases bulging with overnight papers. Later, as the work mounted, the briefcases were retired in favor of a full-sized suitcase.

There was always an early start to beat the rush hour. In the car's rear was a folding table. "My work starts the minute I step in," Burger said. "We go slow enough for me to write. It is valuable time. The next thing I know we go down the ramp." The changing sounds as the car descended the police-guarded slope into the Court's underground garage were the signal to snap shut the suitcase and to head for the elevators for the two-story ride to the floor of chambers.

Inside the courthouse by 7:40 A.M., Burger would breakfast, sometimes taking his turn in the public cafeteria chow line, on other occasions using the refrigerator and the small "pullman" kitchen in his chambers. There was an unvarying rule about soiled dishes. Burger rinsed them in hot water lest the residue harden.

Nine times out of ten, by his count, Burger lunched alone in his chambers. Only occasionally, such as on a Justice's birthday, did he and the other eight make use of the handsome private dining room the architect had built for them. At the anniversary parties it was the Chief's custom to buy the wine, "but not enough to do any harm."

Some Saturdays, with the cafeteria closed, the Chief would become the chef in his chambers, whipping up something in the little kitchen for his law clerks. Bean soup was one of his prides. So was his pumpkin bread and the marmalade he canned at home.

For visitors, the Chief liked to serve tea, carrying on what he understood was Justice Burton's custom in the 1945 to 1958 period. It was a careful ritual. First the Chief Justice would warm the cups. Then a bit would be tipped into his cup. Next a full serving would go to the guest.

Burger's tutor on just how to do it had been Herbert Lewis, a hometown friend who was in later years the editor of the *Minneapolis Tribune*. Lewis had been a correspondent in London during World War II, there learning the proper handling of an Englishman's favorite beverage. A touch of old England was fine with the Chief. Ever conscious that America's legal traditions stem from the English past, Burger was unabashedly Anglophilic.

To serve the tea the antique-loving and history-minded Chief used a silver pot made in 1800 in the era of silversmith Paul Revere whose midnight ride in '75 had "spread the alarm to every Middlesex village and farm." Burger sometimes would point out with pleasure some of the familiar antique features of the teapot, a spout in the shape of a porpoise's head, tiny eyes on either side.

People who saw it often got it wrong. "They think it's a snake," he would say.

The teapot was a gift from former law clerks. It was inscribed: "To Chief Justice Warren Burger on his twentieth anniversary on the federal courts and the two hundredth anniversary of American independence." Despite his strictures against inappropriate luxury at the Court, the Chief accepted the pot.

That proved to be only the first problem. The clerks were in their forties. Many were in firms that might have cases before the Court. There could be no suggestion that there was any conflict of interest should Burger have to sit on such cases.

With agile legal minds at work, a solution was found. The pot would not be Burger's personal property. It would not go with him when he left the Court. It could never be passed on to son Wade Allan or daughter Margaret Mary Elizabeth. It would be a present to the Supreme Court Historical Society, one of Burger's creations, but a gift with a stipulation. So long as Burger was Chief Justice it should remain with him in his chambers.

Pouring tea for the PIO one day, the Chief murmured: "Service by a liveried flunky!" Dressed in a jacket and pants that did not match, the Chief Justice hardly measured up to a flunky dress code, but his ironic reference was to a searing magazine article by one of the Court's persistent media hair shirts, Nina Totenberg. The Court, she charged, was "the last plantation," the final remnant of the ante-bellum South. Blacks, she suggested, were manservants for the Justices, bottom level employees who could hope for little more.

It was true that each Justice had the help of a "Messenger," a factotum available to handle the time-killing day-to-day chores of everyday living that otherwise would drain off energies and moments Justices needed badly for the judging of cases.

Like his brethren, Burger had a Messenger, Alvin Wright. Alvin had started at the Court as a laborer, had been promoted to the position of Chief Justice Warren's Handyman and had come to work for Burger.

Alvin could, indeed, have poured the tea. Helping with food and drink was one of the Court Messenger chores. At noon Justices' messengers joined the tourist lines in the cafeteria filling trays for the Justices, and when the nine used their handsome dining room the same employees would carry in trays, set the cafeteria food on the table and leave.

Like most of the other messengers Alvin was black. Similar to the majority, he seemed happy with his employment.

The "happy black" was, to be sure, part of plantation mythology, but in the case of those working at the Court, many stayed for a lifetime, even bringing children and grandchildren to follow them. Alvin's son was one of those who remained in the service of the law but not as a menial. In a sign that not all were doomed to the social bottom level, he had gone to law school and was an Attorney.

For Burger, serving as the tea pourer not only was a natural act of courtesy but also a mandate in the house of the *Brown v. Board of Education* desegregation decision.

Talking one day about the intricate calculations that went into the presentation of the teapot, Burger said, "We have to be so careful!"

The Court is Caesar's wife. Not only must behavior be proper it must appear to be proper. The same thought was in Burger's mind when others with a similar humble twin cities' origin extended a vacation invitation. They were the Weyerhaeusers, wealthy foresters, whose family scion had begun as a sawman.

Come, relax for three or four days on Puget Sound in the family yacht, the Weyerhaeusers proposed. A boat lover, Burger was tempted. But might it seem compromising? He declined.

The chambers of the Chief Justice consist of a suite of five rooms, an outer office, a room for secretaries, the Justices' Conference Room, a room in which the Justices don their robes and a private inner office for the Chief.

It was in the latter hideaway that the Chief wrote his Opinions. Generally, he composed them standing at a high ledge. The childhood polio had left him with inoperable spinal curvature. Doctor's orders were to stand erect as often as possible. The Opinions were drafted by hand until the fingers tired. Then the Chief would switch to a typewriter using a combined touch and hunt-and-peck system.

Temperature in the inner office was kept at 65°. To maintain it that low with warmer air in the surrounding spaces, Burger sometimes would push the dial down to 60°.

A button-front beige sweater was his comfortable inner office attire.

A half century of the Chief's earlier life was reflected on the private office walls. There were several paintings and sketches, the work of both Burgers. A study of riding boots, a reminder of the Chief's years as a horseman, was one Elvera had done. Also included were several of Burger's own works, a still life of a half grapefruit and a napkin, a portrait of son Wade as a child decked out in a bright vest reminiscent of a Picasso and, significantly, a rendition of books, including one labeled the "Aaron Burr Case," the precedent on which Burger drew to end the Nixon presidency.

Earliest of all the wall decorations was a sketch Burger had done in high school as a class exercise, a "literary map of England." High points of English history were illustrated with cartoon characters including a joke that the boy artist trusted that his teacher would not misunderstand. A child was shown telling another about the climactic struggle of 1066 in which modern England was formed: "There's Hastings where they fought the battle of 1610!"

On the word of Paul Mellon, dedicator of the National Gallery of Art, the Burger talent both in painting and in sculpture was above average amateur quality. Mellon gave his appraisal at the inauguration of a second building for the National Gallery. Burger was present as the gallery's Board Chairman and thus its "boss," but Mellon insisted that had not colored his judgment.

None of Burger's sculptures was in the inner office but his bas-relief of the "great Chief Justice," John Marshall of 1801 to 1835, was on display in the Justices' dining room.

Burger's lifelong avocation as a painter and sculptor was terminated only by his arrival at the Supreme Court. At the Court of Appeals in the 1960s, he had often done busts of fellow judges and, even at the Supreme Court, he had started one of his "brother" Hugo Black. That went unfinished.

The sculpturing had started in childhood with clay carried home in a toy wagon from the Mississippi banks. Some of Burger's works went to the subjects as gifts, some stayed at the small Burger home. Cleaning his garage one day, Burger found a death mask of Dante he had done in high school. It was somewhat the worse for wear.

Even with the paintbrushes, the palette and the sculpturing tools packed away, Burger found his Courthouse days and weeks packed to the seams.

Routinely, work in the chambers ran to 5 P.M. on Saturday and 4 P.M. on Sunday. Often the same went on in the other chambers. Arriving one Saturday, Burger asked the Court police how many other Justices were present, should he need them. "Six," was the answer.

"And the other two probably were at work at home," the Chief surmised.

Homework, the bane of lazy scholars, was common for the Justices. Phoning one day to the PIO, Burger remarked: "I'm here at home going through a stack of certs."

"Certs" are the petitions for *certiorari,* the lawyers' requests that their cases be certified as one of those to be argued and decided. In Burger's time 97 percent were "decertified," rejected, and by the mid-1990s the turndown rate was higher, sixty-nine rebuffs out of seventy.

Combing through them to create a "dead list," those on which the Chief recommended that there be no Court action, was a constant time-consuming chore. Justices used Fridays to sign off on the list and the Chief's preparations sometimes went down to the wire. "I'll be up until 4 A.M. getting ready for tomorrow's conference," the septuagenarian Burger remarked one Thursday.

It was a heavy workload and getting worse. Burger recalled that the great Louis Brandeis, who served on the Court until 1939, was known to complain that fifteen cert requests were too many to handle in a conference. By Burger's time there were one hundred and, toward the end of the century, two hundred.

The cert flow was one way to judge the size of the Court workload. An even better one, in Burger's view, was the number of signed Court decisions handed down each

year. The curve rose through mid-century. When Earl Warren succeeded the deceased Fred Vinson in 1953 the Justices were deciding sixty cases a year. By the middle of the Burger period the total had more than doubled, up to 145 decisions each year. "It's flattering but unreal to think we can do so much more than Holmes, Frankfurter and Brandeis," Burger said.

Some relief came to the Justices when Congress agreed to give the Court broader leeway in rejecting cases so that by the mid-1990s the number of annual signed Opinions rolled back under one hundred, two-thirds of the peak Burger level, but still far ahead of the mid-century total. With each

The playful and artistic side of Chief Justice Burger. Because Burger would not take the time to pose, NBC artist Betty Wells used a photo for this sketch. Burger was so pleased with the result that he asked Betty to do border sketches of big moments from his life: as an amateur artist at his easel (lower right), *as a horseman in his early years* (lower left) *and as a hit-and-run victim while bicycling for exercise at night* (upper left). *The latter seemed funny to him only after a long, painful recuperation.* Betty Wells.

Justice by the mid-1990s required to make a personal decision about the fate of seven thousand cases, the workload for all nine remained immense.

For Burger, the low point each day was at 4 P.M. "What I need then," he admitted, "is a triple martini, but you can't have that here. Instead, I take a spoonful of honey washed down with tea. It goes immediately into the bloodstream. It gives quick energy."

No play makes Jack a dull boy, so the Chief used many weekend late afternoons and early evenings strolling through Georgetown, the original tobacco export riverport section of Washington, or walking around the city's Tidal Basin, another section of the Potomac waterfront.

Thanks to the absence of Courtroom television, he and the other Justices lacked household faces and generally enjoyed anonymity, but once in a while the Chief was recognized, a minor security hazard. "You look just like the Chief Justice," one passerby commented.

"Yes," was the answer, "people have told me that."

A satirist for *Esquire* spotted Burger one day on Wisconsin Avenue in Georgetown and fell in a few steps behind. Burger window-shopped at some antique stores, ever on the look out for early-nineteenth-century additions to the Justices' dining room, and then, according to the reporter, stopped to "drool" at the pastries in the window of a bakery. Burger had no memory of the incident, but, fighting a weight problem, he conceded with a laugh, that perhaps he had drooled.

The question of excess poundage had come up about that time when Burger had a checkup at the Mayo Clinic in Minnesota where he was a trustee emeritus. "I told a lie to the reporters," he admitted blithely. "They asked how I was and I said 5 pounds overweight. The doctors said 15. The truth was 25." Touching on a matter of such personal detail, the Chief Justice did not feel himself bound by the high scruples of the bench.

No longer riding horseback as he once did, Burger got exercise by bicycling near home in the late evening. It was a practice that nearly cost him his life not long after assuming the Chief Justiceship. A local high school night football game had just finished when a car, described as blue and low slung, struck him, causing a concussion, dislocating his shoulder, breaking his nose and five ribs, injuring a foot and inflicting a gash at an eye requiring eight stitches. Ever taking command, the semi-conscious Chief waved away a stretcher and then nearly collapsed as he staggered to an ambulance.

Burger wanted only limited public information to be provided at the time because the Vice President and the Speaker of the House of Representatives were unavailable at the moment, and he was on the very short list to be Chief Executive should anything befall President Nixon. He saw no point in escalating concern about his condition.

The foot injury proved to be the most bothersome. Until he found time for corrective surgery several years later, Burger wore soft shoes, including two valued pairs he found on sale London.

Years of pain came out of the bicycle accident, but Burger found some macabre humor in it. When Betty Wells of NBC-TV did his portrait from photographs, presenting it to him, he asked that she sketch cartoons around the edge highlighting various career aspects, one of him on his horse, one in painter's smock at an easel and one in judicial black robe in flight above the shattered bicycle. Burger gave reproductions to friends.

The childhood "literary map of England" in the Chief's inner chamber was an early reflection of what proved to be a lifelong affectionate interest in Britain. In summer trips to London to visit English barristers and judges, and to sightsee and shop, Burger became a close friend of Lord Chief Justice Widgery who invited him to sit beside him as appeals were argued.

Widgery in turn visited the Burgers at their Virginia farmhouse enjoying a warm hospitality that was put to a test when he and the Lord Chancellor of England were invited to an ABA convention.

The meeting's organizers arranged for a long procession, dignitaries in pairs. Toward the end, as a climax, Burger would walk alone preceded by the two Englishmen. Not at all, the Chief objected. It was no way to treat friends. The whole idea, he said, was to "show that we are together." With all the rest in twos, the three walked side by side.

Not all Yankees shared Burger's affection for the land of the Union Jack, and among those who had reservations was Justice Douglas, a man of America's common folk. Burger was pained when Douglas gave a speech taking the English Lord Justice to task. Douglas, said Burger, "doesn't realize that Widgery is not part of the inherited aristocracy. He has much the same background as I. His father was a coal miner."

In Burger's view, the English and American courts had shared the same roots until 1776, when they branched off from one another. It could be useful to meet periodically in alternate capitals to compare notes on the different experiences of two centuries, learning from one another in the same way the fifty American states were doing at the Burger-backed National Center for State Courts.

The bilateral exchanges were arranged, with Burger an enthusiastic participant. From them he concluded that Americans could learn a lot from the British at the trial level, while this country could teach a good deal about appeals. Barristers, he found, were hard-hitting advocates but exquisitely polite, never indulging in "barroom brawls." The British won that one.

By contrast, the Chief was shocked by London appellate procedures. This country's Supreme Court Justices have all the issues spelled out for them beforehand in briefs so that they can hear a case in sixty minutes. To the contrary, sitting at Widgery's side, Burger saw to his astonishment that members of the English court knew nothing about the case before them as they went to the bench. Long, drawn-out hearings were the result, some lasting two and one-half days.

The Anglo-American legal exchanges were an all-male affair until a woman from the middle level of the Arizona state judiciary broke the sex barrier. She was Sandra Day O'Connor, a self-described Western "cowgirl" who impressed Burger with her talents as a judge, even if it was then too soon to think of her or any other woman as a sister to the High Court's brethren.

Taking his weekend Tidal Basin walks, Burger sometimes would look in at the high-domed Thomas Jefferson Memorial on its banks. For most visitors to the national capital Jefferson is one of the nation's three super greats, all of them past Presidents and each of them immortalized in a monument—George Washington with his obelisk and Abraham Lincoln and Jefferson with their marble shrines.

Perhaps because of Jefferson's feud with his distant cousin, John Marshall, the jurist's hero, Burger had his doubts about the revered author of the Declaration of Independence. "Jefferson," he said, "was a split personality. You see the noble words on the walls of the memorial, and yet Jefferson said 'Hang Aaron Burr,' a former Vice President of the United States!

"He made violently intemperate attacks on others. He had eight mulatto children. He sent two daughters at maturity to New Orleans because they could not be accepted here in the society of the time!"

Himself a strict, devoted family man, Burger found it hard to forgive the great Jefferson's household relationships.

Even more important, Burger could not forget the Marshall-Jefferson struggle over Aaron Burr in the case that served as his precedent in the Nixon Presidential decision. When the federal judiciary cooperated in creating several Supreme Court historical films for public television, Burger saw to it that the fans of Jefferson working on other parts of the script did not handle the Burr trial. He wrote that part of the text himself.

The moral in both the Jefferson-Burr and Nixon cases, as he saw it, was that Presidents like all citizens must come forward with evidence needed in a criminal defense and that, in a system of divided governmental powers, judges, not Presidents, have the last word on that.

Burger was sensitive about overdoing in a democracy, whether the overdoer was a President or a Supreme Court Justice. When aides wanted to design a Chief Justice flag for his limousine, "I put that down hard," he said.

Another time, when the same enthusiasts found volunteer funds to create a large royal purple flag for the Court building, Burger checked with his brethren. Some other departments of the government did have flags of their own. This time the hint of vainglory died at the Conference table. Some of the brethren objected and the flag, already created, vanished into storage.

About the same time the Mint proposed a series of medallions of the fifteen Chief Justices, starting with Burger. How about starting instead at the beginning with John Jay, Burger suggested. An agreement was reached embracing both ideas. The medallions would come out two at a time, working from both ends, Jay and Burger first, followed quickly by Earl Warren and John Rutledge with plans to add the remainder gradually. The medallions served as gifts for visiting dignitaries.

Enamored of good writing, both as a reader and as a composer of texts, Burger tried to keep his Opinions short though he said he could never equal the succinct Hugo Black. "All judges are in favor of shorter Opinions by other judges," he said. In his own case he tried to set an example, but even so, the Opinions that came down from the bench often ran to two-score pages. A lawyer had to read many of them three times before figuring out what they meant, Burger regretted.

Among his papers at the Court, Burger still kept a copy of a signed short story, *The Gleam,* which he had written for his high school publication, a tale about the woes of a newsman as he tried to interview lawyer Barret Meredith.

Confident about language, Burger would insist on phrases like "rip off" when protesting, in speeches, about some raid on the Public Treasury. Not dignified enough, judicial fellows would say.

No, would be their answer. "Rip off" is needed for effect. "Done" was a word Burger liked for its blunt Anglo-Saxon force. When one of the college professors in the judicial fellow corps, changed it to "accomplished," Burger put back "done." The Department of Justice will be reading the speech for directives, the professor argued. "Accomplished" would sound more serious. No matter, was the reply, "done" it was to be.

As for harshness of language, Burger would add, one should read some of the dissents various of his naysaying brethren published routinely. In his view, some brothers' Opinions, especially those of the liberal Bill Brennan, far outstung anything he composed.

Burger used words with a care his old school teacher surely would have appreciated. When one assistant, speaking of the fifteen Chief Justices, remarked that Burger was "last" of the series, Burger told a story of a vain author who, fishing for compliments, asked an acquaintance whether he had read his last book. "Latest, you mean, though I wish it was the last," was the deflating reply.

A lifelong lover of books, Burger's dream as Chief was to have a month away just to go through favorite volumes. While on the High Bench he never got it.

Burger traced his affection for the printed word to a year at home as a child when he was kept out of school because of the polio. His teacher sent him histories and biographies, one hundred of them, as he recalled. It helped form his life, he said.

Generally, in bedtime reading, Burger found himself merely skipping through accounts of current events, looking for episodes of which he had personal knowledge and frequently finding the telling at odds with his own memory. "I'm a book burner," he told a startled author. "Not because I like burning books, but because I have no space at home and even less here at the Court. Sometimes, I get two copies. I may mark up one and toss the other into the fireplace here."

Burger had an amiable and compassionate manner in many of his relationships, but he could also be firm, even harsh. When someone spoke ill of then President

Jimmy Carter, accusing him of being hard on his staff, Burger put himself in Carter's corner. "He should be hard," he said. "How else can he supervise and reprimand where that is needed?"

Not only was Burger quick to dismiss Court employees who fell short of his standards, he had no qualms about turning away thousands of prisoner appeals as "frivolous." Burger visited prisons frequently in this country and in Europe, campaigning for decent conditions of confinement, and for training in job skills that could be used at release, but he had no doubt that incarceration was appropriate for some and that executions did not violate the constitutional ban on "cruel and unusual punishment." He read with approval a sign over the entrance to a Soviet detention center for youths between the ages of fourteen and eighteen who had committed violent crimes. The sign read:

> You are here because you need help.
> We are here to help you.
> We cannot help you unless you cooperate.
> If you don't cooperate, we will make you cooperate.

Burger, the ex-footballer, used no corporal punishment on Court staffers, but he was physical, and he was daring. When a picture-seeking TV crew crowded into an elevator with him on an out-of-town trip, the Chief's heavy shoulder dropped, and the astonished crewmen found themselves catapulted out of the small space.

On a summer's day in London when Burger saw youths pounding another with fists and sticks, he stepped in between them to break it up.

A skeptic, Burger had to be given proof. He said the attitude traced to an experience on his high school newspaper. Assigned to do a basketball feature, he interviewed a classmate who was a star at that game. He was a bright fellow with a playful turn of mind; later, like Burger, a judge.

The young Burger had picked up a false report to the effect that the basketball team was adjusting to some sort of rule change. With tongue in cheek, the interviewee went along with the misapprehension, spinning out a string of fanciful details. "It was all false," Burger recalled.

He fell for all of it, turning in an exciting story.

"The Editor told our moderator that my story was all wrong, but she said: 'Print it! I have always said a second source is needed, and he didn't have one. It will teach him a good lesson.'"

The Chief added: "It did! I never forgot it. As a Lawyer I would take a sworn deposition and never believe anything until I had a second source."

Combined with the ability to doubt was a well-developed sense of caution guiding his actions at the Court. "It is like a church here," Burger would say. "A soft sound is loud."

To marry tact and the possible, on the one hand, to his strong points of view on the other, Burger wrote his Court Opinions in two stages: "In the first draft I am apt to hit hard." Then came the second stage, the one that might well affect the law of the land. Burger would "pull back, do some softening, do some sharpening up."

The Chief spoke to some newspeople off the record, sharing his views so that the reporters might understand them, but forbidding attribution. It was a way to be comprehended at least by a few regulars in the Court press corps, while avoiding the instant controversies his remarks might generate.

An exception was made for the news magazine, *U.S. News & World Report,* because in that particular era, they would go along with the two-stage practice, allowing Burger to review and amend the transcript before publication. Other contemporaries might reject such an arrangement as tampering with the record, but it allowed Burger to report candidly on a wide range of Court issues, saying in final form what he was prepared to live with, and it gave the magazine a scoop on many of the Chief's views.

Burger, in many "state of the judiciary" speeches to the conventions of the American Bar Association, limited himself to reading carefully worded texts. Extemporaneity was out. At the first such encounter, Burger explained: "I've been told by experienced people in our craft that I should never do more than just clear my throat before then using a prepared text!"

The self-reliance Burger learned as a newspaper deliverer, as a schoolboy newsman and athlete and as a night law student, helped him cope with each day's challenges, but it also caused problems. Burger was astonished on a trip one day when a visitor to his hotel room asked archly what lady had shared the night with him.

Monogamously faithful to Elvera, the highly moral Chief was flabbergasted. What provoked such a question?

All that underwear and the socks and the wash-and-wear shirt drying in the bathroom, was the answer. Burger relaxed. No woman had handled that. He always did his own laundry at night, he explained.

Self-reliance at the Court easily segued over to micromanagement and to the second-guessing of aides. They in return, anxious not to cross wires, but unable to chat often enough with the hectically busy Chief, resorted to memoranda, creating a convenient paper record, but also adding to the already appalling pile of lawyers' briefs and other documentation on the Chief's desks and windowsill.

Perhaps aware of his underlings' problems, but also concerned about his own, Burger tried whimsy one day to fend off the flow: "I'm going to send a note to all of you. As Lewis Carroll said in *Alice in Wonderland*: 'The king said, "That is something I will never forget!"

"'Yes, you will,' said the queen, "unless you write a memorandum!'"

No hours night or day or on weekends seemed enough to meet all the demands the Chief faced, many of them self-imposed, such as the judicial reforms, but others such as his role in the leadership of the Smithsonian Institution mandated by law. A museum buff, Burger was not unhappy with the Smithsonian details even though they added to the pressure. When the Smithsonian put up a new building on the capital mall to house the history of aviation and space exploration, Burger agreed to a request that he speak. But, what about?

Anything, said the Smithsonian staff, so long as it runs for three minutes.

The explanation? At the instant the dedication addresses started, a radio signal would be sent to the most distant of the space probes the National Air and Space Authority had in flight. Traveling at the fantastic speed of light the signal would instruct the satellite millions of miles away to respond at once with an order to the great doors to open. The talks by Burger and the others were to last exactly seventeen minutes, the time the outgoing and returning signals would take. As the final word was uttered, with no other action on the part of anyone on the ground, the doors of what proved to be one of Washington's most popular attractions swung ajar. The immensity of space and the technological ingenuity of the generation had been underlined.

A few old acquaintances including judges from the appeals court below, called Burger by his first name, but staffers and even Court brethren who had known him previously invariably addressed him as "Chief." He accepted that as appropriate to his office. His own notes were signed with three letters, "WEB."

Along with what he saw as sometimes necessary severity, Burger had a playful side. It was in evidence one night at the annual dinner of the Gridiron Club, a group of veteran Washington newspeople who "toast but never scorch" capital celebrities.

Burger was assigned a dais seat between Vice President Fritz Mondale who had not yet arrived, and hoary Democratic political leader Bob Strauss. Down the dais was TV journalist Walter Cronkite, who alternated with Burger high on the polls as one of the half dozen most influential Americans. On one side of Cronkite was Elizabeth Dole, the handsome spouse of Senator Bob Dole, and on the other the equally attractive wife of one of the bureau chiefs.

Burger scribbled a note to Cronkite: "How come you get two beautiful women and all I get is Bob Strauss and an empty chair?" Cronkite treated it as a private exchange as well as a rare keepsake, a footnote to national history. He shared it with his table companions and then pocketed it.

As the dinner broke up, Mrs. Dole lamented to Burger: "He won't even let us have a Xerox of your note!" So, Burger related later, "I wrote it again."

His sentimental side also was reflected in an exchange with a lifelong political foe, Hubert H. Humphrey, another Minnesotan. The Republican Burger never doubted Humphrey's political wizardry. When a local Governor, hard-pressed for personal funds, seemed on the verge of upsetting Humphrey as a Senator, Burger marveled at the way the threatened politician got President Johnson to give his rival a federal judgeship. That took care of the candidate's financial needs and eliminated him as a political threat.

But now the former Vice President was dying. On a trip home to the twin cities, Burger went by the Humphrey home to leave his card. The invalid insisted that he come in.

Days later, the Chief Justice was still emotional as he recounted what happened: "He was thin but so full of bounce. He said: 'All this talk of terminal illness. It's not the doctors but someone else up there who decides!'

"We kidded around. He took my hands in both of his and said: 'We have known each other for forty years, political opponents most of that time. We have lambasted one another, but we have been friends just the same.'

"I was tired when I went there but he lifted my spirits. He said we would have to have dinner on October 2. It is the day the Court opens. I do not accept invitations on Court days but, in this case, I will make an exception. Muriel has been in touch with us. We will be a group of old friends for dinner."

As Elvera correctly put it, WEB did have a softer side and was only human.

❊ CHAPTER 15 ❊

PRESIDENTS

On an official visit to France, Chief Justice Burger was taken aside by President Giscard d'Estaing who had twice in previous days sent the Presidential Guard to pay homage to the Chief's visit, a gesture generally reserved for chiefs of state.

The American embassy was impressed, and sent off a cable to the State Department suggesting that the d'Estaing act was a signal that France wanted to dispel the chill in U.S.-French relations that had existed under the imperious Charles de Gaulle.

What's going on in Washington? d'Estaing asked Burger.

In Congress? At the White House? Burger shrugged. He had no idea. "There are two million other Americans who know that better than I," he told the French chief of state. Newspeople, for one group, he suggested. "D'Estaing," he said later, "looked quizzical. He couldn't believe me."

It was one of repeated occasions on which Burger tried to explain to puzzled foreigners the American system of divided governmental powers and of checks and balances, a sorting out of responsibilities that had allowed him to write the Supreme Court Opinion drawing on the Jefferson-Burr-Marshall precedent, driving President Nixon from office.

When a delegation of judges from Communist China visited the Supreme Court on July 11, 1977, and when Burger paid an official visit to the Soviet Union in September of the same year, the Chief made the same protestation of ignorance about U.S. foreign and domestic policy and met the same disbelief.

It was not that the President, the Justices and the Congresspeople did not meet one another on occasion, exchanging ideas and discussing mutual requirements. There was, as Burger put it, "no bright line" setting the boundaries of action of the three branches. There was need, however, in his view, for each of the three to stay within its own bailiwick, respecting the rights of the other two to operate freely.

As Burger saw it, so far as the judiciary was concerned, "Judges have an awful lot of power and should be careful in using it." But, he continued, theirs is the most limited of the three "co-equal" branches and should not have a "direction" as they decide controversies case by case. "Directions," or policy lines and philosophy, he told visitors, are something that should guide only the President and Congress.

With that said, there was a great deal of tangled back-and-forth. The Supreme Court could and did strike down laws passed by Congress and the state legislatures, and as in the Burr and Nixon cases, did pass judgment on Presidents. In turn, the President, with senatorial approval, appointed new Justices, and the Congress decided what funds the Court could have, what raises in pay there should be, when the Court should return to the bench after the summer recess (the first Monday in October) and how many Justices there should be (from six to ten over the years, and nine since the Civil War).

"Isn't it 'disloyal' of the Court to veto presidential and congressional actions?" Burger was asked by a group of visiting foreign correspondents. Isn't there pressure from the two other branches to limit such "disloyalty?"

The answer to the first, in the Chief's view, was that the Court's proper loyalty was to the Constitution, which sets limits on all three branches as well as on the Fourth

Estate, the media. As for "pressure," Burger told the overseas journalists, in the dozen years he had served thus far as Chief Justice: "I have known of no pressure attempted against the Court. There is no way to bring pressure. The Justices are here for life." He added: "Our salaries are not large [just over $100,000 a year at the time], but Congress cannot bring pressure by reducing them as was done in England."

The Constitution gives the Justices and other federal judges salary protection. There can be no cuts. Yet, in the interplay of checks and balances, even that required some qualification, as was evident in the first days of 1977 when a White House staffer telephoned Burger to get his concurrence on a one-third slashing of a proposed increase in Justices' pay.

The caller, a "low rank functionary" in the Chief's judgment, inquired also whether the Justices would agree to a new ethics code provision. As a topper, the presidential staffer wanted to know the minimum the country needed to offer in hiring a Supreme Court Justice. Always at pains to keep his hot temper in check, Burger found more than usual difficulty as he responded. As for the ethics pledge, "We adopted that seven years ago."

On the subject of how cheaply a Supreme Court Justice could be obtained, Burger saw a parallel in the case of the Justices' law clerks, recent top law graduates who were being paid in the $20,000 range, jumping from there to $100,000 in private practice soon after the end of the one-year Court service, and in some cases, after a few further years, reaching the $1 million annual level, nearly ten times the income of their old Court bosses. As for law clerks, Burger said, "We could get them for $5,000, but it would not be honorable."

Finally, as to whether he would "go along" on the suggested White House roll-back of a small proposed pay increase, Burger exploded. The original suggested raise was itself "insulting," he said, "and I won't characterize what you are proposing, but I do reserve the right to speak out on it." The chastened caller hastened back to the drawing boards.

The blistering Court–White House exchange over Justices' pay might seem strange in the light of the lofty, almost paternal, role the Chief Justice played in inducting Presidents into office. The main image most Americans had of Burger was the sight of him on TV as he stood erect, black-robed, his right hand raised beside his silvery hair, swearing in officials. By his count there had been hundreds of them, including dozens of cabinet officers and two Presidents. That he should have to argue with any of these officials about Justices' remuneration might not be what one would expect, but the ingenious system of checks and balances made it so.

How quickly the friction between the governmental branches could be smoothed over, however, was evident a few days later when the Chief Justice was back in his familiar public role swearing in a President, this time, Jimmy Carter from Georgia.

Burger described later how the installation went: "I said, 'Are you ready, Mr. Carter, to take the constitutional oath?' That relaxes them," Burger explained. "They always say 'I am.' Otherwise, I have seen men choke up so badly they could not make a sound. After the oath, I said 'I present the President of the United States!'"

As Burger recalled it, Carter walked over to him twice after the oath taking, the first time to tell him how moved he was to hear himself addressed for the first time with his new title. Before the oath he was Governor Carter. After it, the President!

The second time the new President came over, Burger introduced his wife. "She, rightly," the Chief said, "does not push forward as some others do." What struck Mrs.

Burger was the new President's relaxed, quiet tone as the three chatted, a pleasant improvement over the high-pitched monotone of the acceptance speech. Why could not Carter have talked to the country through TV in the same attractive way? Her husband had an explanation: "He was very moved emotionally."

The Chief, as was his custom, finished the administration of the thirty-five-word pledge by saying, "So help me God," a phrase the Founding Fathers had not appended to the presidential affirmation. Carter dutifully repeated the invocation.

This provoked a brief debate in the media about whether God should be invoked in a secular ceremony. Critics pointed out that it would have sufficed under the Constitution for Carter to "affirm" his good intentions. Although he had administered the pledge to hundreds of public officials, the devoutly Presbyterian Burger had never focused on the fact that there is an alternative to the "oath" of office. Checking on the critics' complaint, he flipped to paragraph eight of the Constitution's Article II and nodded.

"Yes, 'affirm!' " he said with a touch of surprise. There the word was in parentheses in the opening phrase: "I do solemnly swear (or affirm) ... ." Then, from his reading of history, Burger remembered: "That was put in because there were so many Quakers at the time. Ben Franklin was a Quaker." More than that, he conceded, it was still a matter of public debate: "We have a case coming to remove 'In God we trust' from the currency."

When the currency case came to a head later, the Court allowed "In God we trust" to remain on the coins and folding money, but meanwhile, Burger wondered about how deeply faith in a Supreme Being was reflected in the Court's own practices. Was the name of God invoked every time the Justices went to the bench? Burger had heard the opening cry hundreds of times, but try as he did, he could not remember it. Always so busy making his own preparations for the hearings, he never heeded the crier's age-old words.

To clear it up, Burger at once phoned Mike Rodak, the Clerk, whose office and large staff were on the floor below. An easygoing, former football player without pomp, Mike answered the ring, giving the Chief an opportunity to rag him for a moment: "Mike! Don't you have any lieutenant colonels down there to answer for you?"

That out of the way, Burger got his answer. The crier did open every session with a call in the ancient French of the English legal tradition: "Oyez! Oyez! Oyez!, (Hear ye! Hear ye! Hear ye!), the Court is now sitting, God save the United States and this honorable Court." On that basis, Burger's specific invocation of God in inducting top government officials seemed to have support in general national practice even if the Founders had not included it in the Constitution.

Catapulted from the peanut fields of Plains and the statehouse of Atlanta into 1600 Pennsylvania Avenue, the new President seemed as confused as Burger's foreign interlocutors about just what contacts with the Supreme Court were appropriate.

The custom going back nearly two centuries, as Burger had it researched, was for Justices in the early nineteenth century to ride into Washington on horseback after their recesses, dropping by the White House to tell the President that they were back in town.

There was no TV to carry the news, and except for hearings in the Courtroom in the Capitol, the Justices did the bulk of their work out of sight in scattered boardinghouses and other residences around the city.

After the Supreme Court got its own building in 1935, Presidents occasionally reciprocated the Justices' calls, especially when they appointed a new Justice.

Dwight Eisenhower was one who visited the Court, but he did so only after assurances that the Justices as a group, and not just his appointee, Chief Justice Warren, would welcome the encounter.

Until Eisenhower fell ill, the Justices paid periodic White House calls. With the assassination of John F. Kennedy, such visits lapsed. There were one or two in Lyndon Johnson's time, none during the Vietnam War, and none during the Nixon presidency even though Burger felt, despite the Watergate judgment, that Nixon did not get the credit he deserved for opening relations with China and creating a diversion against the Soviets.

Jerry Ford, as President, visited the Court for the swearing in of his one appointee, the moderate liberal John Paul Stevens. Posing for pictures on that occasion created a protocol problem. Who should stand in the middle? A call to the State Department suggested an answer. It was Ford's country, but it was the Chief's branch of the government. Burger took the place in the center.

Ronald Reagan brought the core of his governmental team to meet the Justices, Ed Meese, Jim Baker, the Central Intelligence Agency's Bill Casey and a few others. The dozen or two men met in the Justices' conference room, standing for a half hour, and making awkward small talk.

Carter as President wondered whether there was "any harm" in relaxing the arm's length relationship between the executive and judicial branches, at least to the extent of an occasional handshake and chat. Burger suggested a way it could be done. The twenty-five member Judicial Conference, he said, existed officially to advise the other two branches of Court needs. He, as Chairman of the Conference, could quite properly confer with his old friend, the former Federal Judge Griffin Bell whom Burger had just sworn in as Carter's Attorney General.

With that as an indirect beginning, the President was in direct touch with the Chief Justice several times in the course of the next year, twice of them for diplomatic missions.

One of the exchanges was in May 1977 while Burger was in a meeting with his law clerks. Carter phoned to say, "I suppose you're going to give a Law Day speech." As the law clerks were sent out of the room, the Chief gave his answer: "No, we're too busy here."

"Do you have any ideas for me?" was the follow-up query. Burger's reform agenda was always long. A President could be a great ally on that. A memo of ideas promptly went to the White House, some to be used, and some to be turned on their heads. Carter thought courts were too hard on defendants. The order-minded Burger believed otherwise.

While that effort to establish Court–White House cooperation did not work as well as Burger could have hoped, Carter did not forget Burger as one of his potential aides. In summer 1977 Archbishop Makarios, the one-man government of the strategic East Mediterranean island of Cyprus, died. Secretary of State Cyrus Vance asked Burger to take a leading role in representing the United States at the funeral, but Burger refused. He had just had a long-delayed operation on his accident-damaged right foot, and healing was much slower than he had expected.

The President telephoned next, and his request was something the Chief felt he could not refuse. He agreed and the trip was among the most miserable experiences of his life: "It was a sixteen-and-a-half-hour flight with a two-and-a-half-hour layover in Madrid. There was no chance to take a shower. On arrival we all had to visit the acting president."

Then came the funeral.

"There was a two-and-a-half-hour service with three orations. Then we had to walk a half mile in 137° heat. I didn't know it could get that hot.

"I had been hardly able to get a shoe on. People were falling down, fainting. My wife was on one side of me and the Lord Chancellor of England on the other, supporting me.

"I had to rest. I leaned on the left foot when we stopped. Fortunately, it went slow."

Diplomacy was not the Chief's task in the divided government, but Burger drew some personal comfort from the measure of consolation the international gestures gave the Cypriots: "They are in a terrible situation over there, like small children who have lost both parents. Makarios for twenty years had decided everything."

A few weeks later came a second excursion into international politics, this time to the Soviet Union, and on this occasion, through a foreign rather than an American initiative. It traced to five years earlier, during the Nixon presidency, when Burger attended a Washington reception for Leonid Brezhnev, then head of the Soviet government and Communist Party.

Burger went through the receiving line and was introduced as the Chief Justice. "Yes, I know," Brezhnev said in English. "Much power, much power!"

Burger described what happened next. "He snapped his fingers for [Ambassador] Dobrynin like this." To illustrate, the Chief twisted to one side, leaning backwards. "Then through an interpreter, I heard him say, 'We must get him to Moscow.' " It was part of the intricate diplomatic dance in which the two superpowers were engaging as they worked toward the end of the Cold War.

Burger was not sure he should have a part in it. Court work was mountainous. Still, it would be interesting to see courts and prisons behind the Iron Curtain, he felt. In annual visits to the judiciary and penitentiaries of England and the Continent, he said, "I got what I could never have learned in law school or in any school."

Burger turned the Brezhnev request aside for the time being, but he made a decision. He would make the trip in the national interest if the State Department and the White House approved, and if he was convinced that it was in the interest of the Supreme Court as an institution. Absent any piece of that puzzle he would not go.

The project remained dormant until the Carter presidency when Secretary of State Vance suffered a sharp rebuff from Brezhnev in Moscow on a Carter proposal for strategic arms limitations. As Burger saw it from the sidelines, the new President had tried to deal with the Soviets "like Georgia politicians." It had been, in Burger's view, a move that would have established Carter as a genius like Talleyrand had he succeeded, or as a "country bumpkin" if he failed.

Burger soon found himself in the middle. The Soviet embassy urged him to make the delayed trip immediately, without waiting for the return of the Secretary of State from Moscow. Vance earlier had approved the idea of such a trip, and Zbigniew Brzinski and Henry Kissinger, two top American counselors on foreign affairs, had told Burger that they favored it.

Wait until the Secretary of State gets back from Russia, Burger insisted to the Soviets. He wanted to be certain that he was crossing no wires. After all, this was precisely what Burger had preached, the necessity that one branch of the government stay out of the business of another.

With Vance returned and all in agreement, Burger consented. What followed illustrated the difficulties when a leader of one of the three branches operates in the area of another, however much the other might approve. It also underlined the ongoing problem of foreigners as they struggled to understand American split powers.

Soviet embassy officers called on Burger with preparatory questions. What was his personal background as a man of the people? What was his influence beyond the Court? To the latter Burger tried to convince the baffled interrogators that the answer was that he had none whatsoever in foreign and domestic policy, none more than "any other man in the street."

As Burger saw it, he would be visiting his opposite number, the Soviet Chief Justice, the same as he did in London visits, for example. By the way, he asked in his turn, who was their Chief Justice? The embassy caller had no idea. His embarrassment was visible. That shows how unimportant is their Chief Justice, Burger mused.

One visitor from the embassy, making small talk, assured Burger that in Moscow he need have no worry about a high crime rate like Washington's. While Burger agreed that the capital's murder rate was appalling, the remark touched a patriotic nerve. A difference here, he retorted is that we have freedom of movement.

The visitor bristled. We cannot have that, he said of his country. We have a severe housing shortage. People from all over the Soviet Union would flood into Moscow if they could. His own rank was high, he added, but even so his appeal for a two-bedroom apartment was still unanswered after a five-year wait.

The same difficult dialogue, two worlds mystified by one another, was to persist through the trip and even after it was over.

As plans were put in final form the obscure Chief of Soviet Justice weighed in with a letter. He understood that Burger wished to see the Soviet Union and he had arranged for it. The trip, Burger quickly replied, was not his idea but Brezhnev's. Burger was determined to keep the record straight. In Moscow, Burger told the Soviet dictator that it was his belief that such American institutions as the independent judiciary and the presidency endured because, "We do not mind protest." He recalled later that "the translator tried to soften it, but I could see Brezhnev stiffen."

At the Moscow Institute for the Study of American Affairs, Burger repeated the point, strengthening it by asking the American Ambassador to find out for him which groups of picketers were protesting that day in front of the Carter White House. "There's always someone there," he was sure.

Burger spoke candidly about the problems of American justice, his view that non-lawyer neighborhood arbitration councils could settle many small claims now clogging courts, his concern for new crimes committed by offenders out on bail and his distress about the high rate of reincarceration of unregenerate parolees.

While the Soviet press stayed fairly close to what Burger had to say, the American embassy reported home that the Russian media left the false impression that Burger praised Soviet law enforcement with its street militias, its people's courts and its pre-trial jailing without bail, as superior to the American system.

Although the federally financed trip was not considered an official government-to-government encounter, Carter had not yet met his Soviet opposite number and asked Burger for a fill-in. Sitting across the desk from the President, Burger was dismayed to see the toll customary political attacks had taken on the sensitive Chief of State in the two-thirds of a year since the inauguration. "He was just not prepared for the attacks," Burger said. "I felt sorry for the way he looked. He said, 'Tomorrow is my fifty-third birthday but, you know, for the past eight months I have felt that I was already fifty-three!' "

In the back-and-forth among capitals, each side tried to learn from the other. On an official visit to Tokyo Burger found the Japanese Supreme Court pondering whether it was truly independent. It had vetoed a law passed by the Diet only twice in twenty-five years, very little indeed by American Supreme Court standards.

You are doing the right thing, Burger reassured his Japanese opposite number in a speech in Kyoto. You are in the same stage as John Marshall was in 1805 to 1810, gingerly feeling your way. Even now our cautious Justices carefully list their different shades of opinion.

His comments, Burger learned, were "reported back to the Japanese Chief Justice within three hours."

When the President of Mexico visited the Court (coffee, please, no tea), Burger was impressed to hear how the Mexican high court conducted its decision conference in public. There was never any give-and-take, the Justices locked in on their positions from the outset. Our way, Burger concluded, was better, with Justices free to have second thoughts after hearing other views, and after more mature consideration.

Chinese visitors were curious about how Supreme Court Justices got their powerful jobs. And Chief Justices, they asked, were they promoted from within? Burger explained to his Beijing guests that Presidents propose and the Senators dispose. On a score of occasions, he recalled, the Senate has said no.

One such was in the case of the second Chief Justice, John Rutledge, who had already taken office during a senatorial recess. He had to step down. It had posed a personal question for Burger. Was he the fifteenth or the fourteenth Chief Justice? For numerical reasons as well as for the display of marble busts in the great hallway, the question had to be resolved some way. The Court came down on the side of Rutledge's legitimacy, and his image is on the ceremonial floor now for all to see.

As for the road to the Chief Justiceship, Burger explained, the chances were better than two to one as the twentieth century neared an end that an outsider rather than an Associate would take the central chair when the opportunity presented. By the final decade of the century only five Chiefs had first served as Associates: the ill-fated John Rutledge, an Associate from 1790 to 1800 and Chief from August to December in 1800; Edward Douglass White (Associate from 1894 to 1910, Chief from 1910 until 1921); Charles Evans Hughes (1910 to 1916 as an Associate and 1930 to 1941 as Chief); Harlan Fiske Stone (1925 to 1941 in the ranks and 1941 to 1946 in the chair) and William Rehnquist, Associate from 1971 to 1986 when he became the sixteenth Chief Justice.

As for that word "promoted," Burger told the Asians, perhaps another should be used: "Promoted? My colleagues might not like that!"

After all, when it came to the core work of the Court, the deciding of cases, the vote of the Chief was worth no whit more than that of the most junior Associate. It was one more aspect of the peculiar but vital governmental balancing of powers.

CHAPTER 16

EIGHT OTHER VOTES

Chief Justices are first among equals with many extra administrative duties, but when it comes to the heart of the Court work, the judging of crucial national issues, the Chief's vote is weightless unless he can get at least four colleagues to agree. James Clark McReynolds who was on the Court from 1914 to 1947, remains in Court memory as the arch illustration of how independent an Associate Justice can be. Late for a meeting of the Court he received a note from the Chief urgently inviting his attendance. Back with the messenger went his response: "Tell the Chief Justice I don't work for him."

Recollection of the haughty, ill-natured McReynolds was still so much alive decades later that Potter Stewart at his retirement in 1981 talked about it as an illustration of the autonomy of the Associates.

"He was a man I never knew, apparently quite unlikable, a bachelor. He had never found a woman willing to marry him, or even apparently wanted to.

"He would get up at 11:30 in the morning on those days of Conferences on Saturday and say, 'Gentlemen, I'm leaving now, I'll see you all on Monday.'

"Chief Justice Hughes would say, 'Well, Justice McReynolds, I think we only have about another hour more,' and he would say, 'I didn't say that you should leave, Chief Justice. I said I was leaving.'

"And no power on earth could keep him there, no power except his own conscience and sense of duty which didn't prevail against his desire to go to the Eastern Shore where he had a place and he wanted to spend the weekend."

To make the "Burger Court" something more than an empty name, to make it truly a reflection of Warren Burger as the Warren Court had been of the liberal former Governor of California, Burger could afford to lose no more than four votes as he led the Conference discussion of cases. With four survivors of the Warren Court sitting before him during most of his tenure it was an often frustrating task.

First to respond would be William O. Douglas who had narrowly missed the Presidency toward the end of World War II. When Burger became Chief Justice, Douglas had preceded him at the Conference table by three decades. What Burger knew from the volumes of the *United States Reports,* Douglas had as a personal recollection, not just the printed results but the back-and-forth around the table that had led to them. Often Burger felt it necessary to go to the liberal Douglas for his unique memories.

Where Earl Warren constantly asked pleading lawyers, "Is it fair?" Burger wanted to know, "Is it in the Constitution? Is it in laws passed by the Congress or the states?" With Burger putting the question that way and Douglas at the opposite end of the table phrasing it in another, the vote as Douglas spoke was often one to one, a draw and Burger still needing four.

Crusty on the outside like an oyster shell, but a warm and trusting friend when his confidence was won, Douglas announced where he stood and made no effort to win converts. It was like his view of the media: "I hate the goddam press. They have scorched me and strung me up so many times, making me say what I did not say."

When a TV artist asked him to pose his reply was curt: "No, ask one of the nicer Justices."

The Douglas attitude drew mixed reaction in legal and judicial circles. A Pennsylvania law review studied all thirty votes Douglas had cast across the years in income tax cases. The justice voted against the Internal Revenue Service in all thirty. The IRS might, indeed, have erred on occasion, the review conceded, but surely not 100 percent of the time.

Tensions between Burger and Douglas reached even into the Burger home. When a gift of firewood arrived from Douglas, Mrs. Burger's instinct was to send it back. Her husband vetoed that reaction: "You never turn down an offer of firewood," he told Elvera. A Burger personal, if not judicial, mellowing toward Douglas was under way.

So far as at least one Court staffer, the Librarian Ed Hudon, was concerned, a better appreciation of Douglas could not go far enough. "Douglas," he said, "is truly a Renaissance man. He is a man of all knowledge. He got us to add to the Library a twenty-volume set of the greatest works of Western culture—Montaigne, St. Augustine, St. Thomas Aquinas, Plato, Aristotle.

"I am often in his chambers. He can write an Opinion in one afternoon. He has already written more of them—mostly dissents—than the others will write this term."

Alone among the Justices, with their six- or six-and-a-half day workweeks, Douglas thought that the members of the Court were blessed with "vast leisure."

In his dissents in *Tidewater Oil Co. v. the United States* in 1972 and *Warth v. Seldin* in 1975, Douglas enshrined his views in the enduring volumes of the *United States Reports*. "No Justice," he wrote, "need work more than four days a week to carry his burden." With himself as an example Douglas managed to combine summer hikes in the mountains with the publishing of more than thirty books.

Despite his evidence of himself, Douglas's brethren were stunned at his assertions.

In a talk to the American Bar Association in Montreal on August 11, 1975, Justice Powell delicately replied. Douglas's vision of the Court reality, he said, "assumes an equality of capacity and application that simply does not exist.

"No other Justice works a four-day week," Powell protested. "Each of us must carry his own responsibility in his own way, utilizing time and resources, as well as experience and ability, as best he can."

Along with his somewhat McReynoldsesque, freewheeling manner, the four times married and three times divorced Douglas was without pretense, and he did not lack a sense of humor. In one book he mentioned the answer he got when he addressed one of the honorary "colonels" of Kentucky with that title.

"Don't call me that," he was told, "I'm only a Kentucky colonel. It is as ridiculous for you to address me that way as it is for me to call you 'your honor.'"

As the years together with Douglas went by, Burger told a friend: "You know, we don't always read the Constitution the same way, but we both want the good things for the country."

Next to talk in the Conference in most of the Burger years was another of Earl Warren's solid liberal majority, the cheery, foxy-grandpa William Brennan, a man well liked by all and artful at cobbling together a strong bloc of "fairness" advocates. Tirelessly at work with little social life, a dedicated Catholic, his, in Burger's perception, was an existence with just two focuses, "church and the Court."

Brennan often made the vote one to two with the needed four still well beyond Burger's reach.

A defender of the Constitution as he understood it, Brennan allowed no one, not even churchmen, to instruct him on what the basic national compact meant. It was part

of Court lore that the shirt-sleeved Brennan amiably admitted two priests to his chambers one day, instantly showing them the exit when they tried to influence his votes.

Brennan was one of those voting for the nation-shaking *Roe v. Wade* decision in 1973, allowing abortions freely in the first three months of pregnancy but assigning the fetus strong protection in the final trimester.

Brennan took it as a given that the Court had to provide answers for the country on many of the most hotly disputed questions. This was by no means true of courts in many other democracies, he conceded.

Talking at the Maxwell Air Force base in Alabama on September 8, 1963, Brennan, a World War II Colonel, expressed it this way: "From our beginnings, a most important consequence of the con-

Justice William Brennan. His "rule of five" (five votes out of nine needed to win) achieved many victories for the progressives. National Geographic, Collection of the Supreme Court of the United States.

stitutionally created separation of powers has been the American habit, extraordinary in other democracies, of casting social, economic, philosophical and political questions in terms of actions at law and suits in equity.

"In this way important aspects of the most fundamental issues confronting our democracy end up ultimately in the Supreme Court for judicial determination."

Where judicial conservatives such as Burger argued that the Congress and the White House, as the elected branches of government, should make such decisions, Brennan felt that reality dictated otherwise.

Brennan added in a speech on September 12, 1979, that one "must remember that it is a duty of a member of the Supreme Court not to count constituents but to interpret a fundamental charter of government regardless of his own moral or philosophical or religious or political views."

The Court, he went further, in the startling words of Justice Oliver Wendell Holmes, of the first third of the century, is a "court of laws, not of justice," a place where basic rules of the land are laid down and not one in which each of the thousands of cases clamoring for attention get a final, proper resolution. Physically, there was no time for the latter.

Brennan's and Holmes's words pointed up how empty is the ringing threat of a losing lawyer that "I'll take this all the way to the Supreme Court!" By Brennan's time, the Court turned away nineteen out of every twenty cases and, soon after his time, was rejecting ninety-nine out of one hundred.

With what was known as Brennan's "rule of five," his willingness to concede points in order to get four others to agree on what he considered basic, Brennan was able to win some battles, but in Burger's years, he succeeded more often in just thwarting Burger's conservatives, throwing the decision to the moderates grouped around Lewis Powell, Potter Stewart and, sometimes, Byron White.

Happy-mannered, Brennan was known as one of the few who would greet the dignified John Marshall Harlan of the 1955 to 1971 period with "Hiya, Johnnie!"

Third to talk in Conference was the one other survivor of the Eisenhower appointments, Potter Stewart. In a sign of how little known are the powerful members of the High Court, he was mentioned in a Washington broadcast two decades after mounting the bench as "Stuart Potter."

Far from being a cipher, Stewart was one of the middle-of-the-roaders who dominated in the early Burger years. When Stewart spoke, the vote could be one to three or an even draw.

Stewart was asked at age forty-four whether he was a liberal or a conservative. "I really can't say," he answered, "except that I like to be thought of as a Lawyer."

At his retirement at sixty-six in 1981, reporters asked how he wished to be remembered, and he said the same: "As a good lawyer who did his best."

It was also the Stewart household perception. When in 1973 the newly installed PIO shared with the Justice's wife, Mary Ann Bertles Stewart, his perception of his job: to seek public understanding and sympathy in a necessarily limited way for an institution that does its real talking through the hundreds of volumes of the *United States Reports,* the Justice's spouse shook her head. "I could not disagree more," she said. "These are just nine lawyers doing their law work."

Stewart's background was as elegant as Burger's was plebeian. His father, James Garfield Stewart, had been Mayor of Cincinnati and, for twelve years, an Ohio state Supreme Court Justice.

Unlike the however competent homegrown art on the Burger chamber walls, a van Gogh was on Stewart's.

Far from matriculating in a night school, Stewart had gone East to the exclusive Hotchkiss Prep and from there to Yale where he made Phi Beta Kappa and to Cambridge in England for graduate work. After three and one-half years as a Navy deck officer on a tanker in World War II, Stewart went to Yale Law School, graduating first in his class. In 1954, at thirty-nine, Stewart was appointed to the federal Court of Appeals, the nation's youngest federal judge.

In 1969, before Burger was chosen as Chief Justice, Stewart had such good reason to believe that he might be nominated for the Court leadership that he took the extraordinary step of asking the White House not to appoint him. He knew what the Chief Justiceship entailed and insisted that his sole wish was to stay on as an Associate.

With such different personal backgrounds and with differing ideas on the role of law, it became quickly apparent that it would not be easy to establish a good rapport between a Justice who refused the Chief Justiceship before it was offered, and a new Chief who said that he had never requested the position but had accepted it.

Although Stewart had not been part of the hard core of the Warren majority, he was devoted to *stare decisis,* the concept that matters once decided generally should be left undisturbed. He took umbrage at some Burger Court reversals of earlier rulings. Dissenting in *Mitchell v. Grant,* he protested that "the only perceivable change" from what the Court had ruled earlier was "the membership of the Court," a reference

Justice Potter Stewart. Harris and Ewing, Collection of the Supreme Court of the United States.

to Burger and the three other Nixon appointees.

Making important legal changes on that basis, he objected, was to "invite the popular misconception that this institution is little different from the political branches of the government." He added: "No misconception could do more lasting harm to this Court and to the system of law which it is our abiding mission to serve."

Among the issues on which Burger and Stewart could not agree was media relations. While the Chief saw reporters infrequently, and such other Justices as Douglas and Brennan had bitter memories of rough handling in the media, Stewart's door, a few yards down the corridor from the Chief's, was often open to reporters. As the former chairman of the *Yale Daily News,* Stewart was comfortable with journalists. He thought that those covering the Court had a daunting job. Their task, he said, was like trying to evaluate each move in a hospital operation while sitting at a distance in a surgical theater. Off there, he said, about all you can determine is whether the patient lived or died.

Although the Court never gives even background briefings on the meanings of the sometimes opaque Opinions, Stewart saw no problem with receiving radio, TV and print journalists into the Court building for a farewell press conference when he stepped down from the bench in June 1981.

Interviews on camera or in any other form might well be a problem when a Justice is in the process of hearing cases, but what harm could there be if he was to sit in judgment no longer? That at least seemed to be Stewart's reasoning, and one more TV barrier fell at the Court.

For reporters, regardless of the Stewart future, it was a unique opportunity to peer behind the velvet curtains, and 101 newspeople showed up, including crews from seventeen radio and television services and reporters from forty-two other news organizations.

The Justice was asked what went on in his mind as he cast his votes in the Warren and Burger Courts. To answer that, Stewart cited one case that had caused him distress, *Engel v. Vitale,* the school prayer decision, one whose reception had also nettled Brennan, though for an opposite reason.

Written by Hugo Black, and supported by Brennan and four others, the decision forbade prayers in public schools even if worded in a denominationally neutral way.

Justices Felix Frankfurter and Byron White took no part, but Stewart alone dissented.

Like many of his colleagues, Stewart was religious, an Episcopalian. His dissent brought him two thousand letters and much embarrassment when various of the writers "attributed my Opinion to my religious views." It was not that at all, he said. It was "my understanding of the Constitution." Stewart went on in words paralleling Brennan's: "So far as I am concerned, the mark of a good Justice or any judge is one whose Opinions you can read and, after you have read them, you have no idea whether the judge was a man or a woman, a Republican or a Democrat, a Christian or a Jew, or—if a Christian, a Protestant or Catholic. You just know that he or she was a good judge."

He went further: "It is the first duty of a judge to remove from his judicial work his own social and philosophical and political or religious beliefs, and not to think of himself as being here as some great philosopher-king to just apply his own ideology."

If philosophy or religious values were to enter beyond what the Founding Fathers had provided, the elected lawmakers, responding to the public, presumably would have to take care of that.

No longer in danger of leaking pending decisions or of compromising himself with regard to future Court issues, Stewart coupled the retirement conference with some one-on-one interviews. He made clear how independent he had been, how hard it was for the Chief or any other to count on his concurrence.

"If you begin with the thought that the Chief Justice is or ought to be the boss in a conventional, hierarchical way, you are wrong," Stewart said at the farewell meeting with the media. To that extent at least, the thorny McReynolds, in his view, had been right. Not only could the Chief not dictate a vote, but each Justice was on his own with the responsibility of deciding which of the thousands of annual cases should be heard and how they should be handled.

It was lonely work, Stewart told William Punnill, an Editor of the publication *Litigation*. He said that he had been shocked when he moved up from the comradely Court of Appeals, to learn from Justice Harlan that the Supreme Court was not "one law firm with nine partners" but rather "nine law firms, sometimes practicing law against one another."

It was a fully demanding assignment. Without specific reference to Chief Justice Burger's vast expenditure of time and energy on legal and judicial reform and on the management of the Court building and staff, or of Douglas's thirty books, Stewart was asked what he thought of a Justice taking on extra chores. He disapproved heartily. A Justice, he said, "is so busy at his job, if he is doing his job, that he hasn't got time to be involved in anything." It is, he said, "a full-time job, a very demanding job."

Asked about great Justices, Stewart reached back beyond the Burger Court for his list. He cited:

- Earl Warren, 1953–1969. "He was a fine person and, I think, beloved and admired by all his colleagues. He was not a great legal scholar and he did not pretend to be, either to himself or to others, which was very disarming. He did lead in many ways but it is arguable whether or not he was the leader of the Court."
- Hugo Black, 1937–1971. "Many would argue he was the leader of the Court. He was a very kindly, engaging, lovable person. Up until the end of his life he kept enthusiasm and intense advocacy for causes in which he believed. He never became jaded or old or tired. I loved that quality. He was pretty much a self-educated man, but a well-educated man. He intended to study medicine but he found out it

Justice Byron White. Harris and Ewing, Collection of the Supreme Court of the United States.

was $50 a year more so he went to law school!"

• The second John Marshall Harlan (1955–1971, grandson of the namesake Justice, 1877–1911). "Toward the end of his life, he almost completely lost his eyesight, about which he never complained either by word or deed. It never affected the quality or the quantity of his work output. He was not so much a scholar as he was a lawyer in the best sense of the word. He had humanity and wisdom and compassion that carried him way beyond an ivory-tower academic. He was not so much a conservative as he was a very responsible, conscientious and careful person."

Asked directly about the "brothers" he was leaving, Stewart put it this way: "You don't choose them. It is a little like a ship's company, you don't choose your shipmates. Some perhaps you like better than others. Others you may have a higher opinion of, but it's your duty to work with each and you do."

When he was still on the bench, Stewart turned down an invitation to attend one of the several annual banquets of Washington news personnel, and was asked whether it was improper to follow up by extending the invitation to another of the brethren. "No," he explained Court protocol, "so long as the other is junior."

Stewart's immediate junior, as Burger looked down the table during the 1970s, was Byron White, two years younger than Stewart, but six years behind him in coming to the Court. White, in the center like Stewart, tipped often to Burger's side. On a case-by-case basis, the vote by then might well be two to three either way. In at least one area the Chief, Stewart and White agreed, that even "foolish" laws of Congress ought to be allowed to remain standing so long as they violated no perceived directive of the Constitution.

White's arrival at the Court in 1962 as the first of John F. Kennedy's two appointees was not for him a wholly new experience, for he had clerked for Chief Justice Vinson in the 1946 term and was thus one of the first of the Supreme Court law clerks to make the round trip back to the Courthouse.

Where Chief Justice Burger's relations with Stewart were cool, his admiration for White knew few bounds and enjoyed some reciprocation. Proud of his own schoolboy prowess as winner of multiple athletic letters, Burger had room for little less than awe of a man whose own skills on the playing fields had won him the nickname of

"Whizzer." White had been an all-American football player at the University of Colorado, a "triple threat" able to run, pass and punt. He picked up three varsity letters in football and baseball and four in basketball. Out of college, White played pro football for Pittsburgh and Detroit, leading the National Football League in "rushing," the suicidal plunges through the opponent's beefy line. "He's probably the most fit on the Court," Burger said of White. "Bumping into him is like hitting the side of this desk." When an especially tiring 1975 term drew to a close in July 1976, Burger cited White as a measure of how hard it had been: "Even he told me he was exhausted."

What is known among the Justices' entourage as the "highest court in the land," is a room fitted out for basketball and volleyball just above the ceiling of the Supreme Courtroom. Officially assigned to the care of the Marshal of the Court, it was taken over by Byron White as his private concern. He made busy personal use of it, shooting baskets there with clerks forty years younger. Still fiercely competitive, his stomping across the court's boards left one Clerk with a broken foot.

Late in his sixties White was dismayed to be told by his physician that the time had come for him to give up skiing. It was a low moment, but there was a sequel as White recalled: "I changed doctors. The new one said it was all right and the other one died."

White was the embodiment of the ancient ideal of *mens sana in corpore sano,* a sound mind in a sound body. First in his high school class, he was Phi Beta Kappa at Colorado and graduated *magna cum laude* from Yale Law School. He studied at Oxford University as a Rhodes Scholar. In England he met Jack Kennedy, son of Ambassador Joe Kennedy, beginning a lifelong friendship. The pictures of both assassinated brothers, Jack, the President and Bobby, the Attorney General, Senator and presidential candidate, were on his chambers walls.

With White, Burger was so much at ease that he felt free on occasion even to tease him about Opinions he wrote for the Court. One such concerned a newspaper, *Zurcher v. the Stanford Daily.* Police had been injured in a violent demonstration, and their colleagues searched the newspaper office for photos or notes that might identify the assailants.

White ruled for the Court that despite the strictures of the Constitution's Fourth Amendment against "unreasonable searches and seizures," whether or not in a newspaper office, the police were justified in their efforts to track down criminals.

The four Nixon appointees agreed, Justices Stewart, Thurgood Marshall and John Paul Stevens dissented. Brennan took no part.

As a defender of "law and order," Burger was delighted and ragged White. It was 1978, a presidential campaign year, with the third of the Kennedy siblings, Senator Ted, a possible Democratic nominee, and the media in an uproar against the Stanford invasion of press privacy.

"Now you'll never get the nomination away from Ted Kennedy," Burger told White with a laugh. As it was, Kennedy, too, was passed over. Jimmy Carter won the Democratic nomination and the presidency.

There had been no suggestion that White wanted to be a presidential candidate but, with Chief Justices near the top of the list to replace the Chief Executive in a crisis, and with Taft, Hughes, Douglas, Warren and perhaps Stewart former occupants or near occupants of the White House, a Justice as a potential nominee was not unthinkable.

Fordham University in New York City asked White to accept an honorary doctorate as a model scholar-athlete and was astonished when he refused. "I never accept honors," the master-achiever explained.

White shared with his colleagues an affection for the Court as a basic American institution. When anti-abortion demonstrators waved protesting placards in his face on a visit with Burger to the latter's hometown of St. Paul, White accepted the rebuke without comment. Past the picket line, however, he remarked to a companion: "They don't know I was against that decision." White and Rehnquist had been the sole dissenters in the 1973 *Roe v. Wade* judgment.

Sixth to comment in the 1970s was Thurgood Marshall, son of a Club Steward, and the first of African descent to serve on the Court. In a Brennan-Burger standoff, Brennan routinely could count on Marshall's vote, making it often a one, two, three breakdown—the Chief, two moderates and the Brennan left wing. A Burger majority was still well out of reach.

Brennan and Marshall were both from families with harsh memories of discrimination in the nation's earlier decades, Marshall, black, and Brennan, son of Irish immigrants. The two were so close that when Marshall made up his mind to retire in 1991 the first person he informed outside his family was Brennan, by then also a retiree.

In photos, Marshall wore a dour expression, but a Justice remarked, "He's not like that." In Conference, with a limitless store of anecdotes, Marshall could be counted upon, in tense moments, to lighten the mood with a story.

His language was salty. When Douglas, without support from any of his colleagues, expressed concern that spying might be underway inside the Justices' Conference, Marshall said that, as far as he was concerned, anyone who wanted to do so could even tap his chambers telephone: "All they'll hear is me talking dirty to my wife!"

For all the surface good humor, however, Marshall brought to the Conference table a bitter resentment of the way those of African origin have been treated in the course of American history.

The pain stayed with him even though he had succeeded personally in attenuating much of it. It was he who had argued successfully the *Brown v. the Board of Education* school desegregation case, and as Lyndon Johnson's Solicitor General, the top Department of Justice courtroom advocate, he had won further Supreme Court civil rights victories. The Justice's very presence on the Court was a measure of the nation's, however belated, effort to make racial amends.

But was the sum of it enough? Was it yet time for African Americans to "thank God almighty," in the words of the murdered Martin Luther King Jr., that they were "free at last"?

"I'm not free," Marshall said at a departure press conference at the Court. "All I know is that years ago, when I was a youngster, a Pullman porter told me that he had been in every city in this country, he was sure, and he had never been in any city in the United States where he had to hold his hand up in front of his face to find out that he was a Negro. I agree with him."

When the University of Maryland Law School in Baltimore erected a statue to him as the sole native of that city to join the Court, Marshall was reluctant to attend the dedication. He had been refused admission to that school because of his race although he was a *cum laude* graduate of the all-black Lincoln University in Chester, Pennsylvania. Turned away by Baltimore he matriculated instead at Howard University in Washington, D.C., where he graduated first in his class.

A fighter, Marshall said he wanted to be recalled as one who "did what he could with what he had." In winning the *Brown* case what he had as a playing card was the fact that a predominantly white country had proclaimed as its fundamental belief that "all men are created equal."

Burger tried to bridge the racial gap by asking Marshall what name he preferred for a race variously described as colored, black, Negro or African-American. Marshall's original usage was Negro, but in later years he shifted as did many others. Asked at the Court press conference whether he believed there had been an improvement in the lot of "black people," he flashed back: "I am not a black people. I am an Afro-American."

As for the rest of the question, he said that whether his race had made gains was irrelevant: "So are white people better off since I sat on the Court."

Some critics said that Marshall worked too little as a Justice, often just signing off on Opinions by Brennan. After one attack Burger invited the Justice to his chambers to say that he deplored what had been published to that effect. On that occasion, Marshall shrugged it off. He knew his main belittler well, he said. For six or seven years the attacker had been keeping up a drumbeat of negative remarks. It was hardly surprising, Marshall pooh-poohed the objector; it was sour grapes. The critic, he said, had wanted a place on the federal Court of Appeals, and after that, the Supreme Court. He also wanted to be Dean of the Harvard Law School. He never attained any of the three. Marshall noted that he himself had achieved the first two though he had nothing to do with the third. Despite Burger's efforts to smooth things over, Marshall's frustration mounted as he and Brennan lost battles to the conservatives or the moderates in their struggle to preserve the spirit of a Warren Court that had assured equal voting rights to blacks, had desegregated the schools and had given people in police custody their "Miranda right" to remain silent pending advice from a lawyer. At the farewell meeting with the news personnel, Marshall commented: "For the past four or five years, I asked prospective law clerks how they liked writing dissenting Opinions. If they said no, they didn't get the job."

Marshall's bitterness showed itself in the hostile and sometimes coarse way in which he answered questions at the farewell:

"How do you feel?"

"With my hands."

"Do you have any plans for your retirement?"

"Yes, to sit on my rear end."

Asked about whether a black should take his vacated seat, Marshall said equivocally that race could not be ignored as a factor, but that the selection should not be "on the basis of race one way or the other."

"My dad," he said, "told me way back that you can't use race. For example, there's no difference between a white snake and a black snake. They both bite." The "best" man, Marshall suggested, should be chosen. It was not, in any case, for him to decide, he went on, the Republican President, George Bush, assuming senatorial concurrence, would make the choice.

If by the "best" man, Marshall meant someone in his own liberal image, he was in for another disappointment. Presidents look for like-minded nominees, Republicans generally favoring Republicans, and Democrats those of their own political persuasion. Not all succeed, but all try. Court historians remembered that President Theodore Roosevelt was so upset by Oliver Wendell Holmes's vote in an antitrust case that he swore he could have "carved a better backbone out of a banana." The Republican Eisenhower listed Chief Justice Warren as his great "damfool" mistake.

Bush succeeded where Roosevelt and Eisenhower stubbed their toes. Despite Marshall's remark that race should not be the basis for a choice "one way or the other," it would have been hard politically for Bush to take no note of the fact that Marshall's had, indeed, become a "black" seat.

On the other hand, nothing limited the Republican President to an African American of the Brennan-Marshall type. Tracking on Marshall's farewell words, the President announced that he had found the "best" person, a forty-three-year-old federal Appeals Court Judge and former Catholic seminarian, Clarence Thomas, who felt that the eighteenth-century Constitution should be applied narrowly, as close as possible to what the Founding Fathers had in mind rather than as a document with what Douglas called a "penumbra" embracing many novelties.

The departure of Marshall and the arrival of Thomas was a stride in the direction of a long-delayed, true Burger Court.

When three more Nixon appointees arrived within twenty-eight months of the Burger installation, it seemed to many in the media that a Burger-Nixon era had come to the High Bench, but the forecasts were premature at best. Nixon's luck was more like Teddy Roosevelt's and Eisenhower's than that of Bush.

Harry Blackmun, an eleven-year veteran of service on the United States Court of Appeals, looked, through his early voting patterns, so much like a Burger clone that the two, coming from the twin city area of St. Paul-Minneapolis, soon were known as the Minnesota twins. Not only had they shared the same St. Paul Sunday School class taught by Blackmun's mother and the same Boy Scout troop, but Harry was best man at Burger's wedding to Elvera. At last, it seemed, Burger had a supporting vote and for the first few months he did.

Then a change began. Burger was fourteen months Harry's senior, something that had made a difference when they were small boys, but now, after a separation of almost twenty years, they were together as adults in their sixties, both veterans of long federal judicial service. The sensitive Blackmun resented being seen as the rubber stamp of what had been his domineering boyhood companion. A long drift toward the Brennan-Douglas-Marshall left began.

Called in a demeaning way the Minnesota twin, "did kind of irk me a little," Blackmun admitted to the *Minneapolis Star and Tribune* in a 1986 interview, "for who follows whom on decisions up here." Burger was well aware of his old chum's reaction and tried to overcome it. It made no sense to see Blackmun as a surrogate, he said. "One might just as well say that I am his man. We are co-equals. We are exact contemporaries. We are both judges."

A decisive moment in the Burger-Blackmun judicial relationship came within a couple of years in the clamorous *Roe v. Wade* abortion case of 1972. A broad reading of the Fourteenth Amendment with its guarantee of each citizen's "privileges or immunities" seemed to give women and their doctors broad abortion rights at least in the early period of pregnancy. Faced with a majority so persuaded, Burger signed on, thus getting the right to choose which of the Justices, the hardest liner, or the softest, to draft the Court decision. The deeply religious Burger chose the Methodist-reared Harry, the third most junior Justice, his old friend from Sunday School and one who had many contacts with physicians. For nine years Harry had worked at the Mayo Clinic in Minnesota as legal counsel.

The decision caused decades of public turmoil with hundreds of thousands demonstrating on the Washington Mall on each January 22 anniversary of the Court verdict.

Pro-choice versus pro-life became a perennial political campaign issue to Blackmun's
dismay. "It is a moral, not a political, issue," Blackmun lamented to acquaintances. It was
also a matter on which he was
far from sure he had Burger's full
support. "If you read his concurring Opinion," he noted, "he was
sort of lukewarm. He was
troubled by it."

With such impressive minds
as that of Douglas often in the
opposing corner, Blackmun's
move away from Burger slowly
continued. Illustrative was
whether the United States
should have the death penalty.
Is it the "cruel and unusual punishment" that the Constitution
forbids?

Yes, as currently carried out,
the five non-Nixon appointees
agreed in effect in 1972 in
Furman v. Georgia, Jackson v.

Justice Harry Blackmun, author of Roe v. Wade. Collection of
the Supreme Court of the United States.

Georgia and *Branch v. Texas.* Burger, Blackmun and the two other Nixon nominees at
that time demurred.

States began rewriting their death penalty procedures giving the convicted more
safeguards, and in 1976 the Court tried again. This time with John Paul Stevens
replacing the liberal Douglas, and Stewart with the swing vote changing sides, the
Court ruled seven to two in *Gregg v. Georgia, Proffitt v. Florida* and *Jurek v. Texas* that
executions could resume. Burger and Blackmun were then on the winning side. Only
Brennan and Marshall, with some of the final votes of their long judicial careers,
dissented. Burger told interviewers that he found three or four references in the Constitution that allowed the extreme penalty and that had settled the matter for him,
but Blackmun, after years of thought, now came to the opposite point of view.

In the 1977 Opinions written for the Court by Justices Stewart, Powell and John
Paul Stevens, the Court had gone to long lengths to make sure that the accused had
ample reviews on appeal, but Blackmun, in one of his last Opinions before retiring,
brushed such safeguards aside as inadequate. Dissenting in yet another death penalty
case, he wrote: "From this day forward I shall no longer tinker with the machinery of
death. Rather than coddle the Court's delusion that the desired level of fairness has
been achieved and the need for regulation eviscerated, I feel morally and intellectu-
ally obliged simply to concede that the death penalty experiment has failed."

For Blackmun a long drift leftward on the issue had reached a culmination, but
not all cheered. Tart-tongued Antonin Scalia, a new arrival on the Court, and a man far
closer to the Burger vision, was unimpressed with his senior. The Blackmun comment,

he wrote in reply, "refers to intellectual and moral and personal perceptions but never to the text and tradition of the Constitution." Scalia had little regard as well for Blackmun's historic *Roe v. Wade* Opinion. His own vote was ready to overturn it.

Arguing in 1990 that the Constitution does not address such questions as abortion or the right to refuse lifesaving treatment, the New-Jersey native Scalia said that the Justices were no more qualified to deal with such matters than "nine people chosen at random from the Kansas City telephone directory." In such cases as *Roe v. Wade,* Scalia added as his judgment, that the Court had exercised "self-awarded sovereignty" over "a field where it has little proper business since the cruel questions posed are political not juridical."

Despite the tension as he moved further from Burger, Blackmun had compensations. Given his choice, he picked chambers with a pleasant view of the Capitol and the Library of Congress. Beside the office walls were treasured family keepsakes, the sword in a steel scabbard that had belonged to his father and a silver-headed walking stick from his grandfather. Justices have a private second-floor library that none of the others used; Blackmun commandeered it as his getaway, the place where he composed his Opinions.

There were other perks. The United States Naval Academy, nearby in Annapolis, Maryland, likes to have dignitaries such as Justices of the Supreme Court review the company of midshipmen. On more than one occasion Blackmun did that. "It is very impressive," he described it. "The commandant stands at the side, one step to the rear. An aide is there too. They fire a nineteen-gun salute for a Supreme Court Justice. At fifteen, the aide starts counting aloud."

On one occasion there was a slip: "At sixteen there was a double bang. I could see the gun on a slope above the water. The aide said 'What's that? Sixteen? Or seventeen?' And it got up to twenty.

" 'Migod, a twenty-gun salute,' the aide said. You could hear it loudly where we were, but perhaps it was not heard beyond that."

With his old chum's vote increasingly out of reach, the Chief Justice's quest for a majority had to look next to the two additional Nixon appointees, Lewis Franklin Powell Jr. and William Hubbs Rehnquist.

Confirmed by the Senate in December 1971 only four days apart, with Powell the first to get the nod, Rehnquist was doomed for the next four years to serve as the Conference doorman. The junior Justice sits at the foot of the Conference table next to the senior Associate and next to the door. When a messenger arrives with urgent needs for the sequestered Justices, it is the junior who answers the door. The jurist who was to become the seventeenth Chief Justice was getting his start from the bottom.

With the addition of the two new Justices the voting settled into three equal sections, a strong center built around the newly arrived Justice Powell and the earlier appointed Stewart and White, a solid left of Douglas, Brennan and Marshall and the two allies of the Chief Justice, the strongly conservative Rehnquist and the wavering Blackmun.

The slender, gracious Powell, a son of the old Confederacy, and a proud Virginian, soon took over much of the Court leadership as a peacemaker and bridge between the two extremes.

An example was in 1976 when *Time* magazine proclaimed in a headline that "Justice is in arrears." Burger was indignant. *Time* had pinpointed him and Justices Marshall and Blackmun as the three offenders holding up Court decisions. Although Burger conceded that the quantity of Opinions written for the Court was not a perfect measurement of a Justice's contribution, he argued that it had some indicative value. The day the newsweekly hit the stands Burger released his seventeenth Opinion for the term, five above average. What hurt worst about the *Time* charge was that it is a Court maxim that "Justice delayed is justice denied."

Far from dragging far behind, the Court finished its term one week into July, only seven days or so later than usual. Powell urged Burger not to be so upset: "Chief, you have to expect attacks." It was not for himself that he was outraged, was Burger's answer: "It is for the in-justice to the two other Justices. I don't mind it for myself. I ex-

Justice Lewis Powell, the key man in the middle. Collection of the Supreme Court of the United States.

pect it and pay no attention, I have taken far worse."

His indignation, he insisted, was in behalf of the others. He cited Blackmun. Unlike his own hectic, skin-toughening years as Assistant Attorney General and as a member of the contentious Court of Appeals in the national capital, it had been different for his old twin city friend. Blackmun, he commented, "came here from a cocoon," the quiet of the Mayo Clinic, and a less scrutinized Midwest Court of Appeals, For him the harsh criticism was more painful. Though the Chief held his ground, he could not but be influenced by Powell's calming influence.

Powell came to the supreme bench at age sixty-four after an eminently successful earlier legal career. He had served as President of both the American Bar Association and the American College of Trial Lawyers, two positions in the forefront of his profession. He had made a happy life for himself in Richmond, Virginia, the capital of the old Confederacy where, with great tact, he had chaired the public school board for nine years during the difficult period in which Jefferson Davis's old stronghold adjusted to the classroom desegregation decreed by the Warren Court.

Powell had passed his whole professional life as a member of a prominent local law firm, seeing its name change across the years from Hunton, Williams, Anderson, Gay & Moore to install him as a name partner in Hunton, Williams, Gay, Powell & Gibson. It had been profitable as Powell disclosed when Congress in 1979 directed all federal judges, including the nine members of the Supreme Court, to make an annual disclosure of their incomes, their stocks and other possessions as a reassurance to the public that their rulings involved no conflict of interest. Powell was revealed to be substantially better off financially than the Chief Justice whose holdings were some-what under $730,000, and far above those of Justices Brennan, White and Stevens. Most modestly placed of all was Thurgood Marshall whose sole income was his salary as a Justice, $75,000, and interest of under $1,000 from a savings account.

Despite the satisfactions flowing from so many successes, Powell told the young lawyers sections of the Virginia and American Bar Associations in a filmed interview to be shown to tourists at the Court building, that being chosen for the Court was "very much like being struck by lightning. No one ever quite recovers from the shock and yet one's reverence for the Court remains undimmed." He added: "The Court is the final guardian of the liberties of the people guaranteed by the Bill of Rights. Every Justice is ever conscious of that responsibility."

While Powell never lost that vision, he did become painfully aware of the cease-less flood of papers washing through his chambers in what became a six-and-a-half-day workweek. Powell could be seen often in the next fifteen years striding the corridors of the Justices' area. Without some such exercise, he said, one would "die here of dry rot."

As the archetypal "Southern gentleman," it fell to Powell's lot to cope with an academic crisis brought to the explosion point by the case of the *Regents of the University of California v. Bakke*. It was a grandchild of Earl Warren's *Brown v. the Board of Education*. If schools are to be desegregated in the early grades, how far should society go to make certain that they are desegregated all the way to the top? Should qualified whites be kept out to let less prepared blacks enter?

With fears on the campuses that there would be riots no matter which side won, a throng of the curious huddled all night long in front of the Supreme Court in the hope of squeezing in for the Courtroom hearing. Burger's effort to get a majority was put to the test.

As the decision was handed down on June 28, 1978, with campuses safely empty for the summer vacation, there was good news for the white litigant, thirty-eight-year-old Allan Bakke. He had tried to enter the University of California Medical School at Davis but had been turned away. There were one hundred spaces in the entering class, but sixteen had been reserved for members of racial minorities. Bakke insisted that, solely on the basis of merit, he would have been entitled to one of the sixteen set-asides. The Chief Justice, and Justices Rehnquist, Stewart and Stevens agreed with him, basing themselves on the Civil Rights Act of 1964, which forbade discrimination on grounds of race, color or national origin in any federally funded program. The university received such aid. Hence Bakke could not be excluded merely because he was white. Powell took the same view, making it a decisive five to four. It was what the white Bakke had hoped to hear.

But the Virginian Powell was not finished. Lined up in opposition to the Chief's group were Brennan, Marshall, White and the Chief's onetime best man, Blackmun. Brennan wrote for the four. He saw it as a matter of the Constitution. So long as the government, with such things as the federally subsidized programs "acts not to de-mean or insult any racial group," in this case the white people, but just seeks to "rem-edy disadvantages cast on minorities by past racial prejudice," it was not wrong to "take race into account." Powell approved that, putting it into effect by a vote of five to four with the Burger group dissenting.

Only Powell affirmed what was the controlling middle ground, that state univer-sities could not ban whites from competing for a fixed quota of off-limits seats, but that admissions officers could, on the other hand, consider race along with other factors in accepting students. Neither blacks nor whites had won it all, and Lewis Powell, with the swing vote, had been established as a dominant Burger Court influence.

With four votes in the middle, Stewart, White, Powell and more and more Blackmun and three others on the left, Burger at long last was able to look down the table at Douglas's elbow to a Justice with views largely like his, the Court's youngest member at forty-eight, William Rehnquist.

Bill Rehnquist, like White, was not wholly new to the Court. In 1952 at the wheel of a ten-year-old Studebaker, he had arrived from California to serve for a year as a Law Clerk for Justice Robert H. Jackson (1941–1954), a close political ally of FDR who had supported the President in his ill-fated effort to pack the Supreme Court with six additional Justices of his allegiance.

A devout Lutheran who, as a Justice, served as the strong-voiced chief caroler at the annual Supreme Court staff Christmas parties in the hall outside the Courtroom, Rehnquist arrived as an articulate exponent of archconservative views.

A sergeant in the Air Force in World War II, Rehnquist had made Phi Beta Kappa "with great distinction" as he took both an A.B. and an M.A. in 1948 from Stanford and an M.A. in political science in 1950 from Harvard. In 1952 he graduated first in his class from the Stanford Law School where a classmate was Sandra Day, the future wife of another classmate, John O'Connor.

In his 1987 book, *The Supreme Court, How It Was, How It Is,* and in a 1957 articles for *U.S. News & World Report*, Rehnquist, the unapologetic conservative, left no doubt about what he thought of his fellow law clerks of the 1952 term. The bulk of them, he said, were from Eastern and Midwest law schools, Harvard, Yale, Columbia, Pennsylvania, Chicago and Northwestern. The "liberal point of view," he said, "commanded the sympathy of the clerks I knew." He spelled out what that was as he perceived it: "Extreme solicitude for the claims of Communists and other criminal defendants, expansion of federal power at the expense of state power, great sympathy toward government regulation of business, in short the political philosophy now expounded by the Court under Chief Justice Warren." The words left no doubt that it would be different were he ever to succeed Warren, as indeed he did.

What was it like that year inside the little world of the law clerks? There was no excessive modesty: It would have been "all but impossible," Rehnquist wrote in the 1987 book, "to assemble a more hypercritical, not to say arrogant, audience than a group of law clerks criticizing an Opinion circulated by one of their employers."

When it came time as a Justice to suit his own taste in law clerks, Rehnquist added in the 1987 book, his preference was for "law clerks who seem to have a sense of humor and who do not give the impression of being too sold on themselves."

In the valley between his two tours of service at the Court, Rehnquist first practiced law in Arizona, a state to which his Stanford law classmates, the O'Connors, also migrated. There he became an ardent campaigner for fellow Arizonan, the right wing Barry Goldwater, an activity that caught the eye of Nixon's Deputy Attorney General Richard G. Kleindienst. The latter, in 1969, called Rehnquist to Washington for a two-year stint as Assistant Attorney General in the Justice Department's Office of Legal Counsel, the same section of the government from which Warren Burger and White had made their way to the High Court.

In his Justice Department position Rehnquist quickly became one of the main Nixon spokespeople on Capitol Hill, defending policies, including the wiretapping of

Chief Justice William Rehnquist. The only Law Clerk to eventually serve as Chief Justice, the highly conservative Wisconsonian began his long service at the American judicial summit in 1952, clerking for Justice William Jackson. After a sixteen-year interim in private practice and as Assistant Attorney General, Rehnquist was appointed Associate Justice in 1972, and as Burger's successor to the central post in 1986. Collection of the Supreme Court of the United States.

citizens and tightened curbs on pornography. Confirmed as a Justice by a Senate vote of fifty-eight to twenty-six, Rehnquist first had to explain why, as a Law Clerk, he had written a memorandum for Jackson advocating separate but equal schools for blacks and whites, an idea condemned in the Court's subsequent *Brown v. Board of Education* case. The concept, he told Senators, was his Justice's, not his.

As Rehnquist valued a sense of humor among his clerks, he was able to match it with one of his own. There was an example when he talked to the Bar Association of New York in 1973 about recusals, judges removing themselves from cases where there appeared to be a conflict of interest.

The question came up at a supper in Washington as the Nixon case went through its early stages. Conversation, as often that year, turned to the President's plight. Then someone interrupted: "Wait a minute! We probably shouldn't be talking about this in front of you because it will probably come to the Supreme Court eventually."

No problem, Rehnquist reassured the speaker: "If listening to this conversation were to render me damaged goods for the purpose of adjudication, it is at most harmless error in view of the damage I have already sustained by being exposed to the newspapers and television news."

Then the Justice told a recusal story. When he was practicing in Arizona there was a local Judge with such delicate sensitivity about conflicts of interest that "if he had so much as shaken hands at a political gathering with one of the litigants, he would summarily disqualify himself." The result of such nicety, said Rehnquist, was that on "at least one working day a week he was able to reach the first tee of the golf course before eleven o'clock in the morning, or get home and do some of those jobs that escape the attention of all of us on the weekends."

Despite his jeers at excessive recusals, Rehnquist, unlike the three other Nixon appointees, chose not to sit on the President's case. Different from the three others, his had been a recent intimate involvement with the Nixon administration.

Rehnquist's willingness to discuss issues approaching the Court also was delimited. When, at an embassy reception in 1995, he was asked about the rights and wrongs and security aspects of non-English-speaking immigrants pouring in from Mexico, a matter with judicial implications, the ex-Sergeant Chief Justice suggested tactfully that a Major General who was present was better placed to address strategic questions. He added no more.

With two probable votes, the more and more uncertain Blackmun support, and the occasional help of Powell, White and Stewart, Burger had the makings of an occasional majority. When Douglas withdrew in 1975, replaced by Jerry Ford's one nominee, the moderate John Paul Stevens, the scales tipped further toward Burger, but they were still in a precarious mode. The Powell-Stewart center was strengthened.

A pilot flying his own small plane, Stevens was another of the expanding list of law clerks making the U-turn back to the High Bench. After graduating Phi Beta Kappa from the University of Chicago in 1941, Stevens had served three years in the Navy in World War II earning a Bronze Star for bravery. He took his law degree from Northwestern University in 1947, signing on just after that as a Law Clerk for Justice Wiley Blount Rutledge (1943–1949). Both were mid-countrymen, Rutledge a native of Cloverport, Kentucky, and Stevens of Chicago.

Regionalism may well have gone into Stevens's selection for it certainly had played a big part in Rutledge's ascent to the bench. When, in Rutledge's confirmation hearings, Senator William Langer decried the nominee as inexperienced, adding that "second-best justices or legal mediocrities" can insure justice no better than second-best generals or admirals can win wars, FDR conceded to Rutledge, his eighth and final Court appointee that while "we had a number of candidates who were highly qualified, they didn't have geography—you have that."

If geography helped the young Stevens land his clerkship, other factors went into his confirmation by the Senate. Recognized as a leading antitrust Lawyer and moderate Republican, Stevens had served from 1970 to 1975 on the United States Court of Appeals winning a reputation as a Judge's Judge with careful Opinions suggesting bias neither toward the left nor the right. The Senate confirmation vote was unanimous.

With Stevens settled into his chambers, what served as the Burger Court for most of the tenure of the fifteenth Chief Justice was in place. The vote was two fairly certain ballots for Burger's positions on the right, two on the left and five in the middle. The "Nixon-Burger Court," dolefully predicted by many in the media, had not materialized.

Pollsters appraised the Court. In March 1977, the *U.S. News & World Report* asked 211 federal judges, one-third of the total, 110 judges in the state courts and 187 prominent lawyers, how they rated the Justices.

Powell, the peacemaking Virginian, alone was considered excellent by more than half. Sixty percent gave him that rating. The African-American Thurgood Marshall was treated the most harshly. Only 13 percent found him to be excellent and 32 percent gave him the lowest rank of "poor."

Among the other Associate Justices, Rehnquist, the Chief Justice-to-be, scored highest with 44 percent. The athlete-scholar White was next with 37, followed closely by Stewart with 35. Lumped together at 29 were Brennan and the newcomer Stevens. Lowest was the wavering Blackmun at 14.

The many-hatted Chief Justice Burger for whom the Court of the 1970s was named was rated in the middle. Along with his ideological nemesis Brennan and with Justice Stevens, he was given an excellence score of 29, half that of Powell.

CHAPTER 17

THE BIG SECRET

With the Justices on the bench hearing a case one day, the Marshal at Chief Justice Burger's far left was startled at what he saw in the audience. In the section reserved for members of the Court bar one man's eyes were closed.

The Courtroom protocol is strict: no whispering, no note taking unless you are in the press area and certainly no sleeping.

The Marshal twisted around in his seat and signaled to one of the messengers perched out of sight on small chairs behind the bench. Much of the time the young students seated in back of the Justices are there to fetch copies of the nearly five hundred volumes of earlier Court decisions that are kept close at hand behind the curtains should a Justice need to refer to them during a hearing, but this time the Marshal beckoned for a different purpose. He handed the runner a note for Chief Justice Burger: "A man is asleep. Should I eject him?"

Keeping an ear turned to the lawyer who was arguing, Burger looked down at the dozer. He whispered to Brennan at his side, the two of them in their seventies, and scribbled a reply: "Leave him alone. We will all be there one day."

Still dissatisfied as the hearing ended, the order-minded Marshal walked the "sleeper" down to the PIO office for an explanation. "I wasn't asleep," he said. "I was resting my eyes. Let me introduce myself. I am the past President of the Pennsylvania State Bar Association and I go to my law office in Pittsburgh every day. I am ninety-two years old." A gallant old battler in the legal trenches, the nonagenarian may well have been in the Court that day with still unexhausted vigor for the very reason that he had never surrendered to the temptation to "take it easy."

The incident was typical of the myriad of other considerations going into a Chief Justice's day, not just the quest for four other votes, but what to do about a Lawyer's shut eyes.

The same was true inside the heart of the Court's great secret, the closed Conference of the Justices in which the nine met to decide cases and to set policy on matters calling for more than just the Chief Justice's personal administrative decisions.

A take-charge personality, willing to introduce such novelties as a supportive Historical Society for the Court and museum exhibits for tourists, Burger felt that even two naysayers at the Conference table were enough to kill or at least postpone some of his projects.

When Burger first took his place at the head of the Conference table, he was concerned by the frailty of two of those who had preceded him to the High Bench.

John Marshall Harlan at age seventy was in his fourteenth year on the Court and Hugo Lafayette Black, at eighty-three, was in his thirty-second. The Justices at that time were conferring just on Fridays, but, Burger said later, "Black and Harlan would wilt" toward the end of the long, demanding sessions.

To cope with that, Burger proposed an additional meeting on Wednesdays to split up the work. It was so agreed. Even with that, however, the problem of the two aging Justices continued.

As they debated one day, Harlan absentmindedly lit up a cigarette in violation of a Conference tradition. His gaffe was explained gently, and he at once apologized.

Burger had an allergy to the very smell of tobacco, not just its smoke, but Harlan was at once assured, good naturedly, that there was a new tradition, smoking was allowed—not at the table, to be sure, but in a far corner of the room.

Marshall, Stewart and White joined Harlan as smokers until one fourth of July when White declared his independence of the weed, quitting cold turkey.

Harlan's sight was so bad, Burger recalled, "that he could not read anything that was not in inch high letters. A Justice beside him had to find the cases for him in his notebook."

The aged Black was an even greater source of preoccupation. "We had to pace the conference for him," Burger recalled. "I would get him a cup of tea and put it beside him. I would not ask him because he would say no, but he couldn't get it himself."

Helping the elderly Black caused Burger some problems with media critics. Burger spoke of one such case: "Black came to me one day to say that the drinking water was tepid after an hour. He asked if something could be done to keep it fresh like the water back in Alabama. I got aluminum cups with a pewter finish labeled 'Black, J.' and so forth. A reporter wrote that the Chief Justice now had silver goblets! In fact, before that, the drinking glasses did sit on silver plates. There was no mention of that!"

It was part of the insistence in some of the media that the conservative Nixon had appointed to replace the much-favored Warren was a vain, fussy fellow with a stuffy Napoleonic complex. "I chided the reporter who wrote the story," Burger said. "He flushed but he never retracted."

The same media charge of pomposity followed Burger's effort to protect Black from a dangerous fall, the Chief recounted: "Coming off the bench, Black would stretch his legs, hardly able to move. I was twenty-five years younger, but I felt it sometimes too. From the bench to the Conference Room there are changes in the flooring that are hard to see. I was afraid Black would slip and break his hip."

Abe Fortas had just left the Court after LBJ's unsuccessful effort to elevate him to the Chief Justiceship. There was some yellow carpeting in his vacated chambers. A piece of it was run across the twenty-foot walk from the bench to the Conference room, bright enough for both Harlan and Black to see. Burger now paves his path in gold! ran a news story.

With the deaths of Harlan and Black in 1971, the Conference pace picked up, but a toll was taken by the strain of sorting through a couple of hundred incoming cases a week, and the greater chore of deciding as many as a dozen argued cases, some of them calling for gravest national decisions. It was the custom to break briefly at 11 A.M. for coffee, tea, toast and cookies, and to take off forty-five minutes at noon for lunch.

Even with those respites, when the long Friday conference would go on to 6 P.M., Burger at 1:30 would notice colleagues "beginning to droop." He arranged for a second ten-minute session of caffeine and nibbles. "With the sugar in their bloodstreams," he could see them "freshen up."

Burger sympathized with his colleagues' needs. He shared them even on days in his chambers when there was no conference. In late afternoons, he told a caller, he had a need for a "triple Martini!"

"But you can't have that here," he was quick to add. "What I do is to take a spoonful of honey washed down with tea." He felt an instant lifting effect.

The Justices went to pains to protect the privacy of their sometimes sharp, off-the-top-of-the-head remarks, a type of exchange that allowed them to hammer out and modify ideas without a public record holding them to what might have been ill-considered original statements.

Without law clerks, secretaries, family and friends closing ranks behind each one of them in resenting a colleague's gibe, it also made it easier for most to forgive and forget.

Heavy drapes were in place opposite the door to the Chief Justice's inner work-room, a holdover from the years from 1939 to 1962 when Felix Frankfurter was in the Conference. Frankfurter's voice was high-pitched, and he wanted the baffle for fear that clerks at work beyond the door would hear him.

Justices were satisfied that they could speak freely with scant likelihood that their remarks would go beyond the table. Douglas alone believed otherwise. Ever ready with an original thought, he startled his brethren with an Opinion in case A-335 in October 1973, writing that it was probable that the Conference was bugged. The White House, with presidential approval, was taped as the Nixon case showed, why not the Court Conference?

For the media it was a fun story, and TV and radio begged Douglas or anyone else on the Court staff to go before the microphones reading the A-335 remarks. No one would. It was a Douglas exclusive and all he had was "circumstantial evidence and impressions" plus the memory that in the time of Chief Justice Hughes, with whom he served for two years, there had been some firings of employees for Conference eavesdropping.

That Douglas might come up with an idea shared by no other was not new to the Conference. Rehnquist in a book about the Court during his time as an Associate Justice, said of Douglas that in Conference "we sometimes had the impression that he was disappointed to have other people agree with his views in a particular case be-cause he would therefore be unable to write a stinging dissent."

Douglas, by then, had completed three decades on the Court, and in Rehnquist's view, despite "a brilliant legal mind," seemed "somewhat bored with the routine func-tions" of the institution. Justices, cut off in their "separate law firms," could go a year without setting foot in each of the other eight chambers, so housekeeping chores took Conference time along with judging. Sometimes press leaks were the topic, and one such was when Jimmy Carter became President. An egalitarian Democrat, he seemed to have no objection when his aides said that anyone wanting a seat to see his inaugu-ration could have one for $25, admittedly a budget item for the poor and uninfluential, but an equal tax to be imposed on those in high places.

The Republican Burger grumped, and a gossip item promptly appeared in the press: Burger says that if Carter charges him $25 to be at the inauguration he will bill him $50 to swear him in! Burger was incensed. The stories that he, Marshall and Blackmun were behind in writing their Opinions had broken at the same time.

The origin of such gossip, Burger told others in the conference, "is right here at this table!" He added hotly: "I serve notice now. I am not asking, I'm telling you. The next time it happens I will do something you will not like. And, I won't say what, because that will be discounted beforehand in the gossip columns."

As for charging the new President $50 to administer the oath, that was an under-estimate, he went on. The charge would be $500, enough to pay for seats for all the Justices and their wives plus a pair for retired Tom Clark who, though no longer on the High Bench, was still busy aiding Burger with judicial reform.

When the dust settled, Burger swore in Carter free of charge as he had done for dozens of others, and the White House apologized that it had all been a mistake. Free tickets to the inaugural arrived not just for the Justices and their spouses but even for senior staffers. Getting the tickets proved a mixed blessing. A sharp January wind cut into everyone attending the Capitol steps ceremony.

Another housekeeping chore that brought harsh words from the Chief Justice concerned when to hand down the decision in the sensational *Bakke* reverse discrimination case. The Los Angeles Police Department asked for advance information on when the Court would announce the verdict. Presumably the information would enable them to put out extra patrols.

The Justices came down with no decision while potential student rioters were still on campus for the spring semester, but they stuck to the rule that no one should be told beforehand when any verdict would be rendered. Crowds lined up overnight outside the building on days of major hearings and even greater throngs and demonstrations could be expected if the crucial decision days were to be known in advance.

For reporters, it was a policy adding to their difficulties. If they knew when the big decisions were coming they could bring up extra help, but all the PIO was able to tell them was that on a certain day there would be "three or four" or perhaps "six or seven" decisions, never a precise number, for any Justice was free to postpone a decision up to the moment of the Courtroom release.

"On a rising scale of one to ten, how important will they be?" an occasional journalist would ask. There was never an answer to that. It would be a tip-off for the big days, but in addition, the *Bakke* case was different. As Chairman of the Court, Chief Justice Burger was sure of what could be expected. There would be huge excitement in a racially split country. Burger was determined to keep to a minimum crowd reactions at the Court.

Each Justice usually had a half dozen Courtroom seats at his disposal. Often they invited their wives although it was understood that they should not discuss which cases were coming down. For *Bakke,* the Chief decided that there would be special rules. A mass arrival of spouses would be a giveaway. Therefore Mrs. Burger would not attend and, if the other wives showed up en masse, the case would not come down. Any Justice, not just the Chief, can call back an Opinion up to the moment that it is announced from the bench.

For the PIO, in his office on the floor below the Courtroom, such a last-second reversal would mean a small problem. Seventy copies of the Opinions would reach him two hours before the planned release and would sit face down on his desk waiting for a phone call relayed from the Clerk in the Courtroom that the Chief had announced the judgment. With thirty eager reporters within arm's reach of the still unofficial and secret papers, it was the PIO's job to make sure that none of the copies slipped into circulation.

On *Bakke* day, June 28, 1978, there proved to be no such problem. The Chief saw nothing untoward in the Courtroom and the decision came down.

Only once in nine Burger years was there a last-moment withdrawal. A Justice noticed an error in a date and the Opinion was held over for another day.

Most moments at the Conference table were grave, sometimes sharply combative, but there were also lighter ones, even personal joshing, as Justice Powell mentioned in a speech to lawyers in Dallas. Powell himself was the target of some teasing. Burger taunted him about "your child beating" Opinion. The decision had caused some excited comment about whether parents with impunity could now even "cut off a child's ears!" The point of the decision, Burger pointed out, was very limited, the disciplining of offspring was not a matter of national law on which the Supreme Court should rule. It was a local matter. As far as child abuse was concerned, protective laws on assault and battery were on the books and fully effective.

One Burger remark in Conference in 1973, four years into his tenure, threatened his pocketbook. The Justices, he felt, did not realize how many Opinions they were turning out each year, a book-sized total for each of them, "Up to forty Opinions each." Some were full Court Opinions, others concurrences and dissents.

All at the table knew that the annual workload was heavy but some thought the Chief was overstating it. "Do you have $5 to back up what you say?" asked one.

"No," was the rejoinder, "but I'll buy you a bottle of wine if I'm wrong, and you can get me one if I'm not." The records in the Clerk's office could settle the bet, There was no report on who won, but it was clear that a score or more Opinions, three or more a month from each chamber, were being produced.

Following a custom going back to the time of Chief Justice Melville Weston Fuller, who presided from 1888 to 1910, the nine Justices shook one another's hand one by one as they met for the Conference. The first arrivals would wait as each latecomer sought them out for the greeting. The liberal Brennan spoke of it: "Please don't suggest that this sounds like the preliminaries to a prize fight—the buzzer rings, the fighters shake hands and then proceed to clobber one another."

As for a buzzer, there was indeed one. It sounded in each of the chambers five minutes before the Conference and echoed through the building when the Justices entered and left the Courtroom. But that, said Brennan, was not the point. The handshake, he said, was "a symbol that harmony of aims if not of views was the Court's guiding principle."

In his filmed interview for use in the Court's small ground-floor open theater for tourists, the retired Justice Clark described the Justices' time-honored system in Conference for accepting and rejecting cases: "You look for the federal question. If it's not a federal question, you throw it out; you're obliged to."

Clark added that the Court's role was limited. The Justices could not just issue edicts on problems they perceived; they had to wait until litigants chose to place the matter before them. As the Texan Clark put it: "We can't reach out like a legislature can and say, 'Oh, here is a bad thing over here; let's straighten it up!' We have to wait until we get what we call a justiciable issue, and then it has to involve a substantial federal question." These were seldom slow in coming. The issue then was to apply the laws and the Constitution, even laws Justices such as Burger considered "foolish."

Where apparently mistaken laws were concerned, Chief Justice Burger never forgot what Hugo Black, his Associate for his first two years at the Court, had to say about that: "When practicalities and the letter of the law are opposed, go with the law. Let Congress change the law."

The Constitution posed a more challenging problem. Black kept a copy of it with him at all times. Not all of it has great current meaning as Justice Stewart remarked at his retirement. He asked reporters if they had ever studied the third amendment. Its full text reads: "No soldier shall in time of peace be quartered in any house, without the consent of the owner, nor in time of war but in a manner to be prescribed by law."

There were also constant questions about what some sections meant and which applied where there appeared to be conflicts. Justice Powell discussed it in his 1975 ABA address in Montreal: "The Constitution is a charter of principles and concepts, and not a Code Napoleon. Its meaning is rarely self-evident especially when we are called upon to apply doctrines such as federalism and separation of powers, concepts such as justiciability and standing to sue, and ideals of a free society such as due process and equal protection of the laws."

With the applicable laws and the Constitution on one side there were the facts of each case on the other. Powell spoke of that: "Many cases present extremely close and difficult questions of law. Often these questions are intertwined with sensitive collateral judgments of morality and social policy."

Making up one's mind in many cases is "a lonely, troubling experience for fallible human beings conscious that their best may not be adequate to the challenge." Powell added: "One does not forget how much depends on his decision. He knows that usually more than the litigants are affected, that the course of vital social, economic and political currents may be directed."

To help a Justice as he prepares to cast the decisive vote in a five to four case such as Powell faced in the *Bakke* matter, there were four main aids: the Conference, the lawyers' briefs, the Oral Argument as the Courtroom debate was called and the draft Opinions the Justices exchanged. The Oral Argument and the briefs were open to the press and public, but the rest, until decision, was secret.

With each Justice well aware, as Powell put it, that "the liberty and property and even the lives of litigants" might be at stake, there was often vigorous debate in Conference with what Rehnquist called remarkable candor and give-and-take, some "jockeying, maneuvering and what have you," some ill-conceived comments uttered with no fear of seeing them ridiculed in the next day's media and "occasional short-tempered remarks and bits of rancorous rhetoric."

Each Justice was free to talk as long and as often as he wished but, said Rehnquist, "each member is bound to do a good deal more listening than he does talking unless he is completely arrogant and impervious to any new ideas." Some Justices, at least in earlier years, did fall into the latter category. Powell recalled it: "It is said that a famous Justice, now deceased, often would deliver lengthy and erudite arguments at Conference, pacing the floor and waving his arms. One of his brothers enjoyed deflating the orator, saying at the end of an eloquent peroration, 'I was with you for the petitioner until you spoke at such length. You have persuaded me to vote for the respondent!'"

Some of the Conference Room struggles did meet the public eye in dissenting Opinions in which "we say some outrageous and unflattering things about each other," Powell said in his 1980 talk to the Southwestern Legal Foundation.

Unlike some strong personal antipathies that were known among the Justices as recently as 1947 when John Paul Stevens was a Law Clerk, current battles among the jurists, Powell said in 1980, did not keep those of his era from being "warm personal friends."

On the Monday after two weeks of Courtroom arguments and Conference debates, the behind-the-scenes process of creating a Supreme Court decision goes into a new phase, the writing of Opinions. If the Chief, after all the Conference back-and-forth, declares himself part of the majority, it is his right to choose the Justice who will speak for the Court.

"It's a hard job," Burger told a visitor. His own personal rule, he said, was never to give a case to a Justice who had already produced as many as two Opinions on the same subject: "I give it to one of the others. Otherwise it appears to be one-man justice."

Usually, Burger said, the assignments were accepted without comment, but there were variations: "Just today a Justice who wanted to do an Opinion, gave me a concrete reason why he could not. So I have withdrawn it from him. But I had already assigned Opinions to the others. I will probably end up doing it myself."

It was toward the end of another grueling term, and as he spoke of it Burger looked weary. His Chauffeur was among those who could see his fatigue. "He thinks he's sixteen," the driver said. "I feel sorry for him. I know him intimately. He is a pleasant person."

Tough cases sometimes took two or three conferences to resolve. Even then there might be no majority. "In that situation," Burger said on the Court theater film, "a practice has grown up of assigning it to one Justice to simply prepare a memorandum about the case. And at that time all other Justices are invited if they want to submit a memorandum. And then out of that memorandum usually a consensus is formed and someone is identified who can write an Opinion that will command a majority of the Court."

With the parceling out of the Opinions the Court's big secret dissolves into nine secrets, each of the "law firms" going to work trying to create documents on which at least four other chambers would agree.

As a newcomer to the Court, Powell, the past President of the American Bar Association and member of a large and wealthy law firm, had a list of what he thought would be good innovations. One was to hire a permanent staff of experts on a wide range of legal specializations from labor law to taxation. That was the way they did it back in Richmond and in modern law firms across the country. As a senior partner at Hunton, Williams, Powell told an ABA audience, his job had been not to "look into law books and draft briefs and corporate documents." Others did that. He edited and "made sure the bills went out."

Powell's proposal met a courteous rebuff. His colleagues advised him that "I was being paid to render personal judgments even if they were devoid of expertise."

How bereft they could be came home to the new Justice when he was handed his first case. It was about taxes.

"It had been years since I had looked into the Internal Revenue code, and I had hoped never to see it again," Powell told his fellow lawyers. Back in Richmond it would have been a simple matter for one of his tax partners to turn out the necessary paper in three days. "It took me and a Clerk three weeks," Powell remembered. "Fortunately the case has never been cited since I handed it down!"

Powell had thought the Court would be a place of "consultation and cooperative deliberation" but discovered instead that it was "the last citadel of jealously preserved individualism" with whole terms going by without setting foot in each of the other eight chambers. Memos, phone calls and only occasional face-to-face chats with other Justices were the methods used as each Justice put together his set of Opinions.

Writing Opinions "is not easy work," Rehnquist commented. "It always takes weeks and sometimes months of painstaking research," he said.

Precedents, especially the Supreme Court's own earlier verdicts, are consulted and sometimes the authorities and documents in other fields far from the law are drawn in—history, economics, the social and other sciences.

Rare, said Burger, is it that the first draft makes its way into the law books. Many times a Justice will rewrite an Opinion a dozen times before, as Rehnquist put it with tongue in cheek, he decides it is "unanswerable" and lets the others see it.

Then to the "unanswerable" come the answers. It is often at that time, said Rehnquist, that an Opinion writer finds that his work has just begun. To the extent "feasible," a Justice will recast his Opinion to adjust to the suggestions of the others and "a critical comment from a colleague is accepted routinely," Powell said. What is really dismaying, he added, is a Justice's note: "I will wait until circulation of the dissent." What had seemed like a ready majority when the Opinion writer received the assignment might dissolve in the face of an impressive dissent.

"I have converted more than one of my proposed Opinions for the Court into dissents," Rehnquist admitted. "I have also had the much more satisfactory experience of seeing a dissent become the decision of the Court!" he added.

Some reporters, looking for the scandals that make headlines, would flip quickly to the dissents: one more wrong-headed action by the Court! That did not concern the Chief greatly. Much though he admired the land of his wife's forebears, he did not go along with what the Supreme Court of Sweden had put into effect. It forbade the release of dissents. For all his efforts to put together majorities, Burger remarked: "If we went a year without a dissent, I would feel that we were in serious trouble."

In drafting the Court decisions the Justices leaned heavily on the briefs, the summary of cases filed by attorneys, and on the Courtroom debates. It was a chance to get input from other lawyers and their research of precedents. As the Justices saw it, however, in all too many cases, the outside help was no reed to lean on. For one thing, few briefs were models of brevity. In a Bakke case they could pile up two or three feet deep. "Reading all of it you wouldn't have time to sleep," Burger told a group of foreign newsmen on June 17, 1978.

Lawyers submitting them hoped, of course, that every Justice would savor each phrase, but that was a practical impossibility. "An experienced Judge," Burger said, "can skim. He doesn't have to read every word. Sometimes whole statutes are included when only a small part applies."

In his chambers Burger supplemented his own perusing with instructions to his clerks to highlight what they thought was important. Some speed-read section might need a second look.

Even thus there never seemed to be enough time to cope with the paper avalanche. One day in Court another of the nine became so incensed he exploded at the offending Lawyer. Burger sat silent. "I would never do that during a presentation," he said later. "It would get the Lawyer so flustered he would forget his own name."

Burger had been on the other side of the podium as a pleader and knew the stage fright attorneys can suffer in what may be the high point of their careers.

When the Lawyer finished, however, Burger weighed in. He had done the Court a service, he told the wordy Lawyer with irony. By providing such a horrendous example, he had shown why briefs should be brief. If the other litigants that day had come in at the same length "we would have had twenty-seven hundred pages to read!"

Newspapers jumped on the story of the nonbrief briefs. "To my surprise," Burger said, "it was used all over the country. I got a lot of mail on it."

One letter to the Chief made the point that Justices, too, might better save space. The critic had gone through what the Supreme Court had churned out in the previous year—all twenty-five hundred pages of it! Burger had no quarrel with that. A virtue of reporters, he conceded, was that they knew how to get to the point, while "all Justices think that the Opinions of the other Justices should be shorter."

The Chief's concern about not throwing off the pleading lawyers was well taken, Tom Clark remarked: "After you have argued one or two," he said in the Court film, "you still have butterflies. I did, and I think perhaps it's good if you do. If you get too

West facade of the Supreme Court building. Above the columns is the slogan "Equal Justice Under Law."
Franz Jantzen, Collection of the Supreme Court of the United States.

sure, if you get overconfident, you may lose your case." Clark won all four of his.

The Court has the upper hand on the length of time the attorneys argue. Burger would announce at the outset that there would be a lunch break at midday and at noon the bench would empty. One Lawyer, determined to get across a final point, looked up a bit after noon and was startled to see nine empty chairs.

What the Justices could not control was the quality of the briefs and arguments. A high-caliber presentation in either could help with decisions and Opinions. Instead, half the lawyers pleading before the High Bench were incompetent, Burger remarked on May 11, 1977, adding: "With poor pleading we can miss the point."

The Chief cited a river boundary dispute between two states: "We said federal law controlled. A year later we had another case. Then we said that the other decision just applied in that one instance, that, in general, federal law does not apply in such a matter. It was the fault of poor arguing by lawyers in the first case."

Some of the few times the Justices lunched together, their food brought to them from the public cafeteria by their messengers, was during the midday interruption. Tom Clark, who served eighteen years as a member of both the Vinson and Warren Courts, remembered how the lunch table chatter went in those days. Sometimes the quality of the morning pleadings came up: "That fellow, he didn't know too much about the case, did he?" And, "Why didn't he say this or that or the other?"

Seldom would the rights and wrongs of the issue intrude. That was for Conference. More often in Warren's time the talk would turn to professional ballplayers. "There was a ballplayers yearbook," Clark recollected. "Warren knew more about the players than the book did. And Vinson too. That was one thing they had in common—ballplayers."

While the lunchtime back-and-forth might touch on lawyers' performances only in passing, that was a source of frustration for those on the bench.

Powell, the holder of the strong center position on the Court, might not sign off on the Chief's arithmetic of a 50 percent incompetence level among the High Court pleaders, but he did agree that far too often the attorneys gave little help to the Justices as the nine grappled with national issues.

Powell spoke of it at length in a talk to judges of the federal Court of Appeals in New Orleans. The New York District Attorney was lamenting that he had to send low-paid "boy scouts" on his civil servant staff to plead against high-powered defenders in murder cases, a parallel to what the nine were seeing in their Courtroom.

"There is little doubt that the marked trend of the law toward expanded rights of defendants, a trend so noticeable over the past two decades, has been influenced in part by the representation imbalance before the Court," Powell said.

Most of the lawyers appearing before the Justices were making "one shot" appearances, a far cry from golden earlier years when John W. Davis argued 140 times from 1913 to 1954, or a Daniel Webster appeared on 185 to 200 occasions, or the record holder, Walter Jones (1801–1850), showed up 317 times. With such experience the three knew what the Justices needed in order to create legal precedents.

Too many clients, Powell suggested, ask "a best friend or a neighbor" to argue for them, or choose a Lawyer with nothing but an office practice to try his unhoned skills at the appellate level.

Coming to the Court Powell had expected few mediocre presentations. He was sad to learn differently. The view from the bench too often was bleak.

CHAPTER 18

LITTLE VILLAGE

It was closing time at the Court building, 4:30 P.M. Justices, their secretaries and their clerks were busy in the chambers, but it was time for the stragglers among the annual half a million visitors to head outdoors on Capitol Hill. One couple lingered.

"Time to go," one of the members of the Court's own eighty-person police force told the laggards. "The building is closed."

"We're not leaving," one of the two, a heavy-set middle-aged woman answered quietly. "We want the Justices to allow prayer in the schools. We will not leave until they change their decision on that!" The man at her side nodded but remained silent. The lady was in charge.

In the police area up the hall from the PIO's suite, members of the force talked it over. It was important that there be no charge of male police brutality inside the citadel of citizens' rights. If the lady had to be ejected forcibly it had better be one of the few policewomen to do it. One of them was called.

Next there was the matter of the June 13, 1966, verdict of the Warren Court in the case of *Miranda v. Arizona*. Justices Clark, Harlan, Stewart and White had objected to it, but Warren, Black, Douglas, Brennan and Fortas had the needed five votes to impose on all police, including the Court's own, the requirement that people under arrest be advised of what became known as their "Miranda rights." On the floor above, as the police talked, Chief Justice Burger was sure that in the changed Court then in power there were enough votes to reverse *Miranda*, but, with police by then so accustomed to it, the altered Court was leaving it on the books, merely declining to expand it.

A little group assembled at the side of the two trespassers, and the Court-ordered recitation began. The woman was addressed: "You have a right to remain silent. Anything you say may be used against you. If you need a lawyer, one will be provided."

The woman listened and waived her right to say nothing: "I won't go until the Court changes the prayer decision!"

The man was next: "Sir, the building is closed."

"I won't leave," he finally spoke up. "I'm going to stay here to see that no harm comes to this lady." He had been at the woman's side while she heard her rights, but the police officer read the formula a second time for him. No loophole was left so that his Lawyer could claim later in some court below that he did not realize that what his friend had heard a few inches away applied also to him.

Though the Justices have their police, they have no jail. By that time a District of Columbia police car was waiting in the basement garage. The trespassers, without resisting, were escorted down a flight, and were driven off to D.C. detention pending a morning hearing. The two were soon freed to return to Boston but not before a report came back that the lady had assembled in jail some of the night's haul of street walkers for "Matins," brief morning prayers.

The incident reflected the rarely seen life of a little village inside the Court's marble walls, where a team of three hundred provide support for the nine members of the bench, a family in some sense, and a tiny town in another. Unlike crossroads communities of a similar population, however, this one was housed in splendor a potentate would envy.

East facade of the Supreme Court. The seldom seen rear of the Court building with the slogan devised by Chief Justice Hughes and Justice Van Devanter, overruling the architects' choice. Josh Mathes, Collection of the Supreme Court of the United States.

When the national government moved from New York and then from Philadelphia to the swampy land between the Potomac River tobacco ports of Georgetown, Maryland, and Alexandria, Virginia, there was money enough for the President's White House and the legislature's Capitol building, but nothing for the government's judicial third branch. The Justices borrowed a room in the Capitol where Daniel Webster and others could argue before them and did the rest of their work at home, often in boardinghouses. All that changed in 1935 after Chief Justice William Howard Taft, a former President, convinced Congress that the Court needed a house of its own.

The Court's first order of business when it began its first term, in February 1790, in what is now the Wall Street financial section of New York City, was to hire a staff of two, Richard Wanman as the Crier to announce hearings, and John Tucker, a Bostonian, to be their Clerk.

From that beginning evolved the hundreds helping the Burger and Rehnquist Courts, many of them added when Taft won his fight for a building. It was a victory accomplished just in time as the heavily lawyered, litigious American population inundated the Court of the final twentieth-century decades with appeals to be heard.

Cass Gilbert and John R. Rockart got the contract to design the house for the Justices and they set out to establish that their clients were indeed the equals of the Congress and the President. What they created was a place of magnificence, not without its oddities. Among the latter was a phrase emblazoned across the front of the building which, over the next half century, went down in media and public imagination as a noble, age-old, summation of human rights: "Equal Justice Under Law."

It was ringing and inspiring, but some scholars wondered where it had originated. Was it tucked in somewhere in the mass of language in the Constitution? Was it in Jefferson's Declaration of Independence? Was it perhaps one of the many elements of

Detail of the North Courtroom frieze. Equal time for another of the world's great religions. The Adolph A. Weinman frieze depicts Mohammed holding the Koran. Franz Jantzen, Collection of the Supreme Court of the United States.

the American legal tradition preserved from the English motherland? For that matter was it good English usage? The latter question was raised half in jest, New Yorker to New Yorker, in a letter from Herbert Bayard Swope, a *New York World* Editor, to Chief Justice Hughes, the former New York State Governor. The phrase, Swope objected, was tautological, unnecessarily repetitive. It was verbose. It was redundant. "Justice" not only has no need of the adjective "equal," he said, its inclusion even "robs" the splendid noun of its meaning.

Correspondence in the Court files showed how the Chief Justice tried to reply. The Declaration of Independence aside, Jefferson in his first inaugural address in 1801 talked of "equal and exact justice to all men," two adjectives, not just one. "Is he not still your favorite author?" Hughes challenged the Editor.

Further, Justice Stanley Matthews (1881–1889) spoke of "equal justice," Hughes added, in his decision for the Court on May 10, 1886, in the case of *Yo Wick v. Sheriff Hopkins.* Matthews in his turn had cited as his precedent a San Francisco all-night Chinese laundry case, *Soon Hing v. Police Chief Crowley* (March 16, 1885), where the wordier concept, if not the language, was included: "Equal rights which all can claim in the enforcement of the laws."

That still did not establish a direct precedent for the four-word phrase, so Clarence P. Cowles, a Burlington, Vermont, Attorney and a former pupil in a Sunday School class taught by Hughes, set out to find one. He failed. The fact was that the motto was an invention of the architects. It fit the space they had, and Hughes and his Associate, Willis Van Devanter (1910–1937), had okayed it on behalf of the Court.

The two were not automatic rubber stamps for the designers, however. When the architects suggested "Justice is the Foundation of Liberty" for the seldom-noticed back of the building, Hughes wrote on a 4-by-5-inch pad of a type still in use at the Court years later: "I rather prefer 'Justice the Guardian of Liberty,' CEH."

Still preserved, the note bears Van Devanter's response: "Good, W.V."

The phrase did not capture the public imagination but, a half century later, it still adorns the rear of the structure.

As the architects went to work to give the Justices and their staffs their first house they stinted on nothing and tried to think of the smallest details. Research by a Washington news writer indicated that the four-story structure was at the time of its dedication the largest all-marble building in the country and perhaps in the world. In terms of materials used—marble, bronze, white oak—only one other federal structure was its match, the National Gallery of Art on the capital mall of which Chief Justice Burger was also the overseer.

Seeking to meet all foreseeable needs, spaces were provided for a barber shop (one-hour $7 haircuts by appointment as the century drew toward a close), a laundry to keep police uniforms neat, a nurse, a soon hectically busy telephone switchboard, vast conference rooms suitable for ceremonies, a police station, a corps of messengers and teenage pages, painters, carpenters, printers, electricians, a press area, public eating places and a seamstress to repair wind-tattered American flags and Justices' robes.

Detail of the South Courtroom frieze. An additional representation of the Ten Commandments. Created by Adolph A. Weinman, the frieze depicts Moses holding the sacred tablet. Franz Jantzen, Collection of the Supreme Court of the United States.

Suites of paneled rooms complete with fireplaces were provided for each Justice. There were handsome offices, too, for the senior staffers, the Clerk, the Marshal, the Librarian and the man known as the Reporter of Decisions.

In the upper part of the building there are open-air courtyards, nice for staff snacks and chats in good weather, but a nightmare for older, absent-minded visitors as they try to go from one side of the top floor to the other along corridors twisting around the open areas.

Special touches are everywhere. The bronze front doors weigh thirteen tons and call for good leverage and strong backs as Court police officers open and close them. Carved in the bronze are eight scenes of the evolution of law, starting with a Greek trial scene which, according to the *Iliad,* adorned the shield of Achilles, and finishing with two members of the Court itself, Chief Justice Marshall (1801–1835) and his contemporary, Justice Joseph Story (1811–1845).

Among rare features are two basement-to-roof circular staircases on either side of the Courtroom giving the unnerving impression that each step is supported only by the one below it; pull out the bottom and all would come down like dominoes. It is an illusion. The steps are cantilevered into the wall like diving boards. Gilbert had done a similar staircase, also four stories tall, for the Michigan State Capitol. There are said to be only a few similar flights of stairs anywhere in the world, one in the Paris Opera and another in the Vatican Museum.

The east wall and bench of the Courtroom, with the Ten Commandments and the frieze of eighteen great lawmakers overhead. The Ten Commandments, centered directly over the chair of the Chief Justice, created an eternal problem for the Court's Public Information Office: "What is religion doing in here when we have constitutional separation of church and state?" Franz Jantzen, Collection of the Supreme Court of the United States.

Especially impressive are the first-floor Courtroom and the hall leading to it, both of them forty-four feet high, and also the third-floor library. The Courtroom boasts twenty-four columns of Sienna Old Convent marble, quarried in Liguria, Italy. The walls are Ivory Vein marble from Alicante, Spain, bordered at the bottom with marble from both Africa and Italy. High above the Justices' bench, along with the Ten Commandments, are eighteen lawgivers of history, one from the Court itself, again John Marshall, but also Moses, Mohammed, Confucius, King Solomon, the Draco of ancient Athens's harsh draconian laws, the Roman emperor Augustus and France's Charlemagne and Napoleon.

The animal kingdom is not neglected. A mean-looking panther is in the Courtroom frieze. In the bronze gate to the Courtroom is a snarling lion. Dogs, eagles, an owl and two hunched-down squirrels decorate the great hall. In the ornate, oaken library, there are carved dolphins, butterflies and, above the circulation desk, a flare-tailed turkey.

Among unaccustomed niceties for the Justices after their century of homelessness was their oak-paneled high-ceilinged dining room. For its first decades it was furnished sparsely and modestly until the art-minded Burger arrived. "It looked like Gawler's funeral parlor," he said in a reference to the bleak rooms of a leading Washington undertaking establishment.

Interior view of the reading room of the Supreme Court Library. An example of the luxurious appointments provided by the 1935 architects. Franz Jantzen, Collection of the Supreme Court of the United States.

At Burger's prompting, his new Historical Society got to work and donors, including the families of earlier Justices, began making contributions, many of them prize pieces from the first years of the national history. Included were a 15-foot long dining table of 1790, possibly the work of Duncan Phyfe, sixteen chairs of 1795, two Massachusetts Hepplewhite secretaries of 1780 to 1800, a Sheraton sofa of 1800 and a Philadelphia grandfather clock of 1775 to 1790, which chimes every fifteen minutes. All the pieces were in mahogany.

For the fireplace there were andirons inscribed "O.W. Holmes," originally the property of the first Oliver Wendell Holmes, the author of the classic *Autocrat of the Breakfast Table*. The irons had passed to his Justice son who in turn gave them to Justice Felix Frankfurter.

In addition to the dining room for the full Court there is a seldom-used private eating room named for John Marshall. On one occasion Burger took advantage of that perk. A Senator had come to call and Burger received him there. The visitor noticed two portraits and asked about one of them. "I don't know that Justice," he said.

"I guess you know the other?"

"Yes, James Madison."

The unrecognized, said Burger, was William Marbury. He was not a Justice of the Supreme Court. In fact he even failed to get a job as a Justice of the Peace when he sued the future President Madison for the position. Madison was then President Jefferson's Secretary of State. Theirs was the case of *Marbury v. Madison* (1803), perhaps the most important ever handed down by the Court. In it John Marshall did not

Bas-relief panel depicting Themis ("Blindfolded Justice") on the lampposts of the Supreme Court building. Tourists seek in vain for a free-standing statue of Justice with her blindfold and scales, but must settle for this bas-relief on one of the two giant lampposts flanking the Court's front plaza. Franz Jantzen, Collection of the Supreme Court of the United States.

give Marbury the job but, on his mere say-so, he seized for the Court the right to strike down laws passed by Congress, making the United States Supreme Court one of the most powerful in the world.

Telling the story later, Burger commented that his visitor "got the point." Asked to overrule *Marbury,* thus surrendering the Court's watchdog role with regard to the other branches of the government, Marshall's successors never would do so.

To work off calories absorbed in the occasional lunches in the dining room and to relax from Conference tensions there is in addition to the basketball court favored by Byron White, an exercise room and a steam cabinet, the latter quite popular. Missing, to Burger's disappointment, was a swimming pool. "For $10,000," he said, "they could have included it."

The depression-built structure cost $9,740,000. It came in under budget so $94,000 was put back in the National Treasury. By the time of the Burger Court the replacement cost of the building was estimated at $125 million.

One item for which tourists search in vain is a free-standing statue of blindfolded justice, the popular image of the impartial handling of cases. There is none. Sharpest eyes, however, can find a small bas-relief of the subject on one of the giant marble candelabras on the 100-foot-wide front plaza. There is also a tiny one in the right hand of a massive statue of a female figure called the Contemplation of Justice, which is also on the plaza.

Fifty years after Gilbert and Rockart finished their work, the building and its contents are much the way the architects created them with one large addition, a 2-ton 7-foot-tall bronze seated figure of John Marshall, the admitted "great Chief Justice."

Marshall of the first third of the nineteenth century is never far from the minds of the twentieth-century Justices. A prize Court possession is a Rembrandt Peale portrait inscribed on the back: "Chief Justice Marshall. Painted in Washington about the year 1826. By Rembrandt Peale. From the life." To be sure everyone knew that he had written these words, Peale confirmed it in Latin: *Ipse scripsit,* he himself was the inscriber. The painting dominates the Court's East Conference Room.

Another treasured object was Chief Justice Marshall's chair. Both Lewis Powell and William Rehnquist took turns sitting on it in 1971 as they waited to be sworn in among Marshall's successors. All others since then have done the same.

All Marshall mementos paled, however, in the face of the huge statue. The idea for it dated to the Chief's death in Philadelphia on July 6, 1835. The bar of that city took up a collection, limiting gifts to $10 in a demonstration that the tribute was an expression of many people, not merely of a wealthy few. The idea was noble but impractical. Only $3,000 came in. Not for another half century was the necessary $40,000 raised, half of it from Congress. A son of Justice Story, William Wetmore Story, a sculptor in Italy, was hired for the work, and, finally, with the task completed, was able to incise

The Rembrandt Peale painting of John Marshall, a proud Court possession. Collection of the Supreme Court of the United States.

into the object's right side, "W. W. Story Roma 1883."

There was still a good way to go, however, before the statue took its place as the dominant monument inside the Court building. For nearly a century it sat, little noticed, downhill at the back of the Capitol building, slowly eroding, the bronze becoming so thin that a nail could be hammered through it. Hughes tried to get it for the new building's front plaza, but Cass Gilbert urged against it. It was far too small, he said, to stand before so large a structure.

Where Hughes failed, Burger succeeded. Sounding out the other Justices, Burger found that Earl Warren shared his admiration for Marshall, although there was at least one to disagree. Hugo Black, a stout defender of states' rights, had no taste for Marshall's federalism, his striving for a strong national government. With Black gone by 1971, Burger lobbied for ten years and finally was able to install the statue as a principle adornment of the interior of the Justices' building.

With the Clerk and Crier on board in February 1790 as the first persons employed to help the Justices, the support staff got off to a poor start. If it was Clerk Tucker who took the minutes, he bobbled it. Like someone writing a check in the first days of a new year, the minute taker put down the wrong decade: February 3, 1789. He caught his mistake, making a change to 1790 but, perhaps flustered by his error, neglected to erase the first entry. The two dates on the minutes are still in the Court records.

Whether the first try was clumsy, the Clerk and his successors quickly became a major part of the Court enterprise. The Clerk is the channel through whom lawyers

JOHN MARSHALL

CHIEF JUSTICE OF THE UNITED STATES
FROM 1801 TO 1835

The John Marshall statue. Carved by the expatriate sculptor son of Justice Joseph Story of the Marshall Court, the statue needed more than a century from the time of conception until Burger gave it its prominent ground-floor place in the Court building. William Wetmore Story, Collection of the Supreme Court of the United States.

reach the Court. He arranges to admit members to the Court bar, as many as six thousand new ones each year. He receives forty copies of each of the thousands of annual briefs and, after their use, ships them out to dozens of law libraries that keep full files of them. He assigns dates for cases to be argued before the Justices. He oversees the death-watch when prisoners face execution and a Justice might intervene.

As seen from the audience, the Clerk sits at the far left of the bench during Oral Arguments. He and the Marshal, in swallow-tail coats, take front-row seats along with the Justices when the Court members attend presidential addresses to joint sessions of Congress. And, on occasion, during the mid-century years, the Clerk would hold the Court's two-century-old Bible when Presidents were sworn in.

In the Court's first decades, Justices leaned on the Clerk for other help. An example in the records was a note Justice Robert Cooper Grier (1846–1870) sent on September 8, 1863, to Daniel Wesley Middleton, who had just taken over from William T. Carroll, the Clerk of 1827–1863.

The Justice had trouble:

> I have just received a letter from Mr. Morrison informing me that I have been ejected from my rooms in his house.
>
> I was one of the first who took rooms [there] and did not expect to be turned out first to accommodate a speculating, greedy Yankee woman. But that appears to be the fact.
>
> As I must stay somewhere, I wish you would do me the favor to make the best arrangements for me you can. I am very weak in the legs and do not like the notion of getting up to the third floor, if possible to avoid it.
>
> If I cannot do better, I suppose I must climb.

It was mid–Civil War. The record does not show whether antifeminism or mere pique at being ousted prompted the Justice, himself a Pennsylvanian, to write so disparagingly about a fellow Northerner. Also absent is word about what boardinghouse received him next.

Clerking proved profitable for many years. The Clerk was allowed to pocket as his own all fees paid to the Court. Changes began at the start of the Court's second century and finally, in 1964, Lyndon Johnson and Congress made the Clerk and his own expanding staff regularly salaried government employees. By then it was no boon to the taxpayers. The fees were running at $200,000 and the Clerk and his staff at a quarter of a million.

The next recruit to help the Justices in the final decade of the eighteenth century was a cross between staffer and member of the press corps, an onlooker who wrote down what he could understand from words from the bench and sold the product to lawyers. His reports were collected in book form and the half a thousand volumes of the *United States Reports* began.

The first of the dozen and a half Reporters of Decisions of the Court's two-century history was Alexander James Dallas, a naturalized citizen who had immigrated from Bermuda. He published four volumes known to lawyers as 1–4 *Dall.* Then he found better use for his time, if not for his fame, by taking successive positions as Secretary of the Treasury and of War.

Among attorneys, however, the Dallas name, albeit truncated, is imperishable as they cite early cases. Only the Reporter's son, George William Dallas, Vice President under Polk, did more to celebrate the surname. A Texas city with a powerful late-1990s football team was named for him.

Next to record Court actions was William Cranch, a nephew of President John Quincy Adams. He served from 1801 to 1815, publishing 1–15 *Cranch.* He provided case summaries, including one that has been described as the most significant in the *United States Reports.* It was in the crucial case of *Marbury v. Madison.* Cranch summarized it with no capitals except at the start of his sentence: "An act of congress repugnant to the constitution can not become law."

Taking note of the importance as well as the difficulty of the Reporter's job, Justices, in what they considered "cases of difficulty or importance," began supplementing spoken Opinions with written texts. Cranch was grateful. It helped rescue him, he said, from "much anxiety as well as responsibility."

With the age of the volunteer entrepreneur fading, Justices in 1816 appointed Mr. Cranch's successor. He was attorney Henry Wheaton (1816–1827). Congress gave him an annual stipend of $1,000, and the newcomer produced volumes 1–12 *Wheat.* The $3 a day was a help, but Wheaton needed more to get by. "I pray you bear me in mind for retainers," he begged his friend, Justice Story, when the latter sat on courts below.

Wheaton was so much at ease with Story that he let him know how ill he felt about another on the bench, the blunt-spoken, independent-minded William Johnson (1804–1834) who was known as the Court's first great dissenter.

Issuing one of the *Wheat.* volumes, the Reporter apologized to Story: "I am sorry that there are so many of our friend's crudities in this volume. ... He has unfortunately most concert where he is most deficient. But what can't be cured must be endured."

Justice Johnson outlasted the disapproving Reporter by seven years. Wheaton quit, becoming the Minister to Denmark and later to Prussia.

Richard Peters of 1–16 *Pet.* (1827–1843), was another who got along fine with Joseph Story and picked feuds with other Justices, Henry Baldwin (1830–1844) and John Catron (1837–1865). That got him fired though Story sided with him so fiercely that the Justice weighed leaving himself. In the end he stayed. The good old days of the Marshall Court with its "kind and frank courtesy" were gone, he accepted with sorrow.

Benjamin Chew Howard (1843–1860), Jeremiah Sullivan Black (1861–1862) and John William Wallace (1863–1874) put out 1–24 *How.*, 1–2 *Black*, and 1–23 *Wall.*

With them the Reporters lost their place in the limelight of Supreme Court decisions. Congress stepped in deciding that the nine-decade hand-to-mouth system of the Reporters scrounging to produce the volumes should be replaced by direct government financing. The change was made with an initial $25,000 grant, and the Reporters' names vanished from the titles. The hundreds of subsequent volumes bear mere numbers.

One who regretted the change was Felix Frankfurter. He scolded editors of the *Harvard Law Review* when they tried to cite volumes such as 1 *Cranch* as 5 *U.S.* There should be no tampering with what had become a time-sanctioned way, he said.

Another to lament, with however much tongue in cheek, was Mrs. Henry Putzel, wife of the Reporter of Decisions of most of the Burger years. With his staff of ten, the easy-smiling, kind-mannered Henry, a Harvard Law School graduate and a lover of words, was producing the four or five page summaries of decisions, the *syllabi*, which both reporters and lawyers found an essential guide to Court rulings. He was also serving as the Justices' counselor on proper language. Henry oversaw the word by word production of fifty fat volumes of the *U.S. Reports*, all of which in happier Reporter of Decision days, would have been known in every law office as 1-50 *Put!*

The Reporter's struggle for proper use of the President's English traced to earlier years. On Putzel's wall was a framed letter from Oliver Wendell Holmes to Ernest Knaebel, the Reporter of the 1916 to 1943 period.

A "principle" is one thing and "principal" quite another, and the "capital" of a nation is different from the "capitol" building housing the national legislature, Mr. Knaebel chided the Justice. Holmes prided himself on his command of a language he had spoken and written long before he was wounded on Civil War battlefields, but he knew when he was caught out. Back to Knaebel went the later framed reply: "'Principle,' of course, was a printer's error that I blush to have overlooked.

"'Capitol' was deliberate ignorance—but I see from the *Century* and my old standby *Worcester*, that it should be 'capital' which I never knew before and do a double blush.

"This is one of the few occasions on which I defer to the dictionary."

Worcester, popular in the early 1900s and *Century*, were dictionaries.

Putzel's own running battle with the Justices was over the use of the words "which," "that," "parameter" and "suppletive."

"Good writers," Putzel decided, use "that" when the meaning is restrictive and "which" when it is not. Byron White kept an eye on Putzel's suggested corrections of Opinions and challenged him one day to explain the difference between "that" and which. " The Justice, Putzel felt, was asking "Why are you being so fussy about this?" The Reporter tried to explain, he thought he made some headway, but he gave up the crusade when Justices seemed to pay no attention. From the bench during a December 7, 1976, hearing, White sent Putzel a note asking him the meaning of "suppletive," a word Justice Harlan had used in a concurrence in 1971 in *Labine v. Vincent.*

Odd you should ask, Putzel replied in substance. Putzel had put that very question to Justice Harlan. Should not some other word be used? Putzel checked *Webster's Dictionary.* It said that "suppletive" derives from "suppletion," which in turn means "the occurrence of phonemically unrelated alimorphs of the same morphene whether the morphene is a base or an affix." Even the word-wise Putzel felt at a loss trying to follow that. Harlan's chambers had responded nonetheless by writing *stet,* printer's Latin for letting the word stand as written.

Putzel thought the Justice was off base, but research later by one of the Court's new team of Burger-appointed judicial fellows, Professor Paul Baier, established that Harlan had been right. "Suppletive" is a civil law term meaning "permissive" in the application of a rule rather than "mandatory."

Justices, like their fellow citizens, tend on occasion to use what Putzel called "mod" words, but the Reporter of Decisions resisted. They "cheapen the language," Putzel objected. With that in mind, he tried to keep "parameter" out of the *U.S. Reports.* Look it up in the dictionary, he said, and "I defy you" to hold in your mind what it means.

Putzel thought the word was a military substitute for "perimeter" or "boundary," either of which he preferred. Harry Blackmun, punctilious about texts, signed on with the Putzel crusade. Not quite seriously, he told Putzel that he had read the riot act to his brothers, telling them they would lose his vote in any case where they spoke of a parameter.

Chief Justice Burger placed high value on Putzel's help to the Court, though more than one of the Reporter's predecessors had fared less well with the Justices and the public. The Court house organ, *The Docket Sheet,* in June 1976 cited an example, the case of the Civil War–era Wallace. He telescoped Justices' texts and used headnotes for editorial comments. In his remarks on *Havemeyer v. Iowa County* (3 *Wall.*) he felt free to impugn the integrity of state court judges, a remark that prompted the *New York World Herald* to berate him as "a Supreme Court fool."

Justices seemed to agree. Nathan Clifford (1858–1881) made corrections on the proofs of three Opinions, sending them back with instructions: "Be sure and give a copy of that dissent to the Reporter as I have reason to think that he will omit to publish it if he can find any excuse. Make it certain that he has it."

Justice Noah Haynes Swayne (1862–1881) was of like outraged mind. "My Opinion in 3 *Wall.* is butchered," he protested. "I can't stand it. It shall not occur again. I will do as Justice Clifford does—have the Opinion published in every case as it is delivered to the Reporter." For the *Wall.* era that may have been a revolutionary thought, but by the time of a Putzel, with reporters as the Justices' employees, it could not be otherwise.

On one other point later Justices drew a line: The Reporter's summaries, however helpful as a quick reference for journalists and lawyers, were not official Court pronouncements and could not be cited in court as Supreme Court precedents. Only the much wordier Opinions, which, through the years, came from the mouths, quill pens, fountain pens, typewriters and word processors of the Justices, however unclear or puzzling, were the law of the land.

The third officer to come on board to assist the Justices was the Marshal. In the Court's first decades members of the corps of United States Marshals kept order during hearings, but in 1867, the Civil War just over, Congress gave the Court a Marshal of its own. With the Clerk busy with lawyers and Court paperwork, the Marshal moved beyond security matters to take over as the business manager of the expanding institution. By Burger's and Rehnquist's time, the Marshal was the direct overseer of the bulk of the Court staff. Even the Justices' paychecks bore the Marshal's signature.

Though he kept the title of Marshal and had the eighty-person police force as one of his subdivisions, some traditional functions of a Marshal were rarely performed. What was believed to be the only time a Marshal of the Court served a subpoena was when government officials set out to recapture possession of Martha Washington's will. During the Civil War, soldiers had raided the Clerk's office in the Fairfax, Virginia, courthouse, lifting the historic document. It passed into the hands of J. Pierpont Morgan, the banker, who handed it on to his son. Frank Key Green, who had started at the Court in 1891 as a fourteen-year-old Page, rising to Marshal from 1915 to 1938, subpoenaed Martha's will from J. Pierpont Morgan Jr. who, without further fuss, handed it back.

Green's half century at the service of the Justices was not uncommonly long. Some families contributed as many as three generations to the Justices' service, messengers at the start, law graduates at the end.

Thomas Waggaman, Marshal from 1938 to 1952, was another who began as a Page, in 1911. He took a law degree from Georgetown in 1922.

During much of the Burger period Al Wong, a Chinese-American, was the Marshal. A twenty-five-year veteran of the Secret Service, Al had served as Deputy Chief of White House Security. Ironically, one of Al's assignments from Richard Nixon was to install the tapes that undid the Presidency in the case of the *U.S. v. the President of the U.S.*

A generation after the arrival of the Marshal, the nine-decade-old Court made two additions to its growing team, a Librarian and a Law Clerk, each of whom evolved into major components of the Courts of Burger and Rehnquist.

Chief Justice Earl Warren remarked in 1965 that just as a library is said to be the heart of a university, so is a book collection vital to a court of justice. The late-twentieth-century Chief Justice was sure of that, but Congress, no doubt short of cash, acted in the first decades of the Court as if it thought otherwise. No funds were provided for books for the Courts of Chief Justices John Jay, John Rutledge and Oliver Ellsworth. When John Marshall took over in 1801 and the legislators created the Library of Congress, the question arose whether the Justices at least could use those books. Congress said no. Ed Hudon, the Court Librarian from 1972 to 1976, did research on the era and found that one member of the national legislature had expressed the hope in John Marshall's first year that "the Congressional Library would never be subjected to the abuse books in courts of justice [are] liable to." The naysayer got his way. For more than a decade the Justices of the Marshall Court were kept out of Congress's stacks.

In 1812 Congress relented. The Library of Congress collection of law books by that time was still small, mostly texts from the old English motherland, but John Marshall; Joseph Story; George Washington's nephew, Bushrod Washington and the other members of the High Bench were allowed to see them. There was still no law-book collection of the Court's own. Congress debated whether to fund one and in 1815, 1826 and 1830, said no. John Marshall and his team would have to do without such help. Finally, in 1832, three years before Marshall's death at age eighty, the lawmakers gave in a second time.

The Library of Congress by that time had 2,017 law books. The Justices could have them in their safekeeping but on one condition: Any Congressman who wanted to look at them could do so.

That posed no problem, and Marshall was elated. Story was on vacation in his home state of Massachusetts so Marshall rushed off a letter to him asking him to draw up a list of books needed in the collection. Congress agreed to an annual book fund of

$1,000 to $2,000. In a happy surprise, the Justices found that the slim collection the Library had assembled already included most of what Story had on his list.

Absent a Librarian, the job of looking after the books was handed to William T. Carroll, the Clerk of 1827 to 1863. He let members of the Court bar borrow the volumes, no more than three at a time, and required their return within a "reasonable" period. A fine of $1 a day was assessed for late returns, and loss of a book was punished with a charge of twice the estimated value of the volume.

With the help of the book fund, the collection grew. In 1845 there were enough copies to give Justices of the Roger B. Taney Court (1836–1864) books of their own to ponder at home. A complete set was kept in the Justices' Capitol Conference Room.

When in 1860 the Senate moved into new quarters in the Capitol, the Court played musical chairs. It took over the vacated Senate space as its Courtroom and converted the basement hearing room of the previous half century into its library. By then there were 15,939 volumes in the collection. The library stayed in its new place for the next seventy-five years.

By 1884, with the second in the line of Marshals, John G. Nicolay (1872–1887), on board and a new Clerk, J. M. McKenney (1880–1913), taking over, the librarian chore was shifted to the former. His office kept the overall responsibility for the next half century, but there was at least a tip of the hat to the importance of a library to a precedence-focused Court; in 1887 one member of Mr. Nicolay's staff was given the task of looking after the books as his main job and the Court had its first Librarian. Not for another fifty-one years, however, did Congress raise the Court Librarian to the rank of full Officer of the Court, along with the three predecessors in that role.

The first Librarian, Henry DeForest Clarke, who had started with the Justices as a Porter, had a steadily growing collection of 101,858 books to safeguard both for the Court and for Congress. When the Library of Congress got a building of its own toward the turn of the century, however, Clarke lost two-thirds of the books. Sixty-five thousand, deemed not immediately essential to the work of the nine, were combed out to become the core of an eventual two-million-volume law section of the Library. Clarke was left with 34,860 books.

Next to look after the books was Frank Key Green (1901–1915). He had begun as a Page eight years earlier, and along the way, earned a law degree from Georgetown University. Like many others on the expanding staff, Green served his full work life at the side of the nine. The library chore not yet seen as full-time business, Green doubled for eleven years as the Courtroom Crier. From 1915 to 1938 Green was the fourth in the line of Marshals of the Court.

Succeeding Green as Librarian was Oscar DeForest Clarke, a law graduate, and son of the Court's first Librarian. He had been acting as a Library Assistant since the time of his father's death. After a slow start, it was under his administration from 1915 to 1947 that the Court Library became the crucial aid to the Court that it now is. The turning point was when the Court of Charles Evans Hughes (1930–1941) occupied the Gilbert-Rockart building in 1935. Into his cathedral-like new premises, the second Librarian Clarke moved the 23,000 volumes he had by then in the Capitol basement Conference Room, adding to them 20,000 from the Library of Congress, 7,500 purchased with a $40,000 Congressional grant, and 25,000 from the personal library of former Governor Elbridge T. Gerry of Massachusetts, a nineteenth-century lawyer, humanitarian and bibliophile best remembered for giving the sinister word "gerrymandering" to the language.

In 1938 Congress completed the evolution by passing a law listing the Librarian, Helen C. Newman, as the fourth of the Court's Officers. After a one-and-one-half-century wait, she was also the Court's first woman Officer. At Ms. Newman's death at age sixty-one in 1965, Earl Warren paid her a tribute from the bench and the flag out front flew at half mast for three days.

By the time of the eighth Librarian, Steve Margeton (1985–1988), the Library, with a staff of twenty-four, had three hundred thousand books on its shelves and was deep into computerized contact with other law libraries. Margeton introduced "Oscar," the On-line Supreme Court Automated Resource, a system for tracking every book from the time of ordering, to the desks of borrowers and back to the stacks.

In the Burger and Rehnquist eras, Justices leaned on the Librarian as their answer person, no question so far afield that it could not be posed. Members of the Supreme Court bar also were welcome to use the Library's services. Penny Hazelton, the Assistant Librarian for Research Services recalled in 1984 some of the inquiries:

Q. Has the Court ever ruled on whether a tomato is a fruit or a vegetable?
A. Yes, in *Nix v. Hedden* in 1893; it is a vegetable.

Q. Who said about pornography that "I know it when I see it?"
A. Potter Stewart concurring in *Jacobello v. Ohio,* 1964.

Q. Who for the first time wrote a dissent when the Justices refused to grant *certiorari,* thus turning away a case without a hearing?
A. Apparently it was Felix Frankfurter in *Maryland v. Baltimore Radio Show Inc.,* 1950.

Q. Whatever became of Mr. Marbury in *Marbury v. Madison?*
A. He prospered as a Washington, D.C., businessman.

Along with a Librarian for the Court, the 1880s brought a second major addition to the Justices' entourage. It was an innovation from the Supreme Judicial Court of Massachusetts, and it was something never known in the courts of England—which had provided so many of America's legal ideas—a Law Clerk.

The invention was that of Horace Gray who served later, from 1881 to 1901, as a Justice of the U.S. Supreme Court. Gray had begun at the Massachusetts High Court at age twenty-six as their Reporter of Decisions, serving ten years in that capacity, and then becoming the youngest Justice that court ever had. In 1873 he became Chief Justice, serving in that role for the next eight years. A meticulous researcher, never reversed, and no rocker of the boat, Gray published only one dissent in seventeen years.

Feeling the need for help with research and similar chores, Gray, on the Massachusetts court, hired a fellow Harvard man to assist him. There were no government funds for such a purpose so Gray reached down into his own pocket. The man to whom he gave the job was a bright young student, Louis D. Brandeis.

Appointed to the U.S. Court by President Chester Arthur, Gray brought the law clerk idea with him. It so impressed the other justices of the Morrison B. Waite Court (1874–1888) that Congress, within four years, was induced to pay for one Law Clerk for each of the nine. Thus began a vital institution that spread to lower courts across the nation.

To get the right kind of Law Clerk Congress judged that $1,600 a year would suffice. By the time of the Burger Court law clerk pay was in the $20,000 range, but the money reward was insignificant compared with the other pluses that went with the assignment. Most clerks stayed only for one year, enjoying the country's best postgraduate education in American judicial practice. For those who wanted it the Court salary could be quadrupled immediately in a major law firm. For others it was often a ticket to a career of eminence in government or even in business.

A requirement for the first law clerks was scholarly ability proved in college, preferably at Harvard, but also social skills since the Clerk often moved in as a member of the Justice's household. With law clerks leaving after a Court apprenticeship of a year or two, and their help as researchers and brief readers recognized as invaluable, Justices felt the need of a recruitment system. By the teens of this century, Oliver Wendell Holmes, who inherited Gray's chair in 1902, and Louis Brandeis, by 1916 himself a Supreme Court Justice, shared a talent scout at Harvard Law School. He was Felix Frankfurter who, in his turn, ascended to the Court (1939–1962).

Frankfurter on the High Bench stayed with the Gray-Holmes-Brandeis Harvard tradition, and his own lively law clerk team became known as Frankfurter's "happy hot dogs."

By 1947 Congress agreed to let each Justice have two law clerks. In 1970 the ceiling was lifted to three. By the time of the Burger Court many Justices had four.

Nepotism, or at least its appearance, went into the hiring of some of the early law clerks. The first John Marshall Harlan used his first allotment of law clerk money to employ his own son, John Maynard Harlan. Perhaps he recognized special Court genes, for his Law Clerk son fathered the second Justice John Marshall Harlan. Another son of the first Justice Harlan, James, was taken on by Chief Justice Melville Fuller as his first Law Clerk.

One more taking part in the same early nepotistic practice was Rufus Day (1903–1922). Two of his sons clerked.

As the Court moved further into the new century, with hundreds of law review editors and others at the top of their law classes competing for the clerkships, the Justices faced an embarrassment of intellectual riches. By the Earl Warren and Warren Burger times Harvard, with Yale close behind, was still harvesting a great share of the coveted clerkships, but other schools and regions were winning a share.

How Hugo Black made his selections was explained in 1972 by Kenneth Bass III. He clerked for the Justice in 1969: "The perfect clerk for Justice Black was an Alabama boy who went to Alabama Law School. If that wasn't possible, then someone from the South who went to a leading law school. He tried to convince his clerks to return to the South and a number of clerks still practice in Alabama." Justice Black also liked to find clerks who could give him a good game of tennis.

Justice Charles Evans Whittaker (1957–1962), a native of Troy, Kansas, looked for Midwesterners. Justice Douglas who summered in the mountains of his childhood state of Washington liked to have clerks from the Northwest or elsewhere in the far West. Tom Clark enjoyed hiring fellow Texans; Byron White, a native of Fort Collins, Colorado, chose several from the mountain states.

By the 1960s, despite competition from hundreds of other law schools, Harvard still held on to more than a third of the appointments, 125 out of 361. Adding in Yale's sixty, the two continued to garner more than half.

A second tier developed by the 1970s: the law schools of Columbia, Chicago and Michigan, followed by Pennsylvania, Stanford, Berkeley and Virginia.

As the 1980s began there was a further development, strong preference went to law graduates in their late twenties who had already learned the clerking task at the side of judges in courts below.

Women and African Americans were latecomers to the law clerk corps.

Justice Douglas was the first to hire a woman. In 1944 with the bulk of the twenty-year-old males fighting the war, Douglas hired Louise Lomen who had edited the law review at Washington State University. It was a beginning, but it was not soon repeated. Twenty-two years went by before Hugo Black employed Margaret Corcoran, the daughter of one of Frankfurter's happy hot dogs, Tommy Corcoran. That broke the log jam. By Burger's time women were numerous among the law clerks.

The first of several African Americans was William A. Coleman Jr., who was taken by Frankfurter in 1948. A fellow hot dog that term was Elliott Richardson. It was part of Court legend that the two would use breaks from the research grind to read poetry together.

Both were examples of how the law clerk stint could launch bright careers. Each of them joined presidential cabinets, Coleman as President Gerald Ford's Secretary of Transportation, and Elliott Richardson in a whole range of assignments including Attorney General, a position he lost in Nixon's unsuccessful last ditch effort to save his presidency, a staff bloodletting known as "the Saturday Night Massacre."

Richardson served successively as Secretary of Defense, Secretary of Health, Education and Welfare, Undersecretary of State and Ambassador to the Court of St. James's in Britain.

No Clerk by Rehnquist's time had made it to the presidency, but two served as Secretary of State; Brandeis's Dean Acheson who told the story of his leadership of foreign affairs in his book *Present at the Creation*, and Douglas's Warren Christopher, Bill Clinton's first Chief for the Department of State.

Acheson in *Recollections of Service with the Federal Supreme Court* wrote of his time with Brandeis. He had the happy experience one day of catching the Justice in some small errors and was rewarded with a terse response: "Your mission is to catch my mistakes. And not make any of your own!"

Four by the mid-1990s had made the round trio from Law Clerk back to Justice of the Court, one of them to Chief Justice. They were: Robert Jackson's William Rehnquist, Chief Justice Vinson's Byron White, Wiley Rutledge's John Paul Stevens and Arthur Goldberg's Stephen Breyer.

Among dozens of other eminent graduates of the corps of clerks were:

Holmes's Attorney General Francis Biddle and Irving Olds, Board Chairman of U.S. Steel

Frankfurter's Philip Graham, Publisher of *The Washington Post*

Stanley Reed's Roderick Hills, Chairman of the Securities and Exchange Commission

Brandeis's David Reisman, author *of The Lonely Crowd: A Study of the Changing American Character*

Hugo Black's Charles Luce, Board Chairman of Consolidated Edison and Charles Reich, author of *The Greening of America*

Chief Justice Vinson's Governor Dan Walker of Illinois, and Newton Minow, Chairman of the Federal Communications Commission

Sherman Minton's Congressman Abner Mikva, and Chief Justice Burger's Kenneth Starr, the Special Prosecutor of Clinton administration scandals.

Dozens became deans and professors of law schools, and judges of courts below.

While much of the law clerk history is writ in letters of gold there have been exceptions. One Clerk was indicted in 1919 for leaking Opinions to speculators, a prosecution that later was dropped. Alger Hiss, a Holmes Clerk, and a major State Department official, was convicted of perjury in one of the country's most sensational Cold War trials.

Many Justices presided over an alumni association of their former clerks with periodic dinner meetings. The dramatic play about Justice Holmes, *The Magnificent Yankee*, included a scene of one such party on the occasion of the jurist's ninetieth birthday in 1931. Mrs. Holmes had invited fifteen of the twenty-five Holmes clerks to a surprise birthday party, hiding them at first in the basement in what was described as the coal bin. The cast of the play visited Warren Burger in the Court Conference Room where he told them that the endless Court work was like the travails of the Volga boatmen.

"Which of you are the law clerks?" he asked. Hands were raised by a few young, evidently free, spirits. A good likeness, the sober-sided Burger assured them.

Justice Louis Brandeis, an Associate Justice from 1916 to 1939, was in effect the first Law Clerk of the Court. The top graduate of the Harvard Law School class of 1877, he did so well as a Law Clerk to the innovative Justice Horace Gray of the Massachusetts Supreme Court, that Gray brought Brandeis with him when Gray was appointed to the U.S. Supreme Court in 1881. Harris and Ewing, Collection of the Supreme Court of the United States.

In Burger's time many additions and reorganizations took place in the Court's team. Although Justice Powell had faced a courteous rebuff when he plumped for a team of Opinion-writing specialists such as authorities on the tax code, the Justice from Richmond did win with some other suggestions such as a massive introduction of computers and a proposal to pool law clerks in the initial hunt through thousands of incoming cases for the relatively few raising federal questions worthy of judgment. The clerks sorted through, identifying thousands as frivolous or as too narrow for a Court verdict, and the Justices, with their final responsibility, took over from there.

There was a recurring myth that the clerks made the decisions and wrote the Opinions, but Justice after Justice and former law clerks as well insisted that it was not so. Dean Acheson, for one, said that he composed footnotes for Brandeis Opinions, but that his input ended there.

When Burger convinced Congress that he had to have an Administrative Assistant, Dr. Mark Cannon of Utah, the two took a Page from the White House Fellow system, creating a corps of judicial fellows, many of them university professors, offering them a look inside the judicial process in exchange for the insights they could bring from the social sciences of their specialty.

The Court had never had a personnel officer; the Chief was expected to oversee all hiring and firing. Starting with a Judicial Fellow, the Court created one.

All employees served at the whim of the Justices, a way to protect judicial freedom. Although there were still no unions, an employee grievance system with arrangements for appeal against arbitrary dismissal was placed in effect.

Everyone may need a Lawyer, even the Supreme Court. Who, for instance, could tell the Court police how far they could go in exercising authority inside the building and outside across the lawns and city sidewalks to the curbs? Only a Lawyer. So one was hired.

What should be done about preserving Court history and artifacts? Justices through the decades had been so busy finding rooms in boardinghouses and putting up with the cramped conditions in the Capitol's borrowed spaces that little thought ever had been given to that. "Art Curator" sounded too fancy for congressional budget makers so a slot was created for a "Property Custodian" instead. With time passing and Congress relaxing, Cathe Hetos and her successor, Gail Galloway, became "curators" in title as well as fact as they set about the work of collecting and protecting the artifacts and records of a two-century history.

If the Court staff inside the dramatic Gilbert-Rockart building had become a self-contained small village with its own constables, its eating places, its exercise areas, its laundry, its barber, its carpenters and its painters, the Chief Justice, among all his tasks, was both mayor and father of the family. At Christmastime in the 1970s when, despite separation of church and state, staffers gathered in the hall outside the Courtroom to sing carols, the choir master was William Rehnquist, soon to be Chief Justice number sixteen.

It was a long way from the six Justices of 1790 and their staff of two, yet the Jay, Marshall, Burger and Rehnquist Courts were one and the same, for there had never been a mass replacement of members, there had never been a break in continuity, departures and arrivals had been one at a time and *stare decisis*, respect for what earlier Justices had decided, was an honored doctrine.

Much had changed. Little had changed.

CHAPTER 19

MADAME JUSTICE

Paramount Pictures had a comical idea, a woman on the Supreme Court!

Screen rights had been purchased from two playwrights who, a few years before, had written of such a situation in their *First Monday in October,* starring Henry Fonda as an otherwise liberal male chauvinist doing battle at the Court with its first woman member, a conservative defender of law and order.

"What would you call a woman Justice?" the Paramount researchers asked. The men from far back in Court history had always been Mr. Justice this and Mr. Chief Justice that, just as the occupant of the White House was Mr. President and the chief of the Congress Mr. Speaker. Would she be Madame Justice? Or Mrs. Justice? Or, if unmarried, Miss Justice? The latter had ludicrous, even appalling overtones. "Miss Justice" sounded like "injustice."

Paramount was advised that if, indeed, a woman were to ascend the High Bench she would be known simply as "Justice." Without comment, on November 14, 1980, Clerk Rodak issued to lawyers and the media one of the periodic Orders Lists, announcing various Court actions, an Orders List like all that had preceded it, but with one difference. Without explanation, the "Mr." was dropped from every mention of a Justice. A Court tradition silently had ended.

There was no vacancy on the Court and no woman Justice in the offing, but the feminist movement was strong. Women had more than half the nation's voting power, and even a man's man like the incumbent Ronald Reagan might want to woo feminine support. If the change came, the Justices were ready.

With fun about the title of a woman Justice no longer available to the script writers, Paramount went ahead with its amusing project nonetheless. There seemed to be no doubt that the little joke would keep its savor for a good while to come regardless of pressures from the National Organization of Women and others. History suggested nothing different.

By the 1870s many thousands of men had been admitted to practice before the Supreme Court bar but not one woman. The same was true of state Supreme Courts. Perhaps it was in part because no woman had thought of applying, but finally, as the eighth decade of the nineteenth century began, one woman did make the request. She was Myra Bradwell, wife of Judge James B. Bradwell of Chicago, who had taught her the law.

Mrs. Bradwell asked the Illinois Supreme Court to admit her to their bar, and the court said no. Undaunted, the Judge's wife appealed to the Court of Chief Justice Salmon Portland Chase (1864–1873), but again the response was negative with Samuel Freeman Miller (1852–1890) writing the Opinion.

What put the icing on the bitter antifeminist cake, however, was the Concurring Opinion of Joseph P. Bradley (1870–1892). He wrote: "The natural and proper timidity and delicacy which belongs to the female sex evidently unfits it for many of the occupations of civil life. ... The paramount destiny and mission of women are to fulfill the noble and benign offices of wife and mother. This is the law of the Creator."

Though Mrs. Bradwell had struck out even at the state court level, another woman lawyer, Mrs. Belva A. Lockwood, took aim at the main target, the bar of the national

Supreme Court. She got the same rebuff, but she accomplished a different result. The House of Representatives was a few steps away. She checked in there, got support, and then tried with a reluctant Senate. Finally, with a vote of thirty-nine to twenty with seventeen absent, the Senate agreed and President Rutherford B. Hayes added his signature, ordering the High Court to open its bar to women. On March 3, 1879, Mrs. Lockwood was sworn in, the first woman after eighty-eight years.

A few others followed: in 1885 Laura DeForest Gordon, in 1890 Kate Kane of Chicago who exulted that she was prouder than "a czar of the Russias or a President of the United States" and in 1892 the same Myra Bradwell.

It was progress of a sort, but not until after the turn of the century did a woman plead a case before the Justices. She was again Belva Lockwood. It was an Indian rights case and she won it. Only in 1929 did the one hundredth woman enter the Court bar. By then, twenty-five thousand men had done so.

Joining the ranks of the five hundred federal judges was harder. One hundred and thirty-nine years after the Congress of 1789 created the federal judiciary, Genevieve Clinein became a Court of Claims Judge, the first woman on the national bench.

On the two levels of general mandate in the federal judiciary below the Supreme Court it was only in 1933, FDR's time in the White House, that a woman, Florence Allen, became a Judge of the Courts of Appeals, and in 1949, the Truman era, that Bernita Shelton Matthews ended the male monopoly on District Court judgeships.

The unwritten rule that "men only need apply" also concerned jobs at the service of the Justices of the Supreme Court. It is Court lore that one of the Justices was determined when the Court's building opened in 1935 that men only would work under the roof. The Clerk dared to defy the Justice, hiring a woman. As the legend has it, the lady employee had to hide when she heard the woman-hater coming.

Until the time of Warren Burger none but boys served the Court as pages. Burger and his Administrative Assistant Mark Cannon let Deborah Gelin sign on as a Page, and she did them proud. She got straight As at the Capitol Hill High School for Pages and went on to Radcliffe.

Manning the elevators in the new Court building was just that, a man's job, until 1970, one year into the Burger period, when Hazel Parks, a ten-year veteran of the seamstress staff, was allowed to take over a lift's controls. She, too, did well. At her retirement in 1978 she spoke of the thrills of her final job; even a President of the United States, Jerry Ford, had ridden with her. Two Justices posed on either side of Ms. Parks for a good-bye photo, Justices Brennan and White.

Times gradually were changing. When Evelyn Limstrong joined the Clerk's team in 1939 she was one of two women working with him. When she retired in 1968 there were ten, two-fifths of the staff.

When Congress in 1972 allowed the Justices to hire a few lawyers to help them with emergency applications and other secondary judicial and legal chores, one of the first three taken on was Mrs. Susan Ackerman Goltz, a merry-eyed recent law graduate who had already served as a Bronx County, New York, Prosecutor investigating organized crime.

Some critics had called the Court "the last plantation," a place where blacks had menial tasks and women were on too high a pedestal to be allowed to step down to earn a living. By the early 1980s, however, with the Burger-Cannon reforms, non-Caucasians had leadership positions and women were everywhere except on the High Bench. That was still out of reach.

When Potter Stewart retired in mid-1981 he implied that no woman Justice could be expected soon. He was asked about it. "There are many qualified women," he said, but "there is nothing more antithetical to a good Judge than to think it has something to do with representative democracy."

In short there should be no category seats for women, blacks, Jews, Catholics or any other groups, just seats for good judges. It was a remark paralleling in part what the departing Thurgood Marshall had said about a black seat, though both Justices conceded that it was not for them to decide. The President and Senate with their political agendas would do that.

Paramount's funny idea of a woman Justice seemed safe for a while so the film company pressed ahead. The first tasks were to choose a Director and an actor to play the crotchety "liberal" male Justice, liberal on all matters except having a woman beside him on the bench. Ronald Reame, an Englishman, who had produced film versions of Charles Dickens's *Oliver Twist* and *Great Expectations* was selected as Director. The aging Henry Fonda had played the grumpy male Justice in the stage production, but he was not available. Reame in "Hopscotch" had directed the sad-faced comic, Walter Mathau, and was enthusiastic about him as a versatile actor who could "play anything." Mathau was tapped for the role.

Good jokes need plausibility so it was important for Paramount to film as much as possible around and in the Court building. There the filmmakers hit a snag. The Court was willing to go along with advice on even the smallest details of life inside the Gilbert-Rockart structure but would not permit its interior to be used as a theatrical prop. It was the grave house of ultimate justice and the Court meant to keep it that way.

It was not a new problem for the Justices. Hollywood has an insatiable fascination with the Court both as a place to visit and as a stage prop. Harpo Marx, the pratfall comic, had been a guest of Felix Frankfurter; Joseph Cotten had called on Potter Stewart; Sidney Poitier had lunched with Thurgood Marshall before portraying him in a TV miniseries *Equal but Separate* and Jerry Lewis and Elizabeth Taylor had been among other visitors.

More important to the Los Angeles filmmakers than satisfying personal curiosity, however, was to be able to use the Court structure to lend verisimilitude to their cinematic fantasies. Many others had preceded Paramount in that quest, generally achieving much less than they wished.

An example in 1972, three years into the Burger Court, was when Columbia Pictures arrived with a rollicking yarn, *The Last Detail*, about three sailors so drunk they confused the Supreme Court with the Washington Monument. Columbia wanted to shoot the scene on the front steps, and a U.S. Senator from California, John V. Tunney, son of a former heavyweight boxing champion, urged the Justices to agree. Permission was refused. In real life such a thing could not happen; the Court police would see to that. So far as the Court was concerned what was impossible in fact was not to be portrayed in fiction.

Otto Preminger, the Vienna-born director, was another who tried. In 1976 he wanted twelve to fifteen days inside the Courtroom, a Justice's chambers and the cafeteria to film Max Lerner's story of the life of Hugo Black. Preminger had met Chief Justice Burger at a stag dinner at the White House and had some reason to hope that would help. It had been raining as the party broke up; Preminger had no transportation. The Chief watched him buttoning up against the chill, recognized his plight and gave him a ride to his destination.

The episode gave the Director an "in," but it was not enough. Burger let him sit in a special box in the Courtroom during a hearing to get the flavor of the proceedings but refused to allow actors to be filmed inside the structure.

Bette Davis, in one of her final roles, playing a grandmother, was allowed to do a scene on the front steps during the 1970s. It was sedate, no inebriated seamen involved.

Faced with the same ground rules, Reame set out to make the best of it. With William O. Douglas chosen as the model for the Mathau character, the script identified the player as a mountain climber just as Douglas had been. Douglas for thirty-five years at the bench had used a tufted leather chair that had been a government hand-me-down since the Civil War. It had gone to the Douglas museum in Yakima, Washington. Paramount had an exact duplicate built for Mathau.

With no filming allowed in the Courtroom, the studio built an expensive copy that was so perfect that only Reporter of Decisions Putzel spotted an error. As one of the four officers designated by Congress, the Reporter has a special seat. Hollywood had omitted it.

Jill Clayburgh was chosen to play the first woman Justice. She and her Director were escorted behind the Courtroom's back curtains to see the route through which the Justices approach the bench, the Chief first in line, then in descending order of seniority the other eight. In the reenactment Mathau as the senior Associate would walk second and Ms. Clayburgh would follow at the end.

Behind the rear curtains, at the spot the newest Justice would pass just before entering the Courtroom, the two visitors noticed a water fountain. "Ah, look at that," the director told Ms. Clayburgh. "You're going by here. You're awestruck. Your mouth is dry. You stop for a sip."

"Like this?" she asked. She bent over the fountain, straightened up and then flicked away a few imaginary drops.

"Exactly," the director approved.

Inside the Courtroom the two stood behind the chair at the extreme left of the Chief Justice, the place for the newest arrival. "Can you swing the chair around with your back to the room?" the director wondered. "I can pan across your troubled expression to the lawyers and people behind you."

Not true to Court life, a staffer interjected. Justices going to the bench do not turn their backs on the observers. The director pondered it.

"I think I'm too young to play a Justice." Ms. Clayburgh murmured. Not really, she was reassured. Two members of the Marshall Court were thirty-three, Joseph Story and William Johnson. The actress brightened.

"Good," she said. "I feel better. I'm thirty-seven."

During the filming, Ms. Clayburgh suffered a miscarriage so the climactic scene, the two protagonists reconciled at the end and mounting the front steps, had to be postponed until a bitter wintry day.

Between takes, the two principals shuffled back and forth from the frozen steps to the warmth of their curbside vans.

There was no change in ground rules, outside shots okay, nothing in the building so it was a surprise to a staffer, checking on progress, to find the director and his cameras inside the bronze doors. One final bit of comic business could finish the picture. Mathau's character, a gentleman, could let Ms. Clayburgh precede him as they neared the top, then push in front of her as they entered, his instincts as senior taking over. Mathau with his familiar sad-clown expression was huddled just inside the freezing entranceway awaiting the order to perform.

"They can't enter the building," the staffer reminded the director.

Reame looked distressed.

"Until now," he said, "you have been very good, but now you are naughty." In his London drawl the word hung in the air like an imprecation.

Paramount had meant to release the picture at leisure but instead, with fifty-one-year-old Sandra Day O'Connor of the middle level State Court of Arizona chosen by President Reagan as the 102nd Justice of Court history and with a unanimous confirmation by the Senate, *First Monday in October* was rushed into movie houses while the jest still had some savor.

Sandra O'Connor, a self-styled cowgirl who had grown up on her family's 155,000-acre Lazy B Ranch in Arizona, was no

Justice Sandra Day O'Connor. As a woman, she was unable to get a job as a lawyer when she, her future husband John O'Connor and future Chief Justice William Rehnquist graduated from Stanford Law School. A self-styled Western cowgirl, Justice O'Connor overcame prejudice to become the first woman Justice of the Supreme Court. Collection of the Supreme Court of the United States.

stranger either to Warren Burger or to his successor, William Rehnquist. When Burger took part in an exchange with English judges, each side visiting the other in alternating years to see how judicial practices had changed in two centuries of separation, Judge O'Connor was the first American woman invited to take part. Burger liked what he saw.

When a group of eighteen German reporters and editors visited the Chief some months after the O'Connor arrival, Burger's praise for the Court's first woman was unstinting. "She has adapted as well as any of the Justices I have seen arrive since I came here," he said. "Often I wish she was all eight of the Associate Justices," he added. "Her ideas are often very close to mine."

As Presidents consider the needs of various minorities, would there be another woman on the premier bench?

"Well, for 191 years there were none," the Chief responded. Yet, he added, "I think another woman is very much a possibility.

"I can't speak of women as a minority," he went on. "In fact they are a very powerful majority. They have always had a great influence over men."

William Rehnquist knew Mrs. O'Connor even better. He also knew how Paramount could have discounted the chance of any woman reaching the High Bench.

He and Sandra O'Connor had been fellow editors of the law review of the Stanford Law School. Rehnquist was graduated first in their class of 102 students and Sandra Day was third. Rehnquist's reward was a Supreme Court clerkship. Sandra Day applied at one Los Angeles and San Francisco law firm after another and was rejected as a Lawyer by all of them. Her gender was wrong. One firm offered to take her as a Secretary.

Back home in Arizona, by then married to law-school comrade John O'Connor, the future Justice went into politics, becoming the first woman to be the Majority Leader of a state Senate. From there she went to the Arizona State Court of Appeals, her final position before joining the High Bench.

As Paramount had considered a woman on the Supreme Court an amusing, however improbable, development so did the news media treat the appointment as a sensation. It was the first time a Justice had been appointed from a state bench since William Brennan had come in 1956 from the New Jersey Supreme Court and Benjamin N. Cardozo (1932–1938) had arrived a half century earlier from the New York Court of Appeals. All newcomers to the High Bench attract heavy press coverage, but Mrs. O'Connor's advent broke records, and set precedents in an institution that lives by precedent.

Justices take two oaths, one in the Courtroom with hundreds in attendance, the oath taken by all federal office holders, pledging to support the Constitution, and a second oath to do justice to all without favor. The latter is taken inside the Justices' Conference Room with none but the other eight members of the Court present. Neither oath taking was photographed.

For the arrival of a woman on the High Bench the rules were changed. President Reagan who had closed the Court's gender gap wanted to see both oaths administered. He also liked the idea of standing in with the members of the new Court as their first group picture was snapped. Hitherto none but the Justices were in such a photo. The Justices agreed and two cameramen, one for the White House, and one for the Court, made a unique pictorial record of a Justice's private oath taking and a President with a Court he had just created.

Hundreds of writers, artists, still photographers and television crews, plus the fifteen-person "deathwatch" news team that follows the President wherever he goes, wanted to cover every moment of the woman Justice's installation.

There are no standees at Court sessions, but that rule was broken to allow dozens of artists and writers to squeeze into the Courtroom's small press area for the public oath taking. Not even for the Nixon hearing had that been permitted.

The Court held firm to the historic ban against cameras in the Courtroom but relaxed its resistance against television coverage of ceremonies inside the walls. With the White House planning to pass the costs to the TV networks, the Waco Ladder and Scaffolding Company was hired to build a two-tier stand inside one of the second floor courtyards for a photo opportunity with the three principals, the President, the Chief Justice and the woman who had done what no one had accomplished before.

TV watchers saw the courtyard meeting as it occurred. The Court wanted no unsightly cables running down the marble corridors, out the windows and across the neatly tended lawns, so NBC, White House "poolers" for the month, came up with a way to solve that problem. Their pool camera on the courtyard stand beamed its pictures to a receiver installed at the edge of the roof overhead. The receiver flashed the pictures to the NBC studios miles distant across Washington. By telephone from

Barrett McGurn (center) presenting Congressman Robert McClory (R-IL), ranking judiciary member of the U.S. House of Representatives, to Justice O'Connor in her chambers shortly after her arrival at the Court. Robert McClory.

there, five other networks got the feed for instant showing across the country and out of it.

A job of the Court police is to receive the daily sacks of incoming mail, exceptional floods of it on the January anniversary of the *Roe v. Wade* abortion decision, but much of it all the time. A lioness's share soon poured in for Mrs. O'Connor.

A ten-year-old girl from Medway, Massachusetts, wrote to say that "I guess you find your job a proud one—I would," adding that she hoped to be the first woman President.

A thirteen-year-old girl from the Poindexter School in Moorpark, California, confided that "I think it is about time to have a woman to do the job. It's almost like our Student Body here at Poindexter," she went on. Girls, she said, had the presidency, the vice presidency, the offices of secretary and of treasurer, and "most of our class representatives—which I am one of." Not missing the point of why people are elected or appointed, the writer added that "I can also say we have accomplished a lot for our school."

Chief Justice Burger, too, received part of the mail about the first woman Justice. A writer who signed her note "Sincerely, twelve-year-old Kelly Webb," took the Chief Justice to task because of something she saw on the 6 o'clock news. The Chief's robe reached to his ankles, Mrs. O'Connor's just to her knees.

"I noticed that Justice O'Connor was wearing a short robe," Kelly told the Chairman of the High Court. "I don't think that is fair. Because she should be just like you or anyone else on the bench. Don't you agree. So if you get a long robe so should she."

By return mail, on Supreme Court stationery, went a reply to Kelly: "Please be assured no unfairness was intended.

"Each Justice picks out their own robe. Justice O'Connor had the short one from her previous role as an Arizona judge. They wear out after a while, especially in the sleeves.

"Each Justice buys his or her own robe and can have any length they want. When this wears out Justice O'Connor will decide on something else."

Every corner of national life seemed to have its own angle.

The Bloom County comic strip described a classroom art project, a "marriage of beauty with intelligence and compassion," Sandra O'Connor's head on the Venus de Milo.

Reader's Digest asked verification of a news item saying that a golfing coach told the Justice "not to hit like a girl," that she had good eye-hand coordination, that she goes around courses in one stroke over par and that she drives the ball 100 to 200 yards. The item was accurate.

Washingtonion Magazine was investigating "breakfasts of celebrities." Mrs. O'Connor's morning food was no secret, grapefruit and coffee and little else.

A letter to the editor of the *Philadelphia Inquirer* objected that the O'Connors had a Japanese car and suggested that high officials should be "more sensitive" to the needs of American labor. Was the writer right? Apart from the interpretation, the facts were correct, the O'Connors had a Honda but also a Ford and a venerable Cadillac.

The question of Mrs. O'Connor's judicial gown attracted not just the attention of young Kelly Webb but also that of an Arizona museum and the women's history section of Washington's Smithsonian Institution. Each of them asked before her induction that they be given the instantly historic robe worn that day. Flags are flown above the Capitol dome for a few instants so that their recipients can say they have had that honor. Could Mrs. O'Connor do something similar, donning two robes in succession, one for each collection?

The answer was a regretful no. Mrs. O'Connor had only one robe and, despite its importance as a national artifact, she still needed to wear it.

An Associate Justiceship is one thing and a Chief Justiceship another. Fourteen years into her term on the High Bench, Mrs. O'Connor had a fifteen-minute taste of the latter.

It was April 3, 1995. By then Mrs. O'Connor was second in seniority among the Associate Justices, outranking six and sitting at the bench at Chief Justice Rehnquist's left.

The Justices had an Orders List to release, and 131 lawyers to admit to the Court bar. Justice David H. Souter had a summary of a Court decision to read. Both the Chief Justice and the senior Associate, John Paul Stevens, were away from Washington, so Sandra Day O'Connor presided in one more historic first.

Down the bench from her sat a second woman, Ruth Bader Ginsburg. Justice Joseph P. Bradley of the 1870s would have been stunned.

❧ CHAPTER 20 ❧

DEPARTURES

It was ninety minutes to midnight at Steve Munger's annual New Year's Eve party for fellow veterans of foreign service. In the kitchen the phone rang.

"Operations Center at the State Department," a voice identified himself. One recent staffer of the Department of State was now employed by the Justices and was the only Court contact the caller had. The message was brief: "Justice Douglas has just had a stroke. In the Bahamas." Steve's kitchen phone instantly was busy with outgoing calls. First was to the police at the Court: "Find the Chief Justice. Have him call here."

By 10:40 P.M. the Chief was on the line: "Suggestion. Get the President's help. Make a local call to the White House. They will patch you through. The President is skiing in Vail, Colorado."

Next, a call to the Douglas family physician, Thomas Connolly, in nearby Arlington, Virginia. "I am distraught," he said. "He is seriously ill now. A lot of decisions must be made. I want him in a big medical center." Douglas, an otherwise fit and scrappy seventy-six-year-old marathon hiker, had a pacemaker in his chest to moderate an irregular heartbeat.

The Chief Justice had an idea. The Blackmuns were also in the Bahamas, in Eleuthera, not far from the Douglases. With them was one of the Blackmuns' many Mayo Clinic friends, coincidentally another Dr. Connolly, a former Dubliner who was now an eminent American cardiologist. Might he help?

Not much, said the first Dr. Connolly. What could be done was being accomplished. What the Justice's own Doctor needed to do was to leave at once for Nassau. By 11:30 P.M., he was aboard a special military Air Mission Jet Star out of Washington's Andrews Air Force base. At 2 A.M., East Coast time, he was in Nassau.

Pulled away from the ski resort festivities, the Chief Executive was immediately cooperative. What was all the more remarkable was that five years earlier, as Republican leader in the House of Representatives, Ford had done his best to drive Douglas from the bench through impeachment, which would have made him the first Justice ever to suffer that fate, but Ford had failed. Now it was up to him to help save his erstwhile target.

He would use the Air Force to rescue the jurist, the President told the Chief Justice. To make sure it would work, no mean feat with New Year's bells ready to peel, he would assign a two-star General to oversee the operation. That many shoulder stars should get it done.

The Air Force needed landing permission. The State Department op center plugged air personnel through to the embassy in Nassau, and that was arranged.

Next was to find an air base with a hospital plane, nurses and doctors. Three came to mind. One in Arizona, two in Florida, Pensacola in the North, Homestead in the South.

Homestead, across the Gulf Stream from the Bahamas, was chosen. Lift off of a C-9 medical plane was at 4:30 A.M. On the ground in Nassau at 5:05, the plane was airborne again seventy-three minutes later, reaching Andrews at 8:40. Forty minutes after that Douglas was admitted to the capital's Walter Reed Army Medical Center.

Justice William Douglas. Collection of the Supreme Court of the United States.

Safe behind protective walls, the Justice and his friends soon began coping with a problem every Justice faces, how long to stay, when to leave.

Douglas was paralyzed on most of his left side, there was a hesitancy of speech and some drifting in and out of consciousness, but the side of the brain controlling thought processes seemed to be undamaged. That offered some hope.

Chief Justice Burger, back from the night's work on the phones, was one of the first Walter Reed visitors. Apart from the longer future, what was to be done about the 140 cases awaiting judgment? In a contentious Conference there was often a four to four split with the ninth vote decisive. Four to four does not create the precedent lower courts need as their guide. To meet their requirements, the Court would have to go through the long and trying decisional process all over again in another term. An effective ninth vote was called for.

Building on the positive, and treating first things first, Burger used a sheet of his Chief Justice stationery to scribble a reassuring note to the suffering Justice:

> Jan. 1, 1975
>
> Dear Bill,
> I need hardly say that we are all overjoyed at your progress. Just "hang in there" and relax and contemplate. *All* opinions are just "mark time" until you are ready. Right now only one thing is important: GET WELL!
> Vera sends her love.
> Warren

No Justice ever addressed the Chief by his first name and his communications routinely were signed "WEB," but in this moment of ultimate human reality, Burger reverted to the familial form.

The "all" regarding "opinions" was underlined. Even if a decision was ready to be announced, pending a Douglas comment, it would wait.

Drawing on his sketching skills, the Chief inked in on the margins of his note a cartoon character in courtroom swallow tails pointing to the word "well" and, in a balloon, saying: "He's a tough coot. They can't keep him down long."

With the future of history's eighty-second Justice and one of the Burger Court's staunchest liberals suspended in the balance, two old friends of Douglas were among others who hurried to the bedside, former Justice and one-time potential Chief Justice Abe Fortas who had been Douglas's young New Deal Assistant at the Securities and Exchange Commission, and former Law Clerk and multiple office holder Clark Clifford. With their help recovery bulletins were drafted insisting that there had been no "mental impairment." Protected was Douglas's choice whether to stay on or withdraw.

A battler who asked for no quarter, a Justice who had survived a horse fall that had crushed his rib cage, Douglas quickly made his decision. He would recover and remain. A valiant effort began.

Within days Librarian Ed Hudon received book demands from his "main client." Douglas's Secretary was summoned from the Court to take dictation. "Passive" therapy began, massages for the left arm and leg. "Active" exercise for the leg came next as Douglas regained some small use of it and as he struggled to rise from the bed and move to a chair for brief periods.

Sacks of mail arrived at the Court and had to be carried to the Justice twice a day, much of it warmly supportive from those who saw him as the champion of free people in a free society, an implacable foe of intrusive "big brother" government, while a portion of it raged against Douglas as a reckless libertarian.

One of the latter stripe came from Clearwater, Florida. The writer gave it as his opinion that "membership of the Supreme Court should stop at 65," adding: "G.M. & Ford say out at 65. One must start getting senile at 65. Some start *earlier*. Some at 45." The latter was a misdirected jab at the Justice. Douglas had joined the Court not just at forty-five but at forty, the youngest in 127 years.

"Die, baby, Die," said an anonymous card from Chicago. With mail like the latter, a screening system was set up before missives reached the sickroom.

The left arm stayed helpless in a sling, but the Justice thrust himself into a vigorous physical recovery program, with mood swings between cantankerous ragging of all around him to cheerful periods during which he entertained doctors and nurses with his limitless store of amusing memories.

By March, without bothering with medical counsel, Douglas checked himself out of Walter Reed and, in a wheelchair, went back to his chambers at the Court. He had a bold announcement for the press: He had challenged the naysaying doctors at Walter Reed to join him on one of his celebrated hikes along the Potomac canal, not the usual twenty-five miles but a more restrained fifteen. Reporters were invited to leave their typewriters to come along, too. There was a weird *Alice in Wonderland* quality to the pronouncement. In the PIO's view, if the country was to believe that the Justice was indeed ready, as he insisted, to shoulder his share of the burden in resolving the nation's most contentious problems, he would, as a minimum, have to face a ten-minute televised press conference attended by a dozen of the Court's main correspondents. The Justice, stretched out under a blanket on a couch in his chambers, agreed.

The press conference was a disaster. The Justice struggled to form words.

What about that hike, he was asked. When will it be?

Douglas peered at the questioner and then said April, "The last weekend in April." Four weeks away. "You're all invited."

"Have you walked much already?"

There had been a few steps. "Not much," the Justice admitted.

How about the ten weeks of hearings you've missed? Will you vote on them? Will you listen to tape recordings of the arguments? Will you step out of some of them? The questions came in a flood. The cases? "I'll sit on all of them."

The hike never happened. Douglas never left his wheelchair.

By June as the term ended, reporters noticed that an unusually large number of cases were put aside to be reargued the following term. Douglas was counted as voting in scores of cases but never casting the controlling fifth vote. Either he was in a majority of at least six, or his dissent was overridden by a majority. His vote did not count.

Carpenter Ed Douglas built a ramp so that Douglas could be wheeled to his chair at the Chief Justice's right, but by November, after hearing one morning case, Douglas told Burger at 11 A.M. that he would skip the second hearing and would call on the Chief in his chambers at the noon break. At 12 he rolled into the Chief's suite to say that his condition only was getting worse, and that his retirement letter would go immediately to the President.

It was near the end of a painful drama, but some months later, with John Paul Stevens already the ninth vote, Douglas said he had an announcement for the media. He would make a partial return to the bench. Routine Court matters would no longer be part of his chores, but he would vote in major cases.

"But, that's impossible," an astonished staffer retorted.

"No, it's not impossible!" was the answer.

There was indeed a sort of precedent. Nine was not, in history, a magic number. The Court appointed by George Washington had only six members. At the time of the Civil War Congress raised the ceiling to ten but, before a tenth could be chosen, changed its mind in 1869, moving back to nine, a number unchanged since.

The PIO did not make the requested announcement and Douglas did not remount the bench.

The Justice lived on another five years. There were numerous honors. For the first time in a history dating back before the American Revolution, Columbia University conferred an honorary doctorate away from its campus. The university President traveled to the Court building, there enrolling the emaciated Justice in the ranks of Columbia's honorees. Columbia had a special reason for the action. After riding the rails East hobo-fashion, the penniless, youthful, West Coaster Douglas had taught law at Columbia as one of his first jobs.

At a ceremony in the Georgetown section of Washington, Douglas looked on as the 180-mile riverside canal, America's early highway to the West, was renamed in his honor in recognition of his successful, many-year struggle to have it preserved as a national monument and recreation area. He could no longer hike it.

Justice Douglas's painful withdrawal from the Court was far from unprecedented as the Justice himself pointed out a year before his devastating stroke. In full vigor at the time, he observed at a celebration of his record as the longest-serving Justice, that at least three of his predecessors had to be told by their colleagues that it was time to go.

The Founding Fathers shared responsibility for the problem. They wanted a government answerable to the people but also with some degree of continuity and stability, not dominated by passing fancies. To get the first, the drafters of the Constitution required Congressmen to go back to the voters every two years, Presidents every four and Senators every six. To achieve some stability federal judges, including the Supreme Court Justices, were given life tenure so long as theirs was "good behavior."

With no money for a building for the Supreme Court, the National Treasury also lacked funds for Supreme Court pensions. Coupled with a natural reluctance to surrender power, and the common difficulty to appraise one's own decline, the result in the years up to the Civil War was that two-thirds of the Justices, even so special a one as John Marshall, stayed on the bench until death. There were clamorous examples of disability and incompetence, including that of the Justice whose longevity record Douglas broke, the full-bearded Stephen J. Field of 1863 to 1897. He was one of the three cited by Douglas as having been asked to leave.

In the early volumes produced by the reporters of decisions there are frequent mentions that "Mr. Justice ____ was absent the whole of this Term, from indisposition." Justices Gabriel Duvall (1811–1835), Henry Baldwin (1830–1844), John McKinley (1838–1852), John McLean (1830–1861), John Catron (1837–1865), James Moore Wayne (1835–1867), Samuel Nelson (1845–1872), Nathan Clifford (1858–1881) and Chief Justices Taney (1836–1864) and Samuel P. Chase (1864–1873) all served long after contemporaries

Justice Oliver Wendell Holmes. Harris and Ewing, Collection of the Supreme Court of the United States.

doubted that their fitness of body and mind justified their continued presence on the bench.

Appalling cases were many, but it was left to Robert Cooper Grier (1846–1870), another of the three cited by Douglas, to provide Congress with a mid-nineteenth century last straw. Justice Grier had to be carried to the bench where he would sometimes fall asleep. It was a problem for him to hold a pencil to write. In 1870, *Hepburn v. Griswold,* known as the Legal Tender case, decided the Justice's fate while yielding a boon to the Court. With Abraham Lincoln short of funds in 1862, Congress had helped him to finance the Union Army by allowing the issuance of currency not backed by gold. Was that constitutional?

In Conference, Justice Grier thought it was, causing a four to four stalemate. Then, flip-flopping, he opined that maybe it was not. He agreed to suggestions from opponents that he change his vote. Instead his ballot was eliminated and, by four to three, the Court, for one of the first times in its history, struck down an Act of Congress.

For the legislators it was too much. Using a carrot rather than a stick, Congress gave all federal judges, including those on the Supreme Court and particularly Justice Grier, not only their first pension but an especially enticing one, full pay for life for anyone over seventy who had put in at least ten years on the federal bench. Justice Grier was seventy-six. He had been on the High Court twenty-six years. He qualified and, urged by his brother Justices, took the pension.

Fewer Justices after that stayed until death, but many delayed long before accepting the generous pension. One of the latter was the third mentioned by Douglas, the redoubtable Oliver Wendell Holmes. Court lore is that he too had to be nudged awake on the bench at ninety-two. Chief Justice Hughes asked him to leave and he did, dying three years later.

Though he mentioned the nonagenarian Holmes as one of those who had to be asked to leave, Douglas made a distinction about Holmes in his eighties. Himself in his seventies, Douglas told the celebrants of his longevity record that "I admired Justice Holmes for many reasons," not least of which were the powerful dissents he wrote in his ninth decade.

One that came to his mind was in *Gitlow v. New York* in 1925. The Court upheld the New York State criminal anarchy statute under which Benjamin Gitlow, a left wing Socialist and publisher of manifestos, had been convicted. Seven Justices voted for New York but Louis Brandeis and Holmes, concerned about press freedom, opted unsuccessfully for Gitlow. Holmes, at the time, was eighty-four.

By 1973, in a growing company of conservatives, Douglas was himself a tireless dissenter, sometimes issuing taciturn two-word Opinions, "I dissent." While evidently looking forward to a Holmesian eighties for himself, swimming against a big government and law-and-order tide, Douglas did concede that an "advisory committee can serve a long range need," trusted friends who knew better than a Justice that it was time for him to go.

Douglas recalled Chief Justice Hughes's retirement. He was seventy-nine years old. It was 1941, two years after Douglas had joined the Court and nine years after Hughes had shouldered the repugnant burden of advising Holmes to step down. Douglas's memory of the withdrawal was vivid:

> He called a special Conference at the end of a Term and announced that he had that day sent notice of his retirement to the President.
> He said he felt quite adequate for the job and knew he could continue for a while.
> But with tears in his eyes, he added, "I have always been fearful of continuing in office under the delusion of adequacy."

For Douglas, Holmes and Hughes must have been the conflicting models of recent Court history, guiding his own approaching choice, whether to linger like Holmes, making use of still productive late years, or whether to depart like Hughes when further contributions still seemed possible.

Justice Douglas's brothers on the bench watched his final year with dismay, pondering how to avoid a similar grim termination for themselves or for colleagues. Justices who retire may sit on Appeals Courts below for as much time as they wish, but when one assignment came up for former Justice Tom Clark, Chief Justice Burger, his close friend, talked it over with him. Clark was still eager to serve, but he was aged and ailing, near death.

"I told him I would not assign him," Burger mentioned after Clark's death at seventy-eight in 1977. The former Justice took the refusal well. "I think he didn't want to be like Douglas, and I can understand that," Burger remembered.

Four years after Douglas's departure, Potter Stewart, Douglas's junior by seventeen years, received a letter from Donna Gallus, a junior in the St. Cloud, Minnesota, Technical High School. Writing in a careful, clear script, but misspelling his name as "Steward," Ms. Gallus said that she had learned in the previous several days in her American Scene class that Stewart was eligible to retire. The current pension rules allowed retirement at sixty-five for those who had put in fifteen years of federal judicial service; Stewart by then had been on the national bench twenty-seven years, all but four of it on the Supreme Court.

"I am not saying that you need to retire," Donna noted with an effort at tact, but "what makes you continue to be on the Court instead of retiring is my main question."

Ten days later Stewart replied: "Thank you for your letter. I did not become eligible to retire until last month. Under these circumstances, it has not occurred to me, at least so far, that I have remained a member of the Supreme Court an unduly long time ... ."

Up to then he had overstayed his eligibility to withdraw with pay only by thirty-seven days. Donna's letter set him thinking, however, the Justice said. Within a year he did leave, only one of nine in the twentieth century to

Justice Thurgood Marshall. Hessler Studios, Collection of the Supreme Court of the United States.

step down before the age of sixty-seven. Douglas's fate would not be his.

At his retirement press conference, Stewart said with a smile that although he felt in good health, he had chosen to leave because he had been the country's youngest federal judge at thirty-nine and had decided not to stay until he was the oldest.

For some Justices of recent years the question was what degree of ill health could be endured before stepping aside. Burger spoke of it one day, mentioning practices in the Courtroom and Conference: "Byron White and I have a common flaw, among others, we both have bad backs. He and Bill Rehnquist have both had back surgery. Mine is inoperable. "Doctors tell us to stand up every half hour but hourly intervals is about all we can do. Harry Blackmun also stands to stretch. Rehnquist walks up and down behind the curtain. Potter Stewart goes out for a smoke. I could go out and walk a bit but I must see what is going on."

Like Stewart, Thurgood Marshall was a heavy smoker. Emphysema made breathing difficult. Overweight at seventy-one he fell down the steps of the Capitol, fracturing his right wrist and left elbow, gashing his forehead, but he carried on. Finally, at eighty-three, in 1991, he withdrew.

"Why?" he was asked.

"I'm coming apart," he answered.

Two years later, Marshall died. Like few other Justices before him he lay in state in the great hall of the Court building as thousands of mourners, many of them African Americans, passed by.

Chief Justice Burger had given it as his opinion on one occasion that judges of the District Court bottom tier of the federal judiciary should be removed from the bench at seventy, and judges at the appellate level at seventy-five. A difficult to arrange constitutional amendment might be needed for that, but from his point of view, it would be worth it. Applied to the Supreme Court it would have averted many problems.

Like many advocates of early retirement, Burger was well under the proposed cutoff ages when he made his suggestion. Asked about the limits as he reached them, he pointed out that they had never been enacted and thus were dead letters. The question of a proper retirement time, however, often was on his mind, partly because it was a chronic topic of media speculation, especially at the time of recurring illnesses.

When a Justice, particularly a Chief Justice, catches cold, the course of national policy eventually may be changed. In Burger's case there were many physical problems. In a talk with reporters in March 1977 he mentioned that he suffered poliomyelitis when he was ten, an ailment undetected at the time, causing a curvature of the lower spine. To cope with the defect he wore a built-up right shoe.

Struck down by a hit-and-run driver while bicycling for exercise near home at night in 1973, he suffered two cracked ribs, a slight displacement of the nose, a dislocation of the left shoulder, a broken right ring finger, a gash over the left eye requiring stitches and a near skull fracture. Several years were needed to recover from the bike accident.

A year after the accident, in fall 1974 as the Justices debated the fate of one thousand cases, the longest such list in Court history up to that time, the athletic White could see Burger fading. The Conference still had a half hour to go, but were he to keep at it, White felt the Chief would "not last the day." White urged the Chief to skip the rest of the session and Burger did.

Toes had been fractured in the hit-and-run accident and had healed badly. Surgery was needed at the first convenient moment, but it was another three years in a program of incessant activity before that window of available time was found. An occasional "spot of viral pneumonia" added to the Chief's difficulties.

In April 1977 Burger caught himself "snapping the head off everyone I encountered; my blood pressure is usually 130, it shot up ninety points." He was placed on antibiotics. "They may not heal," he concluded wryly as he accepted the medication. "But they have one effect. They are depressants."

On occasion, like Douglas, Burger would stretch out on a couch in his chambers, struggling to restore his strength. Even opening a bottle of the prescribed medication (press down and twist) seemed too much. A staffer would help.

Justices understand that their health is a matter of public concern because of the potential impact on the course of the law, but they also seek a measure of the privacy other mortals enjoy. Burger wavered between the two reactions. Home with a cold in 1978, he received a relayed request from reporters for a progress report on his recovery. "Tell them I'll live," was the answer.

Retirement kept coming back as a question to answer, either to deny that it was imminent, or to agree that there was some point ahead when it would be appropriate. The end of the Douglas career stayed fresh in Court minds. When Leo Jackson, an African-American Filing Clerk, retired in 1978 after forty-four years of service, Burger presided over the farewell and spoke of retirement. Leo had joined the staff when Hughes was Chief Justice and the others on the bench were Louis Brandeis, Benjamin Cardozo, James Clark McReynolds, Willis Van Devanter, Owen J. Roberts, Pierce Butler, George Sutherland and Harlan Fiske Stone, the various appointees of Herbert Hoover, Calvin Coolidge, Warren Harding, Woodrow Wilson and William Howard Taft. Leo had worked for one-third of the Justices of history.

The Rehnquist Court of today. Left to right, seated: *Justices Scalia, Stevens, Rehnquist, O'Connor and Kennedy.* Left to right, standing: *Justices Ginsburg, Souter, Thomas and Breyer.* Collection of the Supreme Court of the United States.

Not even John Marshall who was Chief Justice thirty-four years or Justice Douglas "served so long," Burger said, adding: "One thing I promise: I'll not stay that long!" By that time Burger had completed twenty-two years on the federal bench, nine of it as Chief Justice, and was seventy-one, eligible for retirement several times over. To a group of reporters at about the same time, Burger insisted he had no thought of leaving. "I don't even have any grandchildren, he said. His daughter, Margaret Elizabeth, a foreign language translator, was unmarried, and there was one son, Wade Allan, a photographer.

To another news group in the same period Burger put it this way: "Retirement? I have no such plans. The two Chief Justices who did not die in office in recent times were Earl Warren who retired at 79 and Charles Evans Hughes who retired at 81. I think 80 is a nice age. Maybe this side of it, 79 like Earl Warren." Burger's thought was clear but his figures were slightly off. Hughes left at 79 and Warren at 78.

Speculative stories about his impending departure kept popping up in the media to Burger's irritation. "These news stories," he protested to a group of journalists, "they are like crows on a telephone line. One goes off and they all follow."

Even so, Burger himself continued to reflect upon the question. An assistant to Administrative Assistant Mark Cannon researched the past: Two-thirds of the Chief Justices stayed on the bench until death, John Marshall the first, and then Roger B. Taney of the dread *Dred Scott* decision, passing away at 87, Salmon P. Chase at 65, Morrison R. Waite at 71, Melville W. Fuller of the Conference handshake tradition at 77, Edward D. White at 75, Harlan Fiske Stone in 1946 at 73 and Fred Vinson in 1953 at 63. The average age at which Chief Justices left office was 70, a figure brought down by the first Chief, John Jay, who resigned at 49, doubting that the position ever would amount to much. From the time of the strong John Marshall up to Burger's arrival the average withdrawal age was 74.

Average length of service was twelve years. From the Marshall era on it was fourteen and one-half years.

Burger took retirement in 1986 at age seventy-nine, a year short of the eighty he had cited a decade earlier as a "nice" time for withdrawal. Burger had served as Chief Justice eighteen years, half again as long as the average, and longer than all but three others, John Marshall, Roger Taney and Melville Fuller, all three of whom died in office. Still vigorous when he stepped down, he went on for another several years as Director of a national celebration of the two hundredth anniversary of the revered Constitution.

Burger had exercised his right to remain on the High Bench nine years longer than the cutoff age of seventy he had once proposed for District Court judges, and four years beyond the seventy-five he had recommended for the federal appellate level, but he had withdrawn before the terminal infirmities that had blighted Douglas's final years and those of two-thirds of his Chief Justice predecessors. He died in 1995 at eighty-eight, like Marshall, lying in state at the Court building.

Unlike two-fifths of the Associate Justices who preceded them in Court history, none of the Burger Court members remained until death. Justice Powell, the Court Moderator, retired in 1987 at age 79; Justice Brennan, after suffering a stroke, left in 1990, at 84; the athletic Byron White retired in 1993 at 76 and Harry Blackmun, who had asked a committee to watch him for any signs of senility, departed in 1994 at 85.

Left in place in the last decade of the twentieth century was the conservative Court Warren Burger had struggled, often with limited success, to create, the Court of William Rehnquist, Antonin Scalia, Clarence Thomas, Sandra Day O'Connor, Anthony Kennedy, Stephen Breyer, David Souter, Ruth Bader Ginsburg and John Paul Stevens.

CHAPTER 21

WHEN IT'S WEDNESDAY

"Tell me when it's Wednesday," Chief Justice Burger instructed his Secretary.

Rushing along on what seemed to him like a treadmill, engrossed in legal and judicial reforms, overseeing the staff of three hundred Court employees, offering leadership to the thousands of federal and state judges and the hundreds of thousands of American lawyers, and doing all that while screening thousands of incoming cases and taking the lead in judging 150 of them each year, Burger left the need for a reminder when his strenuous Wednesdays arrived.

Twice a month on Wednesdays during the nine-month annual term, Burger had to preside over the hearing of four cases between 10 A.M. and 3 P.M., then go to the adjacent Conference Room to choose up sides on the four cases argued on the previous Monday. All days were demanding, but Wednesdays called for a Secretary's special help.

The Chief's perspective on the Court and its work was one of the many different ways Justices, the media and the public viewed the pinnacle of American justice. How the public saw the mysterious, powerful Court was reflected in the sacks of mail arriving each day at number one First Street.

Much of the mail was from various of the nation's one million convicts. For many of them the Court was the last thin hope that their lives might be spared or their freedom regained.

A large share of the prisoner mail came in the form of IFP petitions, requests *in forma pauperis*, free-of-charge appeals as indigents, often scribbled on a sheet or two, asking for a reversal of sentences.

Other convict communications, on the other hand, reflected the belief that the Court was a kindly friend, wise in the ways of the law, which could help untangle them from the meshes of lower level justice.

Prisoner 860557 in Lowell, Florida, for example, advised the Justices that "I am becoming a nervous wreck" trying to find some judicial precedent requiring his release.

A convict in Pittsburgh asked for books on jailbreaks, including the punishment of those recaptured.

A man "locked down in administrative segregation" on Terminal Island, California, filled the Justices in on legal arguments he was concocting in his own behalf and asked for a candid appraisal of whether he was "barking up the wrong tree."

An inmate of the Kansas State Prison provided a pen and ink self-portrait, showing himself behind bars as a wide-eyed, pensive thirty year old. He had one question: What "incentive good time" off is there for someone condemned to life imprisonment?

For most of the writers the answers were bleak. The Supreme Court does not provide legal counsel. It merely decides 50 to 150 specific cases each year, creating precedents applicable in similar disputes. Its role is limited.

Children, autograph collectors and even compilers of recipes looked to the Court from their own points of view. One collector of signatures in Metairie, Louisiana, sent word that his specialty was Presidents and Supreme Court Justices. So far he had

Presidents Nixon, Ford, Carter and Reagan and a dozen and a half Justices including Burger, Warren, Frankfurter, Harlan, Black, Douglas, Stewart, Brennan, White, Powell, Blackmun, O'Connor and Thurgood Marshall. His problem was that Marshall's signature looked machine-made. He wanted one from the Justice's own hand. His request was sent on to the Justice's chambers for such handling as they deemed proper.

The Court with the public cafeteria that feeds both tourists and Justices is not a place of gourmet dining, but recipe collectors tried it just the same. A writer from Browning, Illinois, wanted something to use in a book on "favorite dishes from famous homes," while Mike Philbin in Delta Junction, Alaska, hoped for something culinary from the Chief Justice that he could use in "a Mother's Day present."

Mike added: "It's kind of fun writing to a person I don't know. Thank you." Burger did enjoy using spare moments at home cooking up a batch of preserves, but a staffer answered Mike for him, begging off on recipes, but enclosing a booklet on the Court that "I hope you and your mother will like."

Mike's letter was one of many from children. For the greater share of them the Court seemed to be a way to get extra credit in school, but some appeared thrilled to be able to make contact with a high place in national life. Others saw their letters as a way to exchange ideas about life plans.

An example of the school-focused mail was a note from a fourteen year old who said that the Court could "help me get an A" if it would send biographical material on "my ideal Supreme Court": Chief Justices Taft, Hughes, Vinson and Warren, and Justices Brandeis, Frankfurter, Black, Fortas and Douglas.

More career-centered was a letter from a thirteen year old telling a Justice that since he was "very, very successful at [his] profession," the writer would value any tips on how to become "a very well established lawyer." His earlier ambition, he went on, had been to become a major league baseball player, an idea that was abandoned when his mother said, "You should become a lawyer, you're so technical."

Some children sent letters commending the Justices, some of them part of a class exercise, some hoping to expand a photo collection:

"You are doing a good job. I am seven."

"I believe you are a very loyal, honest and knowledgeable person. May I ask to have a signed picture."

"You and your other Justices are very good about keeping order in our government."

"I'm twelve and I can't wait to tell my friends I wrote to you."

"I plan to be one of the eight [sic] lawyers in the Supreme Court. I'm in the fifth grade."

For some adults there was humor in an institution that wielded such power.

When the owner of a prize Arabian stallion "Chief Justice" handed out buttons honoring his horse at a show in Albuquerque, a Washington, D.C., lawyer snagged one for Burger "to wear at home." Sober-sided staffers confiscated the gift.

A Philadelphia lawyer in the same spirit of fun demanded that Chief Justice Burger make a public apology to the shade of William Shakespeare for suggesting that the playwright said that the first thing one should do is to kill all the lawyers. Not so, said the Philadelphian. Not the bard of Stratford on Avon but one of his characters, the scoundrel Cade in Henry VI favored such slaughter. In Cade's mouth, the words were Shakespeare's reverse tribute to lawyers as the defenders of society. Burger let it go.

Some in the public perceived Court problems where there were none. An artist in Minnesota doing a canvas on fifty great sons and daughters of her state wanted to know whether she could include Burger and Blackmun along with Hubert Humphrey and Mayo Clinic physicians. She was assured that there was no copyright on the Justices' images.

Even advertisers saw the Court as grist for their mill. When former Justice Arthur Goldberg bought an apartment in a Washington condominium, the managers ran an ad illustrated by the Court facade, saying in large type that "a former Supreme Court Justice sits here," and in small print, the prices of units still available. Word passed quietly that there should be no further such ads.

Phone calls to (202) 479-3000, the Court's publicly listed and endlessly busy switchboard, served also to reflect the many ways in which the Court appeared to people. Many had personal problems. "I want some support," said an anguished woman phoning from Cleveland. "It's an emergency, snow removal." Name-dropping that her husband had been an acquaintance of Justice Harold Burton (1945–1958), the woman complained that although generous government funds were provided for nutrition, recreation and transportation, "none of that will do me any good if I drop dead shoveling the driveway." She wanted civic funds to help with the next storm, which was already on the way. Sorry, the Court could not help.

In Tucson an apple grower wanted the Court to get some part of the government to buy and operate his orchard.

In Greenville, Texas, the wife of what she described as a mentally ill veteran, asked for assistance in divorcing him. Conspiratorially, she confided, "He will do what people tell him to do." A word from the Supreme Court might do the trick. To her disappointment there was no such word.

Some of the throngs who checked in wanted merely to share a thought. A woman writing from Charlotte, North Carolina, was happy that the male monopoly on the High Bench had been broken and added that "I am looking forward to the day when one of the girls is Chief." It was not, she was quick to add, that she wished in general for "women to take over," but only that "in all that is equally given we should be equal by law!"

While many puzzled over the Court's role in American life, polls showed that there were few who doubted the Court's significance. Notable were the results of a 1977 *U.S. News & World Report* poll of twelve hundred "key decision makers in politics, business and the professions." They felt that Chief Justice Burger was the country's third most influential person, surpassed only by the President and the Chairman of the money-controlling Federal Reserve Board. Among institutions of influence the Court was rated fourth after the White House, television and labor unions with big business fifth, civil rights groups twenty-third and organized religion twenty-sixth.

Of the various publics pondering, the Court, the news media and television were among those with the most immediate concern.

For reporters the institution was seen as a tough and tantalizing assignment. Lots of news was under the roof during the half year or so between the time the Conference made its initial decision and the moment of the Courtroom announcement, but the Justices and Clerks on their floor did their best, usually successfully, to protect their secrets. The beat was like no other in government, no press conferences at which to study the personalities and philosophies of the Justices, no opportunity to sit in on the fascinating Conference debates, no chance to monitor Opinions as they went through a dozen rewritings, no advance copies of decisions to help prepare for the instant flashes editors expected, and no authoritative spokesperson to explain the meaning of carefully concocted five-to-four decisions.

If that is a goldfish bowl, Aaron Epstein of the Knight-Ridder Newspapers protested, it is made of opaque glass!

Reporters did have a way of getting at Court truth but it was a time-draining, difficult one. They received copies of each of the thousands of briefs at the same moment the legal presentations reached the chambers. Studying them, albeit without a team of law clerks to help, the reporter had the same opportunity as the Justices to learn the facts of each case, both the many turned away as well as the several score accepted for adjudication. At the moment of decision, the journalist had what assistance he could draw from the summaries drafted by the Reporter of Decisions and from the dissents. As Justices Stewart and Powell conceded, the job of the news men and women was no easy one.

For television, rated in the 1977 poll as having a greater impact on American life than the Justices themselves, the Court represented a frustration. Starting with Earl Warren in the 1960s the Justices turned down repeated appeals of the TV to cover Court sessions. Arguments of many kinds were presented:

- The Court was doing public business and the people had a right to observe it, not just the few thousand tourists who get into the hearings each year but the tens of millions who watch on TV.
- The Court allows the print media to cover; competitive fairness should permit radio microphones and TV cameras to do the same.
- Court hearings always, in the American tradition, have been places of instruction and also of entertainment. A hidden, single, silent and virtually invisible camera would suffice to provide pool coverage for all TV.

To each appeal, Chief Justices Earl Warren, Warren Burger and William Rehnquist said no. Few reasons were given, but Burger on one occasion said that there is "ham in all of us," Justices included, and that he had no intention of tempting Justices to play to the camera audience rather than focus on the vital task at hand. "Sleazy commercial TV" with its sex and violence could "seek respectability" elsewhere. "Junk" was one Justice's word for TV newscasts and ten-second news bites.

By contrast with how all the other publics saw the Court, the prisoners seeking escape, the people with problems hoping for a salvific bolt from the blue, the partisans demanding approval and journalists seeking a story, there was the way the Justices saw themselves and their role.

One Chief Justice, at a dinner party with an author who was preparing a book on the Court, listened as another at the table asked for the writer's conclusions about the institution. "Nine human beings with very great ..." he hesitated, "responsibilities."

"Oh," the Chief laughed, "I thought you were going to say 'egos.' "

There was no doubt that there was self-importance on a Court where any member had a decisive fifth vote on evenly balanced issues, a Court that had seen the likes of the preachy, professorial Frankfurter and the ill-tempered McReynolds, but it was also true that the members of the Court were aware of their own sharp limits, both personally and in terms of what they were free to do.

Their job was to apply the particular facts of a specific case to the provisions of state and federal laws and to the Constitution as they understood that often terse and cryptic document. In doing that the Justices worked within the often tight limits of what judges had decided in similar cases before them. John Paul Stevens, the 101st member of the Supreme Court, explained it in a lecture at New York University on October 27, 1982: "The Court disposes of literally thousands of cases each year. Over and over again the Court's action involves nothing more than the application of old precedent to a new controversy." In the closed Conference, Stevens added, "The decisional process invariably involves a study and analysis of relevant precedents. The framework for most Court decisions is created by previously decided cases." The ninety-nine Justices who preceded the members of the Rehnquist Court of the 1990s were, in one sense, still sitting around the Conference table. Their words were in the half a thousand volumes of the *United States Reports* on shelves along the Conference walls.

Even more, unlike the White House, the Court never had experienced a sharp break with the past. Justices would retire or die and others would replace them, but the other eight would still be there. There had never been a time in more than two centuries when at least one of the following nine was not present to explain first hand how previous decisions were reached:

William Cushing (1789–1810),
John Marshall (1801–1835),
James Moore Wayne (1835–1867),
Stephen Field (1867–1897),
Edward White (1894–1921),
James McReynolds (1914–1941),
Hugo Black (1937–1971),
Warren Burger (1969–1986)
and John Paul Stevens (1975).

Burger talked of how much his Court was helped by the recollections of Black and Douglas, going back almost to the first third of the century.

Strengthening the sense that the Court was uniquely an element of continuity and stability in a changing nation was the fact that each Justice of the 1990s traced his or her seat to jurists of the past: Chief Justice Rehnquist to Hughes, Taft, John Marshall and John Jay of 1789; Stephen Breyer to Frankfurter, Cardozo, Holmes, the Horace Gray of the law clerk tradition and the eighteenth-century William Cushing; David Souter to George Washington's nephew, Bushrod Washington and to James Wilson of the first Court; John Paul Stevens to Brandeis and John Rutledge of the original Court; Anthony Kennedy to Powell, Black and John Blair of the initial Court; Ruth Bader Ginsburg to Byron White and Thomas Todd's expansion seat of 1807; Sandra Day O'Connor to Potter Stewart, the first John Marshall Harlan and the new John McKinley seat of 1837; Clarence Thomas to John Catron's 1837 chair and Antonin Scalia to the second John Marshall Harlan and the Stephen Field seat of 1863.

Stare decisis put barriers in the path of pro-lifers seeking to overturn Harry Blackmun's abortion decision. It dimmed hope of police officers that they be relieved of the burden of the Miranda warning while apprehending suspects. It hampered opponents of the death penalty. Yet each Court generation defended the inhibiting doctrine as generally wise.

"Stand by the precedents and do not disturb the calm," was the way Justice Stanley Reed (1938–1957) expressed it in the year in which he joined the Court.

"*Stare decisis* provides some moorings so that men may trade and arrange their affairs with confidence," Douglas agreed a decade later.

"*Stare decisis* serves to take the capricious element out of law and to give stability to society. It is a strong tie which the future has to the past."

"A rule that orders judges to decide like cases in the same way increases the likelihood that judges will in fact administer justice impartially and that they will be perceived to be doing so," was the way Justice Arthur Goldberg put it in 1971.

Even in dissents Justices held aloft the *stare decisis* flag. When the Court flip-flopped on all-white primaries in one-party states such as Texas, permitting it in *Grovey v. Townsend* in 1935 but banning it nine years later in *Smith v. Allbright,* Owen Roberts protested: "It tends to bring adjudications of this tribunal into the same class as a restricted railroad ticket, good for this day and train only."

The Court's genius and the hope of those who campaigned for the reversal of such decisions as *Dred Scott* and the "separate but equal" *Plessy v. Ferguson* racial segregation verdict of 1896, was in the fact that the Justices managed to have it both ways, occasionally though infrequently turning backs on what had been done before.

In one sample twenty-year period, the last decade of Earl Warren and the first of Burger, the Court averaged two or three reversals a year, twenty-three under Warren and twenty-four under Burger. They were few overall, but they left loopholes for a change of minds.

The appropriateness of such periodic reconsiderations was defended by Brandeis in his dissent in 1924 in *Washington v. Dawson & Co.,* when the Court persisted on vetoing a maritime act of Congress: "*Stare decisis* is ordinarily a wise rule of action but it is not a universal, inexorable command."

Stevens in his New York University address a half century later was of like mind: "The doctrine of *stare decisis* creates a presumption that generally should be followed [but] as the nation itself grows older, surviving and adjusting itself to changes in the economy and changes in the temper of its people, it is inevitable that judge-made rules that were fashioned in a different period of our dynamic history, will be subjected to increasingly frequent reexamination."

Apart from *stare decisis* setting boundaries, Justices could not ignore their own personal limitations. Burger explained how he voted on the death penalty and so many other closely argued and difficult questions: "I decide, and at night I sleep." No sense tossing and turning.

In regard to legal executions, Burger offered an insight into how he decided when he spoke to reporters in Stockholm in 1976: "I may feel that there should be an amendment banning capital punishment, but that is not the issue. I read the Constitution and found four or five places where it implied clearly to me that the states have the right to decide to have capital punishment if they wish. That settled it for me."

Constantly through the decades Justices have made the point that their decisions are "infallible" binding precedents only because there is no way short of constitutional amendments or new laws to second guess them.

Justice Brennan enjoyed the gloss Cardozo put on that. Instead of fretting over his own inadequacy, he used human fallibility to ease his mind while challenging other authorities. Said Cardozo: "The persuasion that one's own infallibility is a myth leads by easy stages, and with somewhat greater satisfaction, to a refusal to ascribe infallibility to others."

"We are nine humans." Burger put it on one occasion. "We come with preconceptions. Some of them are subconscious. Inevitably they show up."

"These nine guys," Chief Judge Edward Devitt of the federal District Court of

Minnesota, a lifelong friend of Burger, expressed it in 1979, "are a bunch of human beings, with the same weaknesses and prejudices of anyone else."

Douglas made a similar point in a discussion of his 1939 arrival at the Court. He said he was at first "shattered" by what Chief Justice Hughes confided to him: "At the constitutional level where we work, 90 percent of any decision is emotional. The rational part of us supplies the reasons for supporting our predilections." Hughes was right, Douglas concluded.

With all the historic and human limitations guiding and binding them, the nine Justices faced the avalanche of incoming cases, one thousand a year in the time of Chief Justice Vinson (1946–1953), double that in the Earl Warren years, doubled again in Burger's time, and raised once more under Rehnquist.

In mid–Burger period, in 1972, Powell anguished that if he gave even so much as a quarter of an hour to each new case it would take him half a normal work week. Fortunately for the Justices, though not for the hope-against-hope litigants, a vast share of the cases could be combed out quickly as frivolous, needing no further attention.

One help for the hard-pressed Court, proposed in effect by Franklin D. Roosevelt in his New Deal Court-packing effort, would be to expand membership to fifteen, bringing more shoulders to the judicial wheel. For Burger such a solution would be calamitous. The Justices do not break down into committees, some handling one case, others another. Each Justice handles every case. The already difficult task to get five to agree would be magnified in a quest for eight.

Never resolved has been the question of whether there should be a mandatory retirement age for Justices. The presence of seniors in the Conference provided the advantage of corporate memory but also the drawback of their diminishing powers. Many, though not all, accepted the generous retirement-inducing pension. One who did, at age seventy-two, was Stanley Reed, a former leading member of FDR's New Deal governing team. Like Tom Clark and some others, he filled in for a while after his High Court years as a volunteer Judge on United States Courts of Appeals. Twenty years after stepping down from the High Bench, in his nineties, still receiving the same salary as the active nine, Reed chuckled one day in Johnnie Shaw's ground floor barber shop that "this is the best job in the world."

In 1937 before Chief Justice Hughes defeated FDR's plan to pack the Court with six of his appointees, both Democrats and Republicans agreed in resolutions in Congress that an amendment was needed changing the constitutional life term granted to federal judges and Supreme Court Justices. One resolution called for a cutoff age of eighty, six said seventy-five, one proposed seventy-two and two opted for seventy. Nothing came of the resolutions, but the issue will remain a live one.

In the case of the Burger Court, Stewart withdrew at 66, Clark at 67, Harlan at 72, White at 76, Burger and Powell at 79, Marshall at 83, Hugo Black at 85 and Blackmun also at 85. The Court was not what some prisoners, help seekers, children and unquestioning admirers thought it, nor was it the dangerously secretive, offensive institution some cartoonists, columnists and muckrakers made it out to be.

Burger claimed that attacks on the Court did not upset him. After all half the litigants inevitably lose and are bound to object.

Probably closer to the real reaction of the sometimes vilified Justices, however, was a remark of Oliver Wendell Holmes that Brennan cited: "I get letters, not always anonymous, intimating that we are corrupt.

Well, gentlemen, I admit that it makes my heart ache. It is very painful when one spends all the energies of one's soul trying to do good work with no thought but that of solving a problem according to the rules by which one is bound, to know that many see sinister motives and would be glad of evidence that one was consciously bad.

But we must take such things philosophically and try to see what we can learn from hatred and distrust and whether behind them there may not be some germ of inarticulate truth.

CHAPTER 22

EPILOGUE: ONION LAYERS

There are just so many layers in an onion, Chief Justice Burger, the amateur chef, observed one day. Peel off one and another appears, but the pesky bulb is diminished. After a while there is no onion.

What is true of onions applies equally to constitutional law, the Chief suggested. When the great issues of a generation are tackled successively by such activist Courts as his and that of Earl Warren, there may be some quiet in the time of the successor group and, as one member of the Court of William H. Rehnquist put it in the mid-1990s: "We are getting far fewer constitutional issues. The courts below know where we stand so they decide cases accordingly and they never reach us."

The liberal Warren Court had struck down racial barriers in schoolrooms and voting places, had erected them against misuse of police powers and had bolstered press freedoms by limiting the range of libel suits.

The gradually more conservative Burger Court had begun by allowing a great expansion of abortion, had outlawed and then reinstated the death penalty, and then had set limits to the expansion of the rights of the press and of minorities.

New issues such as assisted suicide were perceived on the horizon, but during the first Rehnquist decade few were yet to arrive. In an often stormy Court there was a relative lull reflected in the makeup of the Court and in its press relations.

On the bench, thanks to a generation of twice as much Republican as Democratic control of the White House, there was a Rehnquist Court far more in the image of Burger than of Warren. Gone was the hard liberal left of Brennan and Thurgood Marshall. Where Burger often struggled almost alone on the conservative right, there was now a commanding traditionalist trio of Chief Justice Rehnquist, Antonin Scalia and the man whom Thurgood Marshall surely never wanted as his successor, the former Catholic seminarian Clarence Thomas.

In the center, frequently ready to side with the conservatives, were the first woman Justice, Sandra O'Connor, and another of the Court's Catholic members, Anthony Kennedy.

What passed for a liberal left was moderate, the veteran Jerry Ford nominee, John Paul Stevens, Bush's David Souter and the two Clinton choices: Ruth Bader Ginsburg and Stephen Breyer.

With a Court so unexciting from a news point of view, there was a changed press corps and different Court procedures. The regular press component of just under thirty newsmen and newswomen were still kept at arm's length by the Justices but, every second year, the amiable but cautious Rehnquist would lunch with the regulars. The talk was all off the record, not for direct citation or immediate use, and there was no discussion of litigated issues, just a repeat of what Burger had called a discussion of wages, hours and working conditions.

Gone from the press corps were such pillars of earlier Court coverage as *Time* and *Newsweek*. Networks had bigger newsfish to fry so CBS, for one, on decision days, often merely sent an intern or a junior producer to pick up whatever PIO Toni House had from the bench. New to the press room as regulars were reporters of the expanding legal and business press, one or two of them even rivaling the all-encompassing Associated Press in the volume of output.

Press snooping was off and limits on the media were lightened. Regulars on the beat were allowed access to the press area and its stacks of legal briefs twenty-four hours a day, seven days a week, but were denied access to the vulnerable library during off hours. By the mid-1990s it was a decade since the last case of media espionage. A TV reporter had asked permission to film in the empty Conference Room. Despite Court nervousness about the television cameras, the exercise seemed innocent enough so the request was granted. Inside the Conference Room, as cameras set up, the reporter on that occasion could not resist the temptation to pry into institutional secrets. Justices take notes as they debate cases, sometimes deciding not to keep them, tossing them instead into the Conference Room fireplace. The reporter was caught combing through the ashes hoping for a scoop. He got none.

By the mid-1990s there was television in the high Courtroom but not what the pictorial media really wanted. Individual Justices were allowed to sponsor groups using the Courtroom for conferences in off hours, and television coverage of such events was permitted. Lectures sponsored by the Burger-inaugurated Supreme Court Historical Society were run on cable television's *Court TV* program and on *C-Span,* but the ban on any cameras of any kind while the Justices were on the bench remained unchanged.

Hollywood maintained its fascination with the Court, but the Rehnquist era stayed in lockstep with the Burger precedent, forbidding any use of the interior of the building as a stage prop and even tightening controls on use of the exterior. Movie companies were allowed to use the front plaza and steps, but only on condition that the story line, as in the trailblazing *First Monday in October,* made the Court an integral part of the production.

Justices continued to listen to cases on the first three days of hearing weeks and to choose up sides in their Conference Room on Wednesdays and Fridays but, in a time of reduced constitutional litigation and fewer cases accepted for debate, rarely matched the Burger total of four cases a day, generally hearing no more than two or three.

The number of decisions shrank, no longer 150 or 200 a year, sometimes as few as 65.

The Court's concern that law clerks not be even inadvertent news sources remained under Rehnquist. The special cafeteria-area room Burger built for law clerk lunches, a place away from the attentive ears of newspeople at nearby tables, was rebuilt in a comfortable ground floor space just off the public cafeteria in what had been the "break room," a rest and storage area for the Court's police. The security force, expanded to a membership of eighty, was given instead a less public area for its breaks, the no longer needed basement print shop.

Chief Justice Burger had taken cautious and deliberate step after step away from the technologically primitive Warren era when the junior Justice made do with the all but illegible eighth carbon copy of Court documents. Burger's gradually expanded use of computers was carried far forward under Rehnquist. Pressure was taken off the telephone switchboard by providing instant phone-in information by computer on the status of the hundreds of cases awaiting a verdict and, at the moment of decision in the Courtroom, a diskette was removed from the house computer and transferred to a sender, providing instant distribution of full texts to major subscribers. There was less excuse for what happened to Justice Brennan's disgust in the school prayer case, criticism not based on knowledge of the Court's actual action and reasoning.

The decision-transmitting system served three Court needs. Major users of the Court decisions did not have to depend on press corps bulletins. There was no pressure on the Court budget; subscriber fees covered all costs. Switching of the diskettes eliminated any danger that subscribers could steal into the Court secrets during the gestation process.

Reporters still got an annual story out of each Justice's personal wealth and could note that take-home from the Courthouse was better than a decade earlier, up from the $100,000 range to $164,000 for each of the eight Associates. As usual, in repayment for his greatly expanded responsibilities, the Chief Justice received $100 a week more.

The Justices, in their reunions with their old law clerks, could still look around the table at men and women often outstripping their earnings by a factor of five. Physically, there were only small changes. Goose quill pens were still put out for pleading lawyers as the Court moved deeper into its third century. There was a small difference, The quarter-of-an-inch-wide plume on the pen used by John Marshall had been replaced somewhere along the line by the flaring inch-and-a-half-wide feather favored by Marshall's nemesis, the Declaration of Independence author and President, Thomas Jefferson.

In the Conference Room area there were new plumbing arrangements. The Justices' rest room with its row of urinals was divided now into two separate facilities for the two sexes.

Behind the bench where once there had been metal spittoons there were ceramic ones now, wastebaskets for a Court without chewers of tobacco, all of them the same with one difference. Eight had a dark green exterior with a white interior. One was light green. In Justice O'Connor's first year someone had stolen her cuspidor and it had proved impossible to get an exact duplicate.

With the lady Justice now a Court senior she had a proper dark green receptacle. The pale green one is passed on now to the Court's latest comer.

With the aging Court now in its twenty-first decade, two women on the bench and another of the gender in charge of the Justice Department as Attorney General, the distaff presence was no longer a novelty and there were even some in the press corps who had a candidate for the first woman Chief Justice, Ruth Bader Ginsburg. Since only a third of the Chief Justices have risen from the ranks, such predictions admittedly were very speculative.

With the traditionally strong Protestant, and now ample Catholic and Jewish representation on the High Bench, religious holidays, despite church-state separation, continued to be celebrated in off hours under the roof. An enthusiastic caroler, Chief Justice Rehnquist continued to lead singing at Christmas parties while, in the Hanukkah season, Justice Ginsburg on at least one occasion had a Jewish group at the Court premises.

To the old debates about banning the television coverage of the Chief Justice's annual state of the judiciary address to the ABA, Chief Justice Renquist found a solution. He eliminated the speech, rarely attending ABA meetings and limiting himself to publishing an annual state of the judiciary report.

Mindful perhaps of Potter Stewart's warning against too much activity, apart from the deciding of cases, the Rehnquist agenda of judicial and legal reforms and involvement in institutions apart from the work of the nine was far less than Burger's.

While the Court caseload might have been expected to shrink in a period of reduced constitutional litigation, it rose in the mid-1990s to seven thousand. Far from being discouraged by the way so many of their appeals are swept aside, prisoners were accounting for three-quarters of the caseload. With many crimes made federal offenses by Congress and new strictures on judges with regard to permissible sentences, prisoners leaped at the opportunity to escape from state judiciaries to the peak of the federal system while also contending that sentences received in federal courts were excessive.

Few convicts received satisfaction, but the screening burden on the Justices was heavy.

After more than two centuries it was still in many ways the Court Congress created in 1789 and that George Washington appointed, a body with appallingly great responsibilities, not always right as its history shows, but deserving appreciation from the media and public nonetheless.

NOTES

PREFACE

x. ... Whittington ... Even before journalist Whittington was taken on, the Justices, late in 1935, felt the need for some help with the media and Ned Potter, a "minute clerk" on the staff of Clerk C. Elmore Cropley, was detailed to handle the job.

PART I: SECRETS

Chapter 2: The Court, the President and the Media

11. ... Teddy White ... He produced the expected book on the fall of the President, devoting the opening chapter to the Court case. For the verdict he preferred the Chief's spoken summary rather than the stiff decision text, and asked for a copy. The Court house organ, *The Docket Sheet,* a product of the Public Information Office, had been running items on hundreds of dollars paid by collectors for some early Court autographs, so Burger, with a smile, said that White not only could have his spoken text but, for twenty-five cents, could have it autographed. White got it signed but did not have to part with a quarter.

11. ... 130 of the media ... Among those shoehorned in were the *National Observer,* the *Dallas Times Herald,* the *New York Post,* the *San Francisco Chronicle,* the *Providence Journal-Bulletin,* the *Chicago Sun-Times,* the *Philadelphia Bulletin, The Boston Globe, The Detroit News,* the *Milwaukee Journal, The Cleveland Plain Dealer, Newsday,* the *Minneapolis Tribune,* the Knight-Ridder Newspapers, the Thomson Newspapers, Landmark Communications, *U.S. News & World Report, Time, Newsweek, The Village Voice,* the *Atlantic Monthly* and the *Congressional Quarterly.*

Chapter 3: Decision

13. ... Richard Kluger ... His book was *Simple Justice, the History of Brown v. Board of Education and Black America's Struggle for Equality,* Random House, 1975.

Chapter 4: Cloudburst

19. ... two books ... *All the President's Men,* with Carl Bernstein, and *The Final Days,* with Scott Armstrong.

19. ... *National Law Journal* ... Interview with Tamar Lewin, December 14, 1979.

20. ... *Newsweek* ... December 10, 1979.

20. ... sitting target ... "The Supreme Court was a sitting target," said full-page book promotion ads cited by Philip C. Clark in a December 19, 1979, broadcast on 225 stations.

21. ... could not resist ... *National Law Journal.* Lewin interview. Ms. Lewin quoted an unidentified former Law Clerk, contemporaneously practicing law in the national capital: "It would have been impossible for me to resist a chance to meet Bob Woodward.

"Being asked to help him on a story is like being asked to help the President on a policy decision or to help Leonard Bernstein figure out how the music should go. Who's going to turn that down?"

22. ... vituperation ... Alleged remarks of Associate Justices, presumably relayed second or third hand by ex-law clerks, describing the Chief Justice variously as abrasive, asinine, a braggart, blustery, dishonest, incapable of moral and intellectual leadership of the Court, manipulative, of mediocre intellect, pompous, tasteless, unable to understand the simplest petition for *certiorari* (a request for a hearing) and uneducated, in short one who puzzled his fellows about whether he was evil or just stupid. (Epithets collected in part, and decried, by Professor Francis P. Kirkham of the J. Reuben Clark Law School. February 29, 1980.)

22. ... silence .. a disappointment ... Woodward interview with William Overend, *Los Angeles Times,* January 28, 1980.

22. ... no smoking gun ... Janofsky address to the Sacramento, California, Bar Association, February 28, 1980.

23. ... thrown out ... The Woodward-Armstrong book said that Thomas G. "Tommy the Cork" Corcoran, a Clerk of Oliver Wendell Holmes, had visited Justice William Brennan in an attempt to discuss *Utah Public Service Commission v. El Paso Natural Gas Company.* It was a conversation terminated immediately by the Justice.

It was "the only episode in the book that [came] anywhere near becoming a scandal and it [was] not a scandal about judicial behavior," noted Professor Bruce Marshall in the *New York University Law Review.*

23. ... doesn't happen ... *Philadelphia Inquirer* interview, December 19, 1979.

Chapter 5: Driblets

24. ... he could read ... Interview with Lou Cornio, the last of the Court's head printers, in the Spring 1984 issue of *The Docket Sheet.*

25. ... split-second interpretations ... Charlotte Moulton, the highly competent reporter for the United Press International, could not forget an incident early in her twenty-nine year tenure. A flood of decisions came down. There were no summaries. Charlotte rushed off a story on each as well as her speed-reading gave her to understand. Hours later when she had time at last to study the documents, Charlotte was horrified to discover that a footnote had reversed what she had taken to be the decision.

27. ... *Herbert v. Lando* ... This was a libel suit brought by Lieutenant Colonel Anthony Herbert against Barry Lando, a producer for CBS's *60 Minutes* news show, and also against correspondent Mike Wallace and the *Atlantic Monthly.* The appellant charged that a TV show segment on "the selling of Colonel Herbert" and a Lando article in the magazine were malicious defamations.

27. ... relatively empty ... The Association of Colleges and Universities invited the Court PIO to lunch at their Dupont Circle headquarters in the capital to express the hope that the Justices would not act with campuses full.

27. ... was on target ... Although Tim's telecast was reassuring to college administrators, the Court's Solomonic decision in *Bakke* would have been unlikely to spawn disorders in any case. This time the baby was sliced in two. Powell made a pair of points. Rigid numerical quotes such as barred the way to the Caucasian were wrong. Four conservatives agreed and that became law.

On the other hand, it was proper to give some extra consideration to members of minorities that had been victims of past discrimination. All four conservatives withdrew their support, but all four liberals signed on. That too became law. Only Powell approved the whole text.

Bakke, said UPI's Charlotte Moulton at a 1978 retirement party, was "what really decided me to quit!"

28. ... the leak ... *Washington Star,* April 25, 1979.

29. ... common market ... Goldberg quoted in *Equal Justice Under Law, the Supreme Court in American Life.*

30. ... best interests ... Cited in the *Columbia Journalism Review.*

30. ... applies everywhere else ... *The New York Times,* April 29, 1979.

Chapter 6: Adversaries

31. ... who enjoyed themselves ... While Justices frequently were appalled by cartoons, there were times when the satiric artists skewered other victims to the pleasure of the jurists. One occasion was when Burger called on lawyers to keep their "briefs" brief. Many of the presumably terse summaries were running to scores of pages. It was a logic that also applied to loosely organized Courtroom speeches.

Garner in the *Commercial Appeal,* to the Chief's amusement, showed one Justice asleep on the bench and another shooting paper airplanes as a long-winded orator droned on before them.

32. ... for a profit ... Denniston comments at a joint ABC-TV and Columbia University Graduate

School of Journalism seminar on national security and press freedom, January 5, 1983, as reported in the *Foreign Intelligence Literary Scene*, February 1983.

33. ... Court of Secrecy ... *American Bar Association Journal*, 1983.

33. ... reject that logic ... *American Bar Association Journal*, 1983.

33. ... closer look ... *Baltimore Sun*, January 19, 1978.

35. ... sort of scandal ... Column in *San Angelo Standard Times*, "High Court Carpentry Criticized," June 11, 1977.

35. ... Anderson's interest ... Jack Anderson's feud with the Chief Justice and his staff took the form of one attack after another. Items included:

- "Burger Accused of Detesting Press," *The Washington Post*, October 27, 1978. (The columnist was right that Burger had many misgivings about some Court coverage, notably including Anderson's. In a footnote in the October 27, 1977, column, perhaps not to appear a common scold, Anderson gave the Chief some quarter: "Burger's defenders insist that he is a dedicated and conscientious Chief Justice." No "defender" was identified but Mark Cannon, the Chief's Administrative Assistant was a fellow Mormon.)
- "Burger Press Aide Faithful Reflection," The Washington Post. (A drubbing for the PIO.)
- "Punishing Critics of the High Court," *The Washington Post*.
- "High Court Now a Top-Secret Agency," *The Washington Post*.
- "A Look Inside the Supreme Court," *The Washington Post*.
- "Burger, Like Nixon, Favors Secrecy," *The Washington Post*.
- "Chief Justice's Scales Tip to Favored Publications," *St. Petersburg Times*. (It was true that Burger gave detailed annual interviews to the *U.S. News & World Report* that allowed him to edit transcripts, going on record only with what he finally wished.)
- And, "The Brethren Can Be Articulate," *The Washington Post*. (The column said that a "furious" Burger had turned down repeated requests for an interview to "get his side of Supreme Court actions.")

Chapter 7: A Chief Justice's View

39. ... sometimes laugh... Chuckling and whispering, to the surprise of some onlookers, was done atop as well as below the bench, but Chief Justice Burger did not feel that what was sauce for the Justices' goose was sauce for the reporters' gander.

39. ... using a large one ... Earl Warren's mahogany desk was "partner's style," big enough for two to work at simultaneously.

40. ... Abe Fortas's chambers ... Fortas, a Justice from 1965 to 1969, was Lyndon Johnson's nominee to succeed Earl Warren as Chief. When conflict of interest charges were raised against Fortas, the nomination was withdrawn and he left the High Bench. He stayed close to Justice Douglas, assisting him in his final illness.

Chapter 8: Rope-a-Dope

44. ... Holmes ... He served from 1902 to 1932.

44. ... Cardozo ... On the Court from 1932 to 1938.

45. ... standing on the Opinion ... Discussed in *John Marshall's Defense of McCulloch v. Maryland*, G. Gunther, editor, 1969.

45. ... forced to speak out ... Brennan address at the Maxwell Airforce Base, Alabama, September 3, 1963.

45. ... [Tom] Clark ... Justice from 1949 to 1967.

45. ... Arthur Goldberg ... On the High Bench from 1962 to 1965.

46. .... *New York Times Co. v. Sullivan* ... Argued January 5, 1964, and decided March 2, 1964.

46. ... Stewart's view ... Yale Law School anniversary address, January 22, 1977.

47. ... unburdened himself ... Powell address to the Southwestern Legal Foundation, April 29, 1980, entitled "What Really Goes on at the Court."

Chapter 9: "Sleazy TV"

53. ... pulled back ... In the early 1990s, federal courts in seven states experimented with TV coverage of hearings. The results were unhappy. Chief Judge Jon O. Newman of the United States Court of Appeals for the New York area, one of those who experimented, said that he had begun with "a bias toward openness" but had ended with the belief that the harm to witnesses and jurors outweighed any public benefit." Reported in *The Washington Post*, September 23, 1994.

The governing body of the federal courts, a twenty-seven judge group known as the United States Judicial Conference, took the same view in the same month. In its regular semi-annual meeting in the Supreme Court Building, with Chief Justice Rehnquist in the chair, the Conference refused to extend the experiment to other districts and banned TV altogether in federal criminal cases.

54. ... judicial lockjaw ... Quoted in A. F. Westin's *Out of Court Commentary by United States Supreme Court Justices, 1790–1962*.

54. ... hedge the soul ... Quoted in G. S. Hellman's *Benjamin N. Cardozo, American Justice*.

56. ... politely be shown the door ... Stern contended later in a letter to the PIO and others that he and his crew had behaved civilly, moving only 5 feet into the room so as "not to intrude on the Chief Justice's conversation or discomfort him with our light."

A transcript of his videotape that he provided showed, however, that after Burger's initial expostulation: "Who is this fellow with the camera; you leave or I leave," the NBC camera kept shooting for twenty-seven further questions and answers as Stern asked innocently what possible objection the departed Chief could have had.

57. ... TV was still absent ... Although the Courtroom ban on TV stayed in effect, Burger finally in his last decade made his peace with electronic journalism away from the Courthouse. When the ABA in April 1979 opened all its functions to TV coverage, Burger went along, permitting the filming of his annual speech, merely setting a few conditions such as a ban on blinding lights.

Later as leader of the celebration of the bicentennial of the Constitution, he wooed TV's useful support.

PART II: INSIDE THE GOLDFISH BOWL

Chapter 10: Two Chiefs

62. ... Lafayette Park ... The Federal Judicial Center and the Administrative Office of the United States Courts moved in 1992 to the new Thurgood Marshall judicial office building at the edge of Capitol Hill.

65. ... $3.5 million ... Private foundations with some help from the Law Enforcement Assistance Agency shouldered the bulk of the cost.

Chapter 11: Fifteenth Chief Justice

66. ... we are infallible ... The same thought was expressed earlier by Robert Houghwout Jackson (Justice from 1941 to 1954). In a Concurrence in *Brown v. Allen* in his final year on the Court, he wrote: "We are not final because we are infallible. But we are infallible only because we are final."

69. ... night classes ... Burger reminisced that he was a University of Minnesota dropout, not because of lack of academic skills, but because he learned he needed no college diploma to go to law school. He graduated from the latter *magna cum laude*.

Chapter 12: Other Chiefs

72. ... Where's God ... Justice Clark's reminiscences were recorded in a film on the Court produced by the Young Lawyers Association of the ABA and of the Virginia Bar Association. The film was shown for years in a small ground floor theater at the Court.

72. ... a philosophical court ... Although Librarian Ed Hudon thought of the Holmes, Brandeis and Frankfurter eras as their "courts," none was a Chief Justice. Holmes served under four Chiefs from the time of Melville Fuller in 1902 to that of Charles Evans Hughes in 1932. He and Brandeis were in the Court of Edward D. White (1910–1921) and of former President Taft (1921–1930). All three on Hudon's list were Associates in the Charles Evans Hughes period (1930–1941).

Frankfurter, after the Holmes and Brandeis retirements, remained to serve on three more Courts, those of Harlan Fiske Stone (1941–1946), Fred M. Vinson (1946–1953) and Earl Warren (1953–1969).

Chapter 13: Fixing Cracks

75. ... forgive his brother ... The Jay letter was dated September 17, 1782, in Paris, written one year before he and others in the American delegation worked out a treaty with Britain ending the state of war and obtaining London recognition of the colonies' independence.

The letter reflected the bitterness Jay and others among the Founding Fathers nurtured toward Americans, including closest relatives, who supported the Revolution at the outset and then switched sides. Addressed to Peter Van Schaik, a Tory who had never wavered in his support for the English King, Jay said he could respect that but that he could not stomach Americans who turned coats midway. He wrote: "You mention my brother. If after having made so much bustle in and for America he has, as is surmised, improperly made his peace with Britain, I shall endeavor to forget that my father had such a son."

77. ... signing the certificates ... Whether to use a pen or a machine to certify new members of the Court bar was not Clerk Rodak's sole problem with the induction documents. It was established practice to follow the attorney's name with the honorary "esquire," a term tracing back to the Middle Ages in Europe when the *scutarius* was a shield-bearer doing man's work on the battlefield. There were some pursed lips and shaken heads among some feminine members of the staff when Mike refused to list the many new women lawyers as esquires, choosing instead to strike off the appellation for everyone.

80. ... "single" calendar ... The idea of a "single" calendar dated back to 1940, but it was another of the innovations pressed forward by Tom Clark and enthusiastically carried further by Burger.

81. ... Constitutional bicentennial ... The two hundredth anniversary of the Constitution coincided with Burger's eightieth birthday. With still youthful vigor, Burger retired from the Court to lead a several-year celebration of the nation's basic law.

Chapter 14: Only Human

84. ... don their robes ... On taking over as Chief in 1969, Burger found an extra use for the robing room. In it he installed the first Xerox copying machine the Court ever had.

89. ... Barret Meredith ... By odd coincidence, much like Warren Earl B. succeeding Earl Warren, the young Burger chose Barret M. with one "t" as the fictional lawyer studied by the reporter, while a half century later he appointed Barrett M. with two "t's" to be the house journalist pondering the jurists.

90. ... instant controversies ... Growing more confident with the press in his later years, Burger finally agreed to "background" press conferences at the time of his ABA speeches. The talk was limited to the issues raised in the address, was not for attribution and was designed to help the reporters better understand the points he was making.

Chapter 16: Eight Other Votes

109. ... they both bite ... While Marshall left the Court in low spirits, his memory was enshrined on Capitol Hill.

Chief Justice Burger, his sometime nemesis, had lobbied successfully for a vast new judiciary office building a few blocks distant next to the District railroad station. Justices White and Blackmun moved into retirement chambers there, the first such outside the 1935 Courthouse itself. The structure was named for Thurgood Marshall, making him, along with Thomas Jefferson and a half dozen others, the only figures of national history so honored on Capitol Hill.

110. ... a Burger clone ... The "Minnesota twins" were look-alike only in the way their early Supreme Court votes tracked. Physically, Blackmun was elfish beside the Chief's more bearish bulk.

111 ... executions could resume ... When the first convict was to be put to death under the Court's new dispositive, the PIO sat with the Court Clerk, Mike Rodak, as the appointed hour approached, 10 P.M. Washington time. Mike was on the line to the Warden in a Utah prison where a firing squad was in position facing the condemned man. Should a Law Clerk or a Messenger come running from a chamber saying that a Justice had relented, Mike was ready to call off the killing. At a snail's pace, a clock's minute hand moved toward the vertical, finally standing erect. It was 10 P.M. Mike put down the phone. The warden had spoken. Two thousand miles away, the convict was dead.

114. ... $1,000 from a savings account ... The ethics law required members of the federal judiciary including the Justices to make an annual disclosure of assets within broad limits.

By 1995, Ruth Bader Ginsburg was the Court's wealthiest member with assets of more than $4,170,000. In descending order there were Breyer reporting more than $3,170,000, Sandra Day O'Connor above $1,400,000, Stevens over $965,000, Souter under $1,100,000. Scalia below $780,000, Kennedy below $635,000 and Thomas under $275,000.

In the spirit of total revelation, Justice Thomas recorded that Rush Limbaugh, the far-right talk show host, had given him cigars worth $100. Thomas had performed a wedding ceremony for Limbaugh in the Thomas family home in Virginia.

115. ... made their way ... White served as Deputy Attorney General and Burger as Assistant Attorney General in charge of the civil division.

117. ... didn't have geography ... Quoted in *Congressional Quarterly's Guide to the Supreme Court,* 1979.

Chapter 17: The Big Secret

118. ... young students ... Many of the messengers are college graduates taking a respite before going on to law school or other postgraduate studies.

120. ... a stinging dissent ... *The Supreme Court, The Way It Was, The Way It Is,* William Morris Company, New York, 1987.

121. ... personal joshing ... Address to the Southwestern Legal Foundation.

122. ... clobber one another ... Speech at the Maxwell Airforce Base.

122. ... considered "foolish" ... A law Burger applied while finding it ridiculous was that of the snail darter, a rare fish whose presence upstream caused the temporary suspension of use of a dam that had cost scores of millions of dollars. Pushed by environmentalists, Congress had left no loopholes when it banned the elimination of any species.

123. ... spoke of that ... See "personal joshing" above.

123. ... bits of rancorous ... Address at Washburn University, January 27, 1977.

123. ... vote for the respondent ... August 11, 1976, address to the ABA.

124. ... doing it myself ... April 3, 1978, remarks.

125. ... non-brief briefs ... The Court finally solved the problem by banning briefs of more than fifty pages and petitions that exceeded thirty.

127. ... Powell spoke ... See "vote for the respondent" above.

Chapter 18: Little Village

130. ... still adorns ... "Slogans to fit the occasion," *Yearbook 1988, Supreme Court Historical Society.*

131. ... largest all marble ... Dana Bullen, *Washington Star,* August 2, 1964.

131. ... materials used ... Statement of Mario E. Campioli, Assistant Architect of the Capitol, who worked on both. Quoted in *The Docket Sheet,* May 1981.

131. ... $7 haircuts ... The barber shop included a thronelike high chair for shoeshines, but Johnnie Shaw, the Barber of most of the final quarter of the century, never had occasion to make use of it from the time he signed on in 1974. He employed it instead as a little shrine to the memory of Justice Douglas, the jurist's manly image propped on the back of the seat and ferns decorating the foot rest.

At least one Justice of the century's last half did have memories of shines given there. Potter Stewart recalled footwear getting a high gleam in the shop on at least a few occasions after his arrival in 1952.

132. ... Ten Commandments ... The architects presumably did not foresee the passions aroused in late-twentieth-century years by issues of the separation of church and state. Some protesters could be mollified by the explanation that the divine injunction was "an example of written law."

133. ... andirons inscribed ... Court Curator Gail Galloway in *Yearbook 1978, Supreme Court Historical Society.*

134 ... $125 million ... Estimate by George M. White, Architect of the Capitol, who shared with the Marshal the maintenance of the building and grounds.

136. ... joint sessions ... In recent years, the Chief Justice's Administrative Assistant as well as the Clerk and the Marshal have accompanied the Justices to hear the President's State of the Union address.

141. ... twice the estimated value ... *Yearbook 1978, Supreme Court Historical Society.*

141. ... sinister word ... *The Docket Sheet,* November 1978. In 1812, during Gerry's governorship, a northeast Massachusetts electoral district was carved out in the shape of a salamander to assure victory at the polls. Thereafter, such manipulations did dubious honor to the Gerry family name.

142. ... some of the inquiries ... *The Docket Sheet,* Fall 1984.

142. ... no rocker of the boat ... *Congressional Quarterly Guide to the U. S. Supreme Court,* 1979.

143. ... a number ... still practice ... *Yearbook 1980, Supreme Court Historical Society.*

144. ... Congressman ... Mikva ... Later Mikva served also as a federal Circuit Court Judge and as Counselor to President Clinton.

144. ... Starr ... He, too, was a Circuit Court Judge. In the Bush administration he was Solicitor General, the government's lawyer in Supreme Court pleadings.

Chapter 19: Madame Justice

147. ... *First Monday* ... The title of both the play and the film referred to the date on which the Supreme Court begins its annual term.

The Hollywood script writers, in their first draft, understood correctly that it was Congress that assigned the date to the Court but assumed mistakenly that the instruction was included in the original Judiciary Act of 1789. The congressional decree was much later, September 5, 1916.

147. ... law of the Creator ... *Bradwell v. Illinois,* 16 Wall., 1873.

148. ... the first woman ... "A Century of Women." *The Docket Sheet,* May 1979.

148. ... she won ... Alice O'Donnell, "Women and Other Strangers Before the Bar," *Yearbook 1977, Supreme Court Historical Society.*

148. ... good-bye photo ... *The Docket Sheet,* May 1979.

148 ... organized crime ... *The Docket Sheet,* November 1974.

149. ... playing anything ... Roderick Mann interview, *Los Angeles Times* ... July 10, 1980.

Chapter 20: Departures

159. ... doubted their fitness ... *Harvard Law Review,* "The Retirement of Federal Judges," January 1938.

159. ... took the pension ... *Harvard Law Review*, "The Retirement of Federal Judges," January 1938.

160. ... Holmes at the time ... Another late Holmes dissent Douglas admired was in *U.S. v. Schimmer* in 1929. The Court denied citizenship to a fifty-four-year-old pacifist, a Yale Divinity School Professor. Holmes was eighty-eight.

160. ... delusion of adequacy ... Douglas speech of November 3, 1973, in Washington, D.C.

Chapter 21: When It's Wednesday

168. ... opaque glass ... Letter to the *American Bar Association Journal*, April 1983.

169. ... expansion seat ... With Congress making the decisions, the official size of the Court has ranged from the original six in 1790 to as high as ten in 1863.

After the first expansion to seven in 1807, to eight in 1837 and nine in 1863, Congress zigzagged from a new official total of ten back to seven in 1866 and finally up again to the present nine in 1869. The death of James Wayne in the latter year temporarily shrank the Court to eight, but no tenth Justice was ever nominated.

170. ... infallibility to others ... Quoted by Brennan in his talk on August 7, 1944, to a conference of state Chief Justices in New York City.

171. ... bunch of humans ... Quoted in the *Duluth News Journal,* December 13, 1979.

171. ... decision is emotional ... In volume 2 of Douglas autobiography.

171. ... already difficult ... How hard it was to get five votes was reflected in a Burger comment on January 24, 1974, as he recuperated after a Conference in the Court's steam bath. "It was a terrible day," he said, "a struggle every instant."

171. ... opted for seventy ... Discussion in the *Harvard Law Review,* January 1938.

INDEX

ABOUT THE AUTHOR

Barrett McGurn was a reporter for the *New York* and *International Herald Tribunes* from 1935 to 1966, serving sixteen years as Bureau Chief in Rome, Paris and Moscow, where he received journalism awards as the year's best foreign correspondent for his coverage of the French North African war of 1955 and the Hungarian Revolution of 1956.

Joining the government in 1966, he was Press Attaché of the American embassy in Rome, Counselor for Press Affairs and Embassy Spokesman in Saigon, Assistant Press Officer of the Department of State and from 1973 to 1982, Public Information Officer for the Supreme Court.